Peer Mediation

Peer Mediation

CONFLICT RESOLUTION IN SCHOOLS

REVISED EDITION

Program Guide

Fred Schrumpf

Donna K. Crawford

Richard J. Bodine

RESEARCH PRESS
2612 North Mattis Avenue, Champaign, Illinois 61822

RESEARCH PRESS
PUBLISHERS

The definition of peace on page 127 is quoted from "Gifts, Not Stars" (p. 553),
by George E. Lyon, in *Horn Book*, September-October, 1992.

Adaptations of the Red Riding Hood Story appearing on pages 157–159 are based on a retelling
in Individual Development: Creativity, by Leif Fearn, 1974, San Diego: Education Improvement Associates.
Published by Magic Circle Publishing, P.O. Box 1577, Spring Valley, CA 92077.

First edition copyright © 1991 by Fred Schrumpf, Donna K. Crawford, and H. Chu Usadel

Copyright © 1997 by Fred Schrumpf, Donna K. Crawford, and Richard J. Bodine

14 13 12 11 10   21 22 23 24 25

Copies of this book may be ordered from the publisher at the address given on the title page.

Cover design by Linda Brown, Positive I.D. Graphic Design, Inc.
Printed by McNaughton & Gunn

ISBN 978-0-87822-368-8

Library of Congress Catalog Number 96-69186

To Anneke, Vincent, Michael, Dawn, Dirk, and Mike

Contents

Figures & Tables

FIGURES

TABLES

Preface

It was almost 10 years ago that we trained our first group of peer mediators at Urbana Junior High School in Urbana, Illinois, and 5 years since we published *Peer Mediation: Conflict Resolution in Schools* (Schrumpf, Crawford, & Usadel, 1991). Since the publication of that program, it has been our collective good fortune to have accelerated and broadened our experiences in conflict resolution program development and training. These experiences have provided us a considerable expansion of our perspectives and knowledge—hence this revised edition of *Peer Mediation: Conflict Resolution in Schools*. During this time we also produced *The Peer Mediation Video: Conflict Resolution in Schools* (Schrumpf & Crawford, 1992). This videotape program discusses program background and procedures, shows sessions in which program developers train potential peer mediators, and depicts how peer mediators conduct the six steps in the mediation process. Suggestions for using this video are included throughout this revised Program Guide; however, the video is not required in order to conduct the program.

Significantly, the Illinois Institute for Dispute Resolution (IIDR) was created in 1992 by a grant from the U.S. Department of Education. This resulted in the establishment of a highly successful conflict resolution in schools project. Through the IIDR, we have trained nearly 6,000 teachers, administrators, students, and support staff in the skills of conflict resolution. This training was either aimed at the development and implementation of school-based peer mediation programs or directed toward the development and implementation of comprehensive conflict resolution programs, the latter including peer mediation as a significant component. These trainings, although largely concentrated in Illinois, were provided by IIDR in many other states, as well as in Canada and Australia.

The interest in and commitment to peaceful conflict resolution has been gratifying. The conflict resolution in schools profession has grown substantially, especially in the last 5 years. Conflict resolution in schools programs, the most popular rendition of which continues to be peer mediation, are evident all over the United States, Canada, and Australia. Although a far cry from commonplace in schools across the country, conflict resolution programs in schools appear to be a genuine emerging trend.

Interest on the part of schools in conflict resolution may not be entirely altruistic, but rather due to the perceived elevation of youth violence. Violence prevention programs, safe school plans, community resource police officers, and tighter security are now frequently part of the secondary school environment. Legal worries also have forced schools to look seriously at their modus operandi, resulting in new policies that focus not only on safety in the school but also on issues of equity. For example, to ensure respect for individual differences, schools are adopting antiharassment policies. Regardless of the initial motivation, once implemented, conflict resolution programs have been widely heralded as worthwhile.

In these updated, revised, and expanded materials we share what we have learned over the past 5 years about conflict resolution in schools, and especially about peer mediation. The following overview summarizes our new knowledge.

First, peer mediation programs work! Schools that have implemented peer mediation programs generally have experienced success. Schools rarely have dropped the program because of lack of success, and most report some improvement in overall school climate based upon reduction in suspensions, fights, verbal attacks, property disputes, and so forth when peer mediation is available.

Peer mediation is only one component of a comprehensive conflict resolution in schools program. A comprehensive program involves extending training in the foundation skills and the problem-solving strategies of conflict resolution to all staff and students, integrating conflict resolution education into the school curriculum and daily learning opportunities, aligning school policies—especially those concerned with behavior management—with expectations to honor diversity and develop self-responsibility, and developing a school culture of cooperation. Why train only 30 or so students in mediation skills? The larger the number of students and teachers who learn to use the problem-solving strategies of conflict resolution—negotiation, mediation, and group problem solving—the greater the impact on the school climate. Our program *Creating the Peaceable School: A Comprehensive Program for Teaching Conflict Resolution* (Bodine, Crawford, & Schrumpf, 1994) exemplifies such a comprehensive conflict resolution program for schools.

Although only one component, peer mediation represents a viable starting point in developing a comprehensive program of conflict resolution, especially in secondary schools. Even if a school chooses to focus on developing a comprehensive conflict resolution program, it will want to include peer mediation. If peer mediation is the starting point, it is hoped that it will not be the end of a school's effort to provide education in conflict resolution.

Peer mediation programs require administrative and faculty commitment of time and resources. Programs may start strong but then fade. Each year is new, and the program must be continually revitalized and rejuvenated. Without continuing efforts to increase faculty awareness and support, a peer mediation program may fail to realize its potential—even to survive. Program promotion is required, and student mediators should not be solely responsible for promoting the program among the student or adult school community.

Peer mediation training requires a high-quality initial effort and should include provisions for quality training beyond initial or basic training. Peer mediation programs may be part of a leadership class or a peer helper program and, as such, ongoing training is logistically convenient. If such is not the case, provisions should be made to bring student mediators together for periodic extended training opportunities. This advanced training should include the development of advanced mediation skills to facilitate expanded application of program services. Ongoing training should also afford mediators opportunities to learn from their collective experiences in conducting mediations and to continue practicing behaviors learned in their basic training.

Peer mediation is appropriate for a wide assortment of disputes, including disputes rooted in cultural differences and social diversity. Disputes may appear to be arguments or name-calling, or they may be typified by threats, rumors, or property issues. Because such conflicts are often characterized by, or based upon, harassment according to race, class, gender, or sexual orientation, diversity training and cross-cultural understanding should be included as part of the basic training.

Peer mediation is not a reactive tool. It is not designed as a response to violent incidents in the school, nor are student mediators trained to react in such situations. Clear delineations must be made between the conflict resolution program and the discipline program. Mediation is a proactive approach to help students choose and develop alternatives to self-destructive and violent behaviors when confronting intrapersonal, interpersonal, or intergroup conflicts. It is not well suited for dealing with a dispute after it has gotten out of hand unless some other intervention has taken place and the parties have agreed to mediation in order to plan behaviors that might lessen the likelihood of similar future occurrences. Additional school programmatic efforts beyond mediation to fashion complementary ways for promoting peace and preventing violence are advised. Choosing mediation before a conflict escalates is dependent upon a broad-based student acceptance of an ethic of peace.

Peer mediation is frequently used because the students involved in a dispute have not learned how to negotiate. Because the ability to negotiate is a life skill everyone needs, it seems logical for the school mission to include teaching negotiation skills to each member of the school community. If a negotiation breaks down—and there are numerous valid reasons this might happen in any dispute—mediation could then be used. Also, for some disputes, mediation may be a wiser choice than negotiation as the initial conflict resolution strategy.

Peer mediation programs can be an excellent link in a home-school-community approach to violence prevention. Mediation is a tool students can use in each of these settings. Peer mediation might be the stepping stone needed if safety and peace are to be achieved in any or all of these settings.

We believe peace is a realistic and attainable goal. We believe that in order for students to embrace this belief they must experience the condition of peace in a life context significant to them. We believe school can be that context. We believe peer mediation can significantly contribute to creating the condition of peace in the school. We believe that to coexist peacefully students need skills to express their needs and wants adequately and to create boundaries for themselves in a responsible manner. This revised, expanded, and updated Program Guide and the Student Manual that accompanies it describe our knowledge of how to develop and implement a peer mediation program to help middle, junior, and high school students acquire these skills and deal constructively with school-based conflicts. We hope that in the process of teaching students these skills, adults who work and live with these youth will also learn the skills to travel the road toward peace.

Acknowledgments

This book began with a commitment to a vision of peace and our awareness of the educator's responsibility for creating an environment where students can learn to participate effectively in the global community. We have been blessed by the presence of many individuals who have strengthened our ability to pursue this vision.

Through our experiences with colleagues and experts in the field of conflict resolution, we have learned significant lessons that have enhanced our work. We deeply appreciate the support, perspectives, challenges, and friendship that Judy Filner, Pamela Moore, Annette Townley, and William Kreidler have provided.

We are grateful for the opportunities that have emerged in our lives over the past few years and wish to acknowledge the following individuals: Dennis Rendleman, Donna Schechter, and Cheryl Niro (for their efforts and commitment to advocate for our work through the Illinois State Bar Association); Judy Hatswell, Jenny Fielding, and Joy Nielsen (for our consulting and learning experiences in Australia); Roger Fisher and Bruce Patton (for generously sharing their time, expertise, and sanctuary on Martha's Vineyard); and Shay Bilchick, Donni LeBoeuf, and Robin Delany-Shabazz (for the challenges that have expanded our vision and abilities to use our own conflict resolution skills through our work with the U.S. Department of Justice Office of Juvenile Justice and Delinquency Prevention).

We especially want to acknowledge Golie Jansen of Washington University, Seattle, for sharing her knowledge of diversity and social justice, and for contributing chapter 4, on diversity and conflict resolution. We also thank Chu Usadel of the Urbana, Illinois, School District for her work in developing the Common Ground Program and for writing the case study presented in Appendix C. Our gratitude goes to Ann Wendel, President of Research Press, for recognizing the importance of revising the original *Peer Mediation* publication.

Special recognition goes to our colleagues: Mike Kotner (for being a great mentor, spiritual friend, and catalyst for our involvement in the field of mediation); Topper Steinman (for translating our vision in his teaching with clarity, humor, and dedication); and Vernessa Gipson (for her inspiration, reality therapy, and harmonious challenges).

CHAPTER 1

FOUNDATIONS

We learn, remember, and think. We also plan, solve problems, and use language. We can—and usually do—learn to modify our behavior when confronted with new situations. We are capable of generalizing prior learning to different circumstances. We pursue the acquisition of concepts and strategies to cope with both current and anticipated events. This flexible, adaptive character of human behavior illustrates the significance of learning and provides the basic rationale for learning about conflict and conflict resolution. Through learning, we acquire the capacity to behave in a variety of circumstances, always driven by the goal of attempting to attain satisfaction from the experience.

Because conflict is perpetually present, nearly every circumstance affords the opportunity to manage conflict, and we are each required to do so. In short, we each learn to do something with conflict. This is true for students as well as teachers. Unfortunately, many students have no personal experiences upon which to draw and no models from which to learn anything but the mostly dysfunctional approaches to conflict of "flight" or "fight." Their only alternative, then, in order to try to gain satisfaction from experiences involving conflict, becomes to try harder at what they do know—flee faster or farther, or fight longer and harder.

When students encounter conflicts, often they react with verbal or physical aggression, try to ignore the situation, or attempt to withdraw from it, frequently blaming themselves for the problem. If students bring their conflicts to teachers or other staff members, often they are advised to "ignore it" or "walk away." When students bring their conflicts to their friends, the response is typically "get 'em back." If conflicts reach the level at which the principal or another administrator is involved, detentions or suspensions often result. In fact, some of these responses can actually escalate the conflict. Escalated conflicts may turn violent. None of these common responses resolves the underlying conflict. Unresolved conflicts often result in hurt feelings, loss of friends, or increased anger and frustration.

Children are not born violent; violence is learned behavior. If violent behaviors can be learned, alternatives to violence—peacemaking behaviors—also can be learned. Because there appears to be a lack of observable, consistent, omnipresent examples of peacemaking behavior from which youth can learn, peacemaking must be taught. Mediation is a peacemaking behavior, and mediators are peacemakers.

Mediation is one of three strategies of conflict resolution: mediation, negotiation, and group problem solving. Mediation is a communication process in which the individuals with a problem work together, assisted by a neutral third party, to solve the problem. The mediator is the neutral third party who facilitates the problem-solving process and helps the disputants negotiate an agreement. In the mediation process, the mediator creates and maintains an environment that fosters mutual problem solving. During the mediation, the disputing parties listen to each other's points of view, identify interests contributing to the conflict, create options that address the interests of both of them, evaluate these options according to objective criteria, and create an agreement. Although the mediator is responsible for controlling the process, the disputants control the outcome. Participation in mediation is voluntary, and the mediator does not judge, impose a decision, or force a solution. The power of mediation lies in the recognition that:

▼ Conflicts cannot actually be resolved if the disputants themselves do not choose to do so.

▼ Disputants are the best judges of what will resolve the conflict.

▼ Disputants are more likely to execute an agreement if they possess authorship of it.

In short, the disputants are responsible for creating a solution; the mediator is responsible for helping them work together to do so.

Students can often fulfill the role of mediator and help resolve disputes between peers. Such disputes commonly involve jealousies, rumors, misunderstandings, bullying, fights, misuse of personal property, and the ending of friendships. In addition, students and adults may serve together as co-mediators to resolve disputes between students and teachers that might involve personality clashes, respect issues, behavior issues, and other conflicts that diminish student-teacher relationships. Student-teacher mediations are often an outgrowth of established peer or adult mediation programs.

Peer mediation programs have emerged as one of the most widely used types of conflict resolution in schools. This may be due to the fact that educators perceive peer mediation as a conflict resolution tool that involves little risk because it is used in addition to disciplinary actions such as suspension and detention. In addition, peer mediation obviously takes educators out of the time-consuming role of arbitrating sanctions that rarely resolve the real conflicts among students. More significantly, peer mediation programs are present in schools throughout the nation because students themselves offer particular qualities that make these programs work:

▼ Students are able to connect with their peers in ways adults cannot.

▼ Peer mediators are capable of framing disputes in the perspective, language, and attitudes of youth, making the process age appropriate.

▼ Students perceive peer mediation as a way to talk out problems without fear that an adult authority will judge their behaviors, thoughts, or feelings.

▼ Peer mediators are respected because they honor the problem-solving process and their peers in the dispute by the way they conduct mediation sessions.

▼ The self-empowering aspect of the process appeals to youth and fosters self-esteem and self-discipline.

▼ When students come up with their own solutions, they feel in control of their lives and committed to the plans of action that they have created to address their problems.

Peer mediation programs send an important message to students: *Our school is a place where we can talk over our differences. We don't have to fight to get justice.* Peer mediation offers the opportunity to attack the problem and not the person. Whereas a peer mediation program offers every student a constructive means of resolving conflict—generally resulting in an improved school climate—the peer mediators themselves often gain the most because they acquire and internalize conflict resolution skills that will benefit them in their present and future lives. Specific life skills like self-control, anger management, communication, problem solving, critical thinking, and planning form the basis of the mediation process. These are skills that all students need to learn. Students who participate in mediation often, as a result of learning these skills, feel an increased sense of internal control and self-esteem.

The peer mediation approach described in this book is based on an understanding that conflict is a natural life condition and can be a positive force to stimulate personal growth and social change. To assist fellow students to deal constructively with conflict, a trained peer mediator facilitates the process of communication and problem solving toward resolution. Peer mediation is explained to students as "an opportunity to sit face-to-face and talk, uninterrupted, so each view of the dispute is heard. After the problem is defined, possible solutions are created and then evaluated. When an agreement is reached, a commitment to a plan of action is obtained."

Considering the competitive nature of our society, it is not surprising that conflicts are frequently viewed as contests in which there will be a winner and a loser. This win-lose attitude may adduce a significant block to constructive conflict resolution. Through the mediation process, conflicts are redefined so no one has to lose. In searching for a solution, disputants become partners and share in a dialogue about the quality of their lives.

Benefits of peer mediation are as follows:

▼ Peer mediation can enable students to see conflict as a part of everyday life and as an opportunity to grow and learn.

▼ Peer mediation can be more effective than suspension or detention in promoting responsible behavior.

▼ Peer mediation can help reduce violence, vandalism, and absenteeism in schools.

▼ Peer mediation can help reduce the amount of time teachers and administrators spend dealing with conflicts among students.

▼ Peer mediation is a life skill that empowers students to solve their own problems through improved communication and understanding of differences.

▼ Peer mediation can be a force for promoting mutual understanding of various individuals and groups throughout the school community.

PEER MEDIATION AS LEADERSHIP DEVELOPMENT

"Students helping students" is an important concept in the secondary schools that often finds expression in peer-helping and/or peer leadership programs. But, due to the increasing complexity of the social and emotional problems that today's teenagers experience, the sponsors of peer-helping programs often find themselves faced with increased liability. Peer mediation differs from other peer-helping programs in that the mediators are taught to handle a clearly defined, formal process. They act as facilitators between two peer disputants. They do not take sides, give advice, or assume responsibility for solving the dispute. They are trained only to assist those in conflict to solve their own problem.

Peer mediation can be added to a currently established student leadership or helping program. In doing so, a school can extend its services to improve the atmosphere of the whole school community. Peer mediation, however, requires the acquisition of new skills. Peer mediation is not counseling, but rather a service to help individuals plan need-fulfilling behaviors. Generally, a program that offers a better alternative to resolving school conflicts will have no difficulty finding enthusiastic support from school staff.

TOWARD A CLIMATE OF PEACE

Creating a school climate conducive to peace is a major challenge for everyone involved—students, teachers, administrators, parents, community members, and so forth. The manner in which a school community views and manages conflict will have a profound effect on the overall school climate. A school community may use conflict to teach important life skills, promoting peace and fairness. A peer mediation program alone cannot provide a climate of peace, but peer mediation can be an important component of any comprehensive effort to create such an environment. Peer mediation offers an alternative to self-destructive, violent, and other dysfunctional behavior often chosen in response to conflict, but the impact on the lives of students is dependent upon the degree of organizational internalization of the ethic of peace. The organizational mission and its observable operation must support and exemplify peacemaking.

Youth involvement in and with violence is a pervasive problem that touches every school and neighborhood, cutting across race, religion, and gender. Feelings of frustration and hopelessness have become deeply ingrained among educators and other adults directly involved with youth. These individuals increasingly find themselves overwhelmed by students who are hostile, aggressive, violent, and disconnected. Physical aggression and intimidation are often youths' first responses to problems and disagreements.

Violence is behavior by persons against persons that threatens, attempts, or inflicts physical or emotional harm. Although the act of physical violence captures our attention and mobilizes our concern and outrage, the predominance of more subtle psychological violence may well be the more devastating factor in efforts to combat violence. Undoubtedly, some schools think they have far more than their fair representation of violent youth, whereas others think that youth violence does not impact them. The issue for schools is not only serious and violent crime. Unkindness and transgressions toward and among youth have a long history. Such interchanges are universally observable, appearing wherever youth interact. Every child, and thus every school, is affected by violence, whether or not physical harm is evidenced (Bodine & Crawford, 1995).

Tools that allow students to deal constructively with interpersonal conflicts, cultural differences, and the violence embedded in our social fabric are often absent from the day-to-day school experience. While youth are particularly vulnerable to the effects of violence, they are also resilient and reachable. School counselors, social workers, deans, psychologists, teachers, principals, administrators, and superintendents are in important positions to create primary prevention programs. Educators are often discouraged by the notion that prevention is impossible without total social reforms to end problems such as poverty, racism, and substance abuse. The error in this view is that it can justify inaction when there are "doable" interventions that can make a significant difference in breaking the cycle of violence (Bodine & Crawford, 1995).

The American Psychological Association's (1993) Commission on Violence and Youth reports:

> We overwhelmingly conclude, on the basis of the body of psychological research on violence, that violence is not a random, uncontrollable, or inevitable occurrence. . . . Although we acknowledge that the problem of violence involving youth is staggering . . . there is overwhelming evidence that we can intervene effectively in the lives of young people to reduce and prevent their involvement in violence. (p. 14)

The report recommends that schools play a critical part in any comprehensive plan for preventing youth violence. It calls for inclusion of school-based curricula and teaching strategies to build youths' resistance to violence. Given the climate of violence that surrounds our nation's youth—both as perpetrators and as victims—educators must be fully cognizant of their roles as initiators of peace and nurturers of the peacemakers of the future. They can play an important role in reversing patterns of conflict and aggression by implementing comprehensive conflict resolution programs in schools—programs that are characterized by students' resolving their conflicts both with and without adult involvement.

Just as it is important that all schools attend seriously to violence prevention, it is also important that conflict resolution be included as an integral component in that prevention framework. Although conflict resolution in and of itself will not prevent violence, it has a significant place in any violence prevention strategy. When considering the role of conflict resolution, school decision makers need to understand that conflict resolution is not a reactive tool, but a proactive tool. In other words, conflict resolution is not a program for reacting to violent incidents in school but rather an approach to further the educational mission of the school to develop and promote a responsible citizenry. The relationship to violence prevention is that a conflict resolution program affords youth the understanding, skills, and strategies needed to choose alternatives to self-destructive and violent behaviors when confronting intrapersonal, interpersonal, or intergroup conflicts.

Conflict resolution is not a quick fix: It takes time. It takes time for adults in schools to integrate conflict resolution into their own lives and to use it consistently when under pressure, especially in the workplace. It takes time for adults to learn to translate the concepts of conflict resolution for their students. It takes time for students to integrate conflict resolution into their lives and to use it consistently when under pressure, especially from peers who are choosing other behaviors. It takes time for even the most effective school and classroom instruction to have a significant impact upon individual behavior and upon the collective climate of the school. Obviously, time is an issue, but if time is not invested in developing programs to provide youth with alternatives to self-destructive and violent behaviors, time will be invested continually in reacting to those behaviors.

Conflict resolution takes time because the employment of its problem-solving strategies does not occur in a vacuum. To be effective, conflict resolution must be viewed not as isolated interactions between individuals, but as a pervasive, systemic cultural change. Thus, more is involved than providing a few students with the foundation skills and the problem-solving strategy of mediation and making the services of those students available to others. To sustain and expand a program, attention must be directed toward systemic changes in at least three domains: prevalent practices, policies, and rules of the school. The implementation of those practices, policies, and rules often provides a powerful contradictory message to the peaceful resolution of conflicts. Three areas that require specific examination are the degree of competition promoted or demanded within the system, the system's response to issues of diversity, and the manner in which behavioral expectations are taught and enforced.

Cooperative Context

Conflict resolution is problem solving for mutual benefit; thus, cooperation is an operational value of conflict resolution. Johnson and Johnson (1993) assert that "it makes little sense to teach students to manage conflicts constructively if the school is structured so that students have to compete for scarce rewards (like grades of 'A') and defeat each other to get what they want" (p. 1). The nature of the reward system is an extremely important dimension of the classroom and school context. The primary reward system of nearly every classroom and school is grades. Grades exemplify a competitive context: "It makes no sense to talk of constructive conflict management in schools structured competitively. The first step in teaching students the procedures for managing conflicts, therefore, is creating a cooperative context in which conflicts are defined as mutual problems to be resolved in ways that benefit everyone involved" (Crawford, Bodine, & Hoglund, 1993, p. 210).

Diversity

Society is becoming increasingly diverse, and schools are usually among the first of the community institutions required to deal with the changing demographics. Issues of multiculturalism—cultural and social diversity—frequently are imbedded in conflicts that surface in schools, and these issues often present formidable barriers to cooperation. Proactive processes for capitalizing on the benefits of diversity and the contributions of cultural and social differences are important in establishing and preserving the ethic of peace.

Behavior Management

Also noteworthy is the fact that most school discipline plans are based not on discipline, but on punishment. Such programs are designed more to gain student compliance to externally imposed behavioral expectations than to teach responsible, need-fulfilling behaviors. These programs are obedience training, not education. They place the adult in the system in the role of enforcer, and the enforcement can occur only through coercion. Thus, the most significant observable behavior—the behavior of the adult model—is contrary to the message of respect, tolerance, and appreciation for differences. Table 1 contrasts punishment practices and discipline practices.

If the desire is for students to choose not to coerce others, educators must model a truly orderly, productive system accomplished through cooperation and persistent pursuit of quality behavior rather than a system that maintains a semblance of order through actual or implied force. Further, students must be provided with alternative ways to behave—not just told, "Don't do that."

Prerequisite to making this notion operational is the need to make clear the behavioral expectations for the system. Often conflicts occur because the individuals involved interpret differently what is expected, or one or both believe that pursuing their behavioral choice is worth the risk because the behavior has gone undeterred in the past. A successful conflict resolution program, and likely any program of behavior management, is dependent upon students' ability to evaluate their own behavior and generate alternative behavioral choices, ones accepted in the system. Each student must fully understand the behavioral expectations of the school and be fully cognizant of the consequences of choosing to behave otherwise. Such understanding is simplified when expectations make sense to the student. Expectations make sense when there is a logical explanation for their existence;

Table 1. Punishment versus Discipline

PUNISHMENT	DISCIPLINE
Expresses power of an authority; usually causes pain to the recipient; is based upon retribution or revenge; is concerned with what happened (the past)	Is based on logical or natural consequences that embody the reality of a social order (rules that one must learn and accept to function adequately and productively in society); concerned with what is happening now (the present)
Is arbitrary—probably applied inconsistently and unconditionally; does not accept or acknowledge exceptions or mitigating circumstances	Is consistent—accepts that the behaving individual is doing the best he or she can do for now
Is imposed by an authority (done to someone), with responsibility assumed by the one administering the punishment and the behaving individual avoiding responsibility	Comes from within, with responsibility assumed by the behaving individual and the behaving individual desiring responsibility; presumes that conscience is internal
Closes options for the individual, who must pay for a behavior that has already occurred	Opens options for the individual, who can choose a new behavior
As a teaching process, usually reinforces a failure identity; essentially negative and short term, without sustained personal involvement of either teacher or learner	As a teaching process, is active and involves close, sustained, personal involvement of both teacher and learner; emphasizes developing ways to act that will result in more successful behavior
Is characterized by open or concealed anger; is a poor model of the expectations of quality	Is friendly and supportive; provides a model of quality behavior
Is easy and expedient	Is difficult and time consuming
Focuses on strategies intended to control the learner's behavior	Focuses on the learner's behavior and the consequences of that behavior
Rarely results in positive changes in behavior; may increase subversiveness or result in temporary suppression of behavior; at best, produces compliance	Usually results in a change in behavior that is more successful, acceptable, and responsible; develops the capacity for self-evaluation of behavior

Note. Reprinted from *The School for Quality Learning: Managing the School and Classroom the Deming Way* (p. 187), by D.K. Crawford, R.J. Bodine, and R. Hoglund, 1993, Champaign, IL: Research Press. Copyright 1993 by the authors.

when rules are few and simple; when expectations are predictable and can be applied in new situations; and when consequences for inappropriate behavior are known, nonpunitive, and consistently applied. The concept of organizing expectations as rights and responsibilities is teachable and understandable to students because it is based on a logical system of thought—a system fundamental to our democratic traditions. Rules allow everyone to know his or her responsibilities and safeguard the rights of all by making explicit the relationship between rights and responsibilities. Such a logical and fundamentally simple notion provides students with a framework they can use to determine what is and what is not acceptable behavior—a critical requirement in evaluating behavioral options in any conflict resolution process.

In brief, a *sense-based system* for determining acceptable and unacceptable behavior reduces rule confusion, concerns regarding the uniform enforcement of rules, and the willingness to risk getting caught behaving inappropriately. Most schools, however, employ a *rule-abundant system* characterized by many complex rules that appear unconnected and unrelated, expectations that are not easily applied to new situations, and consequences for inappropriate behavior (usually punitive) that are neither understandable nor consistently applied. Table 2 contrasts these two types of systems.

Students cannot resolve behavioral conflicts within a system absent of behavioral norms. This problem is not alleviated by the presence of confusing and ambiguous norms. If the authority and justification for rules are the domain

Table 2. Characteristics of Sense-Based versus Rule-Abundant Behavior Management Systems

SENSE-BASED SYSTEM	RULE-ABUNDANT SYSTEM
Has a logical organization.	Lacks organization.
Rules are few and simple, predictable, and generalizable.	Rules are many and complex, lack predictability, and cannot be generalized (situation specific).
Consequences for inappropriate behavior are known and consistently applied.	Consequences for inappropriate behavior are unknown and/or inconsistently applied.
Authority derives from system.	Authority derives from those in charge.
Reduces rule confusion.	Is characterized by rule confusion.

Note. Reprinted from *Creating the Peaceable School: A Comprehensive Program for Teaching Conflict Resolution* (p. 23), by R.J. Bodine, D.K. Crawford, and F. Schrumpf, 1994, Champaign, IL: Research Press. Copyright 1994 by the authors.

of the adults in the system, students will be severely hampered in any efforts to engage successfully in conflict resolution unassisted by those adults (Bodine et al., 1994). Conflict resolution is facilitated by clarifying behavioral expectations and the consequences of not meeting those expectations. This information becomes a standard of fairness and constitutes the major criteria for selecting options upon which to build an agreement.

Still another strong argument for developing a sense-based system is the understanding that conflict resolution is about designing future acceptable behaviors and must not involve fault finding and punishment for past behaviors. When consequences for unacceptable behavior are clear, it is more apparent which conflicts are appropriate for student-assisted resolution. The application of the consequence is not an issue for mediation or negotiation. Conflict resolution helps those who have chosen a behavior that resulted in a negative consequence plan for a more acceptable future behavior, thus avoiding similar future consequences. Conflict resolution itself, however, should not be a consequence. Conflict resolution is a choice. For example, if the consequence for fighting is suspension, one should not be allowed to escape or reduce the suspension by choosing to mediate. Mediation is appropriate in this scenario if offered as an opportunity for the individuals involved to plan a way to behave toward each other that avoids future fighting, is acceptable to each of them, and is viewed as acceptable by the school.

Creating a culture within the school that embraces the ethic of peace requires systemic changes. Peer mediators are trained to serve the school as peacemakers. Without the systemic changes that support peacemaking, peer mediators will struggle in their efforts, not unlike United Nations peacekeepers operating in a warring world.

RATIONALE FOR PEER MEDIATION

Two principal reasons for establishing conflict resolution programs in schools are to counteract school violence and to develop responsible citizens.

Conflict Resolution and Violence Prevention

Kids are crying out to us to do something. When their anguish was quiet, or self-directed, we did not respond with sustained vigor and concern. But now their feelings are turning outward. They are enraged and disenfranchised, and they feel they have little to lose, no future to compromise. The problem is there for us to see: School must be a place where all students feel valued, useful, and needed (Elias, 1995). If youth are not in a supportive environment, and many are not, then schools and other youth-serving agencies must develop effective ways to compensate, even as other systems work to change the problematic conditions. What proactive measures can we choose to try to improve our current state of affairs? Focusing concern and actions on the occurrence of violence, the modus operandi of many schools and other agencies, is treating a symptom and offers little for the future. Focusing concern and actions on educating students about violence in all its various forms and about alternatives to violence offers hope that those alternatives will be the behaviors students more and more frequently choose.

The best school-based violence prevention programs seek to do more than reach the individual child. They instead try to change the total school environment, to create a safe community that lives by a credo of nonviolence and multicultural appreciation (DeJong, 1994; Moore & Batiste, 1994). One short-term goal of educational institutions must be to move students from simply recognizing that they live in a multicultural, often violent society to feeling prepared to contribute and to live peacefully in their diverse communities. Looking ahead, educators and educational systems must challenge young people to believe and act on the understanding that a nonviolent, pluralistic society is a realistic goal. It is not just what youth are taught in the classroom that will reinforce the messages of nonviolence and respect for diversity, it is also what they experience as the commitments and values of their institutions and the adults who are a part of them (Moore & Batiste, 1994).

Schools alone cannot change a violent society. Schools can, however, achieve the following goals:

▼ Stop making the problems worse.

▼ Teach alternatives to violence.

▼ Teach students to act responsibly in social settings.

▼ Teach students to understand and accept the consequences of their behavior.

▼ Improve the quality of learning.

The goal of making the school a safe haven in which youth can gain respite from violence in order to think and learn is a good one, but it cannot be created apart from improving what and how teachers teach, changing how principals administer school rules, and creating a nonviolent vision shared by everyone in the building. Making school a safe haven is unlikely to stamp out violence in society, but that should not deter us from the effort (Haberman & Schreiber Dill, 1995).

Education is living, not the preparation for living. Students must be involved in dealing with real problems in order to learn what they need to know now and later. The fact is, students are involved with real problems constantly. When the school does not accept this fact and commit to giving students the tools to deal with those problems, students and the school disjoin. Conflict resolution can serve to prevent this disassociation—students can learn to resolve problems constructively in need-fulfilling ways. If students are able and encouraged to solve their own real problems in the school environment, they will become more accepting of the school's effort to expand their repertoire of information and skills.

Three principles are paramount to any program to counteract school violence:

1. *Whatever is illegal outside of school cannot be treated as if it were not a crime inside of school.* Making schools a safe haven for

youngsters does not mean creating a medieval sanctuary where civil authorities may not enter. . . . Crimes are not transformed into something else because they are perpetrated in schools.

2. *The process of school management and discipline is more important than the outcomes.* Repeatedly demonstrating that thinking, reasoning, and working through problems are respectable alternatives to violence are the behaviors to be reinforced and learned. . . . If school officials begin by assuming they do not have enough time or person power to administer individualized, careful processes, they are, in effect, conceding that they cannot decrease the violence. Indeed, we can be certain that a system of only enforcement and control, impersonally administered, with an emphasis on punishments will make matters worse. It will play into the limited view of the world held by most youth . . . that power is everything and it is the school's responsibility to make them behave in much the same way as it is the school's responsibility to make them learn.

3. *Problems of school violence are not intrusions on the school program: They are an integral part of the school program.* Making the building safe is a necessary but incomplete condition; teaching students to care about and predict the consequences of their behavior is the goal. Options to violence . . . must be actively modeled every day in every class. (Haberman & Schreiber Dill, p. 155)

It is important to understand clearly that not all behaviors arising from conflict can be handled through peer mediation or the other problem-solving strategies of conflict resolution. Actions that are illegal, actions considered immoral or unethical by local or societal standards, and actions that are clearly against institutional policy should not be considered conflicts to be resolved solely through the employment of these conflict resolution strategies. Conflict resolution programs do, even with this limitation, provide a proactive means of addressing these principles for counteracting school violence. Conflict resolution especially offers a means for individuals to address the far more pervasive, but frequently institutionally ignored and often institutionally perpetrated, issues of psychological violence. The problem-solving strategies of conflict resolution are better suited for allowing individuals to confront issues of psychological trespass than issues of physical trespass. The expectation is that by constructively addressing issues before physical engagement, the incidence and intensity of physical engagement will diminish.

Conflict Resolution and Responsible Citizenry

The ability to express and resolve conflicts is central to the peaceful expression of human rights. The skills and strategies of conflict resolution are also the skills of peace. Conflict resolution and peacemaking can be viewed as responsibilities inherent in citizenship in a democratic society. When persons are able to express their concerns peacefully and seek resolutions to problems that take into account common interests, they not only promote the values of human dignity and self-esteem, they also advance democracy. A conflict resolution program provides the theoretical understanding and practical experience necessary for youth to become effective, balanced, flexible adults. The school whose structure and teaching enable learners to behave peacefully truly serves the highest ideals of education—the individual acceptance of responsibility to guarantee the universal rights of all. Democratic society relies on the acceptance of individual self-responsibility; it is democratically incompatible to believe responsibility can be mandated and then enforced.

Schools must be places from which viable, positive future pathways for young people can be built. They must, above all, be places where youth can learn to live and get along with one another, as well as to become ready to assume their future roles as responsible citizens of a democracy, as parents, as community members and leaders, and as productive members of the work force. Many students have no other place from which to gain these experiences. Only schools can extend these possibilities equally to all students—this is the constitutional mandate to the schools.

How we "get along"—that is, how we live in civil association with one another—is important to us. Citizenship and how we live in civil association with one another are intricately related. Citizenship might best be understood not simply as membership in a state but as the condition of people participating in the exercise of governing themselves and with the capacity to carry on the public's business effectively. We act as citizens not in private, but together, in relationship with one another, our community, and our country. However, our relationships with one another are impacted by how we live our lives in the modern world, and many forces are at work making these relationships problematic. Conflict resolution skills are increasingly needed to let us lead successful public lives in our schools, communities, and workplaces. This need involves more than complex problem-solving processes; it suggests that our ability to deal with larger issues depends at least to some extent on how we regularly deal with one another. Building effective relationships among citizens is important not just for reaching agreements, but also for how people choose to disagree (Amsler, 1994).

Education can be a force for reducing intergroup conflict. It can serve to enlarge our social identifications in light of common characteristics and communal goals. It can seek a basis for fundamental human identification across a diversity of cultures in the face of manifest conflict. The question is whether human beings can learn more constructive orientations toward those outside their group while maintaining the values of group allegiance and identity. It seems reasonable to believe that, in spite of very bad habits of the past and very bad models of the present, we can indeed learn new habits of mind:

> It is not too late for a paradigm shift in our outlook toward human conflict. Perhaps it is something like learning that the earth is not flat. Such a shift in child development and education . . . might at long last make it possible for human groups to learn to live together in peace and mutual benefit. (Hamburg, 1994, p. 15)

Since we are, in fact, a single, interdependent, meaningfully attached worldwide species, effective citizenry is both a national and global issue of personal safety and national security. Where will effective citizenry emerge if not in our schools?

An attractive behavioral alternative to violence or acquiescence and a basic life skill is assertiveness. Assertiveness is knowing how to take advantage of opportunities without victimizing others, knowing how to resist pressure or intimidation from others without destroying relationships or isolating oneself, and knowing how to resolve conflicts in ways that make use of a full range of nonviolent opportunities. Assertion skills combat violence and are required for a quality life. Such skills are fostered by conflict resolution programs and can be taught in schools. At the very least, peer mediation programs provide a viable means for students to practice assertiveness within the purview of the school. That alone is a starting point on the path toward peaceful coexistence.

CHAPTER 2

UNDERSTANDING CONFLICT

Conflict is a discord of needs, drives, wishes, and/or demands. Intrapersonal conflict involves an internal discord, interpersonal conflict involves discord between two parties, and intergroup conflict involves discord within a group or between groups of people. Each of these types of conflict impacts schools.

Conflict is a natural, vital part of life. When conflict is understood, it can become an opportunity to learn and create. The synergy of conflict can create new alternatives—something that was not possible before. Examples of such synergy exist everywhere in nature: In the forest, the nutrients provided by decaying leaves support the growth of enormous trees. In the sea, a beautiful pearl is the synergistic result of sand irritating a sensitive oyster inside its shell.

The challenge for people in conflict is to apply the principles of creative cooperation that can be learned from nature in their human relationships. When differences are acknowledged and appreciated—and when the conflicting parties build on one another's strengths—a climate is created that nurtures the self-worth of each individual and provides opportunities for fulfillment to each.

PERCEPTIONS OF CONFLICT

Without conflict, there would likely be no personal growth or social change. Unfortunately, when it comes to conflict the perceptions of most people are profoundly negative. When asked to list words or phrases associated with conflict, most adults, as well as most children, respond negatively: "fight," "hit," "argument," "it's harmful," "yelling," "war," "hate," "get even," and so forth. These negative attitudes about conflict are likely the result of assimilated messages from the media, parents, teachers, friends, government officials, and most others with whom one experiences conflict.

Negative perceptions and the reactions they provoke are extremely detrimental to successful conflict resolution. However, before they can be replaced, they first must be understood. To start, think about your own attitudes toward conflict: Does denying the existence of conflict help you resolve it? Does accusing or defending help you to cooperate? Can you make a conflict go away by not thinking about it? Are you really able to force another person to change? Does assuming there will be a winner and a loser help?

15

In every conflict each individual has a choice—to be driven by these negative perceptions or to take control of the situation and act in a positive way. With more personal awareness and better understanding of available choices, one becomes able to approach conflict knowing that it can have either destructive or constructive results. When conflict is perceived as a positive life force, those in conflict become responsible for producing a result in which relationships are enhanced and individuals are empowered to control their own lives in ways that respect the needs of others. In brief, the power to create resolution lies within each person. However, perhaps largely because of the absence of observable models, this power is most often not utilized. The purpose of a conflict resolution program such as peer mediation is to provide students and adults with the knowledge and skills to unleash this power (Bodine et al., 1994).

It is important to realize that students' success in developing an awareness of the positive potential of conflict is an outgrowth of the endeavors and commitment exhibited by the adults in the school to approach conflict in a positive way. Teachers who integrate positive ways of resolving conflicts into their classrooms and school will see results that have a powerful effect on their own lives and work, as well as on the lives and work of their students.

ORIGINS OF CONFLICT

As Dr. William Glasser explains in his exposition of control theory, conflict originates from within (Glasser, 1984). Control theory explains why (and to a great extent how) all living organisms behave. According to this theory, everything we do in life is behavior, all of our behavior is purposeful, and the purpose is always to attempt to satisfy basic needs that are built into our genetic structure. Control theory is based on the assumption that all behavior represents the individual's constant attempt to satisfy one or more of five basic inborn needs. In other words, no behavior is caused by any situation or person outside of the individual.

Accepting this idea requires a paradigm shift on the part of those, including most educators, whose prior training supports the view of life according to stimulus-response theory. According to the stimulus-response paradigm, behavior is caused by someone or something (the stimulus) outside the individual: The action following is the response to that stimulus.

According to the control theory paradigm, people or events outside us never stimulate us to do anything. Rather, our behavior always represents the choice to do what most satisfies our needs at the time. When we repeat a choice that is consistently satisfying, we exercise less and less deliberation in making that choice. Even a quick action, however, is chosen and not automatic.

Basic Psychological Needs

All individuals are driven by genetically transmitted needs that serve as instructions for attempting to live our lives. These basic needs are the physiological need to survive and four psychological needs, as follows:

1. The need for *belonging*—fulfilled by loving, sharing, and cooperating with others

2. The need for *power*—fulfilled by achieving, accomplishing, and being recognized and respected

3. The need for *freedom*—fulfilled by making choices in our lives and being safe

4. The need for *fun*—fulfilled by laughing and playing

The needs are equally important, and all must be reasonably satisfied if individuals are to fulfill their biological destiny. The individual has no choice but to feel pain when a need is frustrated and pleasure when it is satisfied. When any need goes unsatisfied, there is a continual urge to behave. This urge is as much a part of human genetic instructions as is eye color. Instructions related to survival—such as hunger, thirst, and sexual desire—are relatively distinct. Individuals quickly learn that a particular discomfort is attached to a particular survival need, and it is plain what they must do to satisfy the instructions. The nonsurvival, or psychological, needs are challenging because it is often less clear what an individual must do to satisfy them. Psychological needs, like biological needs, have their source in the genes, even though they are much less tangible and the behaviors that fulfill them are more complex than the physical behaviors used to fulfill the survival needs. Glasser holds that we are essentially biological beings, and the fact that we follow some of our genetic instructions psychologically rather than physically makes neither the instructions less urgent nor the source less biological.

The needs seem to conflict with one another, and the constant challenge to satisfy them requires continual renegotiation of balance. For example, when a person chooses to work long hours, his or her accomplishments may help to meet the power need, but the person may not be involved with friends and family in a need-fulfilling way. Perhaps another individual derives a sense of freedom from living alone but loses a sense of belonging when exercising this choice.

Even though individuals may not be fully aware of their basic needs, they learn that there are some general circumstances that strongly relate to the way they feel. For example, people behave lovingly with their parents because it feels good, they realize that when people pay attention to their words or actions they feel powerful, by making choices they feel the importance of freedom, and through laughter they learn about fun.

Even though human needs are essentially the same for everyone, the behaviors through which individuals choose to satisfy those needs may be quite different. Beginning at birth, individuals have unique experiences that feel either pleasurable or painful. Through these experiences, individuals learn how to satisfy their needs. Because individuals have different experiences, the things they learn to do to satisfy their needs will be different as well. Each individual has memories of need-fulfilling behaviors specific to his or her unique life experiences. These pleasurable memories constitute the individual's *quality world* and become the most important part of the person's life. This quality world is composed of pictures (or, more accurately, perceptions) representing what the individual has most enjoyed in life. These perceptions become the standard for behavior choices. Unlike the basic survival needs, which are the same for everyone, the perceptions in each person's quality world are very specific and completely individual. Individuals choose to behave in different ways to fulfill their needs because their quality worlds are different. It is important to realize that the choice the individual makes in each situation is the choice he or she believes offers the best potential to meet basic needs. In short, each person is doing the best he or she knows how to do to satisfy basic needs. One individual's choice, however, may limit or disrupt another's choice. This is one significant source of conflict, especially in social situations like school, where the choice not to associate with one another is nearly nonexistent. To be in effective control of one's life means integrating this knowledge into the way one deals with others. *Making responsible choices that protect one's own rights without infringing on the rights of another is a basic precept of conflict resolution and the essence of effective citizenry in a democratic society.*

Thus, even though all people are driven by the same basic needs, each person's wants are unique. Wants are like pictures in an album: It is impossible for two people to have the same picture album because it is impossible for two people to live exactly the same life. To understand conflict and perceive it positively, the knowledge that no two people can have exactly the same wants is central. For example, if two individuals wish to satisfy their need to belong through a friendship, they must learn to share their commonalities and respect and value their differences. As long as people have conflicting wants and as long as one person's needs can be satisfied in ways that may conflict with another's, the need to renegotiate balance will persist. Driven by our genetic instructions, we will inevitably experience conflict, and therefore we must learn how to deal with it constructively.

Diagnosing the origin or source of a conflict can help define a problem, and a definition of the problem is the starting point in any attempt to find a solution. Almost every conflict involves an endeavor by the disputants to meet the basic psychological needs for belonging, power, freedom, and fun. Limited resources and different values may appear to be the cause of conflicts, but unmet needs are truly at their root. Conflict resolution is next to impossible as long as one side believes its psychological needs are being threatened by the other. Unless unmet needs are expressed, the conflict will often reappear even when a solution is reached regarding the subject of the dispute.

Limited Resources

Conflicts involving limited resources (time, space, money, equipment, property) are typically the easiest to resolve. People quickly learn that cooperating instead of competing for scarce resources is in their best interests. In cooperation, disputants share in problem solving, recognize each other's interests, and create choices. This process usually provides satisfaction because the psychological needs of belonging and power, perhaps even of freedom and fun, are addressed in the equitable allocation of limited resources.

It is important to realize how conflicts over unmet psychological needs are played out against the backdrop of limited resources. For instance, the student who is upset over the fact that his friend has not repaid a loan may really want to know his friend respects him (a power need). He may not easily accept a payment solution unless his need for recognition is addressed in the process. Limited resource conflicts may not be resolved because the resource itself may not define the problem. When solutions are crafted that deal only with the limited resource that seems to be the source of the conflict, the real problem is not solved, and the conflict will return.

Different Values

Conflicts involving different values (beliefs, priorities, principles) tend to be more difficult to resolve. When a person holds a value, he or she has an enduring belief that a specific action or quality is preferable to an opposite action or quality. This belief applies to attitudes toward objects, situations, or individuals. The belief becomes a standard that guides the person's actions.

When the terminology used to express a conflict includes words such as *honest, equal, right,* and *fair,* the conflict is typically one of values. Many times disputants think in terms of "right or wrong" or "good or bad" when values are in opposition. Even conflicts over differing goals can be viewed as value conflicts: The source of a goal conflict relates either to the goal's relative importance for each disputant or to the fact that the disputants highly value different goals.

When values are in conflict, the disputants often perceive the dispute as a personal attack or as a serious conflict between a trusted family belief and an alternative way of viewing the issue. They tend to personalize the conflict because their whole sense of self feels threatened and under attack. Strong stances on principle are therefore characteristic of value conflicts. When people feel attacked, they typically become defensive and stubbornly cling to their own convictions. The conflict exists because the disputants are governed by different sets of rules. Because the disputants evaluate the problem and each other according to conflicting criteria, resolution can be especially difficult.

Values disputes may be rooted in issues of social diversity (differences in cultural, social, or physical/mental attributes), often expressed as different beliefs, convictions, and/or principles, but they often also involve prejudice. Although complex, these conflicts can be resolved by increased awareness, understanding, and tolerance. When a conflict is rooted in prejudice or bias against a fellow student—as a member of a group that is perceived as inferior, unfamiliar, strange, even dangerous—ignorance, fear, and misunderstanding often guide behavior toward that person. Also, an unexamined sense of status or privilege may inadvertently hurt someone else through lack of recognition, exclusion, isolation, and so forth. Verbal expressions of this sense of ascendancy or privilege may even constitute racial or sexual harassment.

Psychological needs are enmeshed in value conflicts. For example, a person may be in conflict when a friend does not keep a promise. The person's picture of a friend is that of someone who is reliable, and her sense of belonging is threatened because her value system includes the assumption that friends do not make promises they cannot keep.

Rigid value systems can severely restrict one from meeting the need to belong. The more one adheres to any value, the more one's belonging is limited to others who hold the same beliefs and the less exposure one has to diversity. Inflexible values are also almost always destructive to our need to be free. We see others as wrong if they do not hold our beliefs, and we see situations as bad if they do not meet our standards. When this is the case, our options in life to satisfy our needs for freedom, fun, and power, as well as our choice of friends, become limited.

Resolving a values conflict does not mean the disputants must change or align their values. Often a mutual acknowledgment that each person views the situation differently is the first step toward resolution. If the disputants can learn not to reject each other because of differences in beliefs, they will be better able to deal with the problem on its own merits. This is one of the fundamental principles of conflict resolution: to deal separately with the relationship and substantive issues of the conflict. To resolve values conflicts, the disputants must look for interests that underlie their conflicting values. Again, psychological needs are enmeshed in values conflicts, and those needs likely frame the interests of each disputant.

RESPONSES TO CONFLICT

Responses to conflict can be categorized into three basic groups: *soft responses, hard responses,* and *principled responses.* For both soft and hard responses, participants take positions or stands on the problem. They negotiate these positions, either trying to avoid a contest of will or trying to win a contest of will. Soft and hard negotiations either bring about one-sided losses to reach an agreement or demand one-sided gains as the price of the agreement. For principled responses, participants use conflict resolution strategies designed to produce wise agreements. According to Fisher, Ury, and Patton (1991), a wise agreement is one that addresses the legitimate interests of both parties, resolves conflicting interests fairly, is durable, and takes contextual interests into account—in other words, how others besides the disputants will be affected by the agreement.

Soft Responses

Soft responses usually involve people who are friends or people who just want to be nice to each other because it is likely the contact between the parties will continue. In either case, they want to agree, and they negotiate softly to do so. Avoiding conflict is often the first soft response. People attempt to avoid conflict altogether by withdrawing from the situation, by ignoring the problem, or by denying that the conflict matters. When people choose to avoid conflict, it is usually because they are not interested in maintaining the relationship or they lack the skills to negotiate a resolution. Accommodation—when one party adjusts to the position of the other without seeking to serve his or her own interests in the relationship—is a common soft response. Soft responses, especially avoidance responses, may have some merit in the immediate situation—for example, they may help a person control anger or offer protection from the immediate danger posed by someone who responds aggressively. However, the soft response typically results in feelings of disillusionment, self-doubt, fear, and anxiety about the future. Many compromises are, in reality, soft responses to conflict. The parties agree to something that addresses only some of each of their needs in order to escape from the continuing confrontation.

Hard Responses

Hard responses to conflict usually involve people who are adversaries and whose goal is victory. Hard responses to a conflict are characterized by confrontations that involve threats, aggression, and anger. Hard negotiators demand concessions as a condition of the relationship and insist on their positions. They often search for a single answer to the problem—the one the other side will give in to. Hard negotiators frequently apply pressure to win a contest of will. They use bribery and punishment (for example, withholding money, favors, and affection). When these intimidating tactics cause the other side to yield, the hard negotiator feels successful. Hostility, physical damage, and violence often result from this type of response to conflict. Furthermore, this attitude is always detrimental to cooperation.

Principled Responses

Principled responses involve people who view themselves as problem solvers and whose goal is a wise outcome, reached efficiently and amicably. These problem solvers have developed communication and conflict resolution skills. Principled negotiators comprehend that communication is fundamental to cooperative interaction and understand what it means to participate in developing a common understanding. Principled responses to conflict are characterized by first seeking to understand the other side, then seeking to be understood. Principled negotiators are skilled, active, empathic listeners. Principled negotiators get inside the other person's frame of reference to see the problem as the other person does and to comprehend that person emotionally and intellectually. Principled responses to conflict create the opportunity for each participant to get his or her needs met. Principled responses to conflict are also proactive, not reactive. When people behave proactively, they do not feel victimized and out of control—they do not blame other people or circumstances when in conflict. Instead, they take charge of their actions and feelings and use their principled negotiation skills to make resolution a possibility.

Outcomes of Soft, Hard, and Principled Responses

The three types of responses to conflict produce different outcomes. Soft responses may be considered a *lose-lose* approach to conflict. When both parties deny the existence of the conflict or when they will deal only with superficial issues and not the interests at the root of the problem, neither person gets what he or she wants—they both lose. In those situations where one side accommodates the other, a *lose-win* outcome may result. A person who avoids a conflict by accommodating the other person loses in the sense that he or she is intimidated and has little courage to express feelings and convictions. When conflicts are avoided, basic psychological needs are either unacknowledged or unmet. Thus, people who avoid conflicts are not in effective control of their lives; they see themselves as victims, and their relations with others invariably suffer.

Hard responses may be considered a *win-lose* approach to conflict, where the more aggressive person wins and the adversary loses. This interpretation of winning and losing is usually in relation to the limited resource involved in the conflict. Often hard responses becomes *lose-lose* when the desire to punish or get even provokes adversaries to take vindictive actions that harm themselves as well as the opponent. These confrontations often are characterized by each party's viewing the other as the enemy and each being driven to vindictive actions to punish or get even with the other. Hard responses produce stressful situations when the negotiators are required to continue to interact in some manner, perhaps even to continue to work together toward common goals.

Both soft and hard responses are characterized by reactive communication indicating the individual is attempting to transfer responsibility and is unable to choose a response: "There is nothing I can do—I am not responsible."

Principled responses to conflicts change the game and the outcome. Principled methods produce wise outcomes efficiently and amicably. This type of response focuses on interests instead of positions and brings people in conflict to a gradual consensus on a resolution without the transactional costs of digging into positions and without the emotional costs of destroying relationships. Principled responses are characterized by proactive communication indicating that the individual takes responsibility for his or her actions and has the ability to choose a response. Principled negotiation is considered a win-win response to conflict.

The actions people choose when they are involved in a conflict will either increase or decrease the problem: When conflict escalates, the problem remains unresolved, and the effect can be destructive. As a conflict escalates, threats usually increase and more people become involved with, and take sides in, the conflict. Anger, fear, and frustration are expressed, sometimes violently. As a conflict escalates, people become more and more entrenched in their positions. Conflicts deescalate when differences and interests are understood. People remain calm and are willing to listen to opposing viewpoints. Those involved focus on the problem rather than on each other, thus creating the opportunity for resolution.

In summary, conflict in and of itself is neither positive nor negative. Rather, the actions chosen turn conflict into a competitive, devastating battle or into a constructive challenge where there is opportunity for growth. One always has the choice, when in conflict, to work for resolution. It is not our choice to do away with conflict—conflict is an inevitable part of life. Our choice concerns how to deal with that inevitability.

CHAPTER 3

PRINCIPLES OF CONFLICT RESOLUTION

The principled negotiation theory delineated in the book *Getting to Yes* (Fisher et al., 1991) provides the foundation for learning any problem-solving strategy of conflict resolution. Problem-solving strategies of conflict resolution based on principled negotiation theory include negotiation, mediation, and consensus decision making. In each of these strategies, the disputants work through a cooperative, collaborative procedure that incorporates four basic principles of conflict resolution. By implementing the principles of conflict resolution, the procedure enables the parties to maximize the chances that a resolution will be crafted to satisfy the interests of each party in dispute.

Although terms are often used interchangeably in conflict resolution literature and practice, they are defined here for the purpose of clarity:

▼ *Negotiation* is a problem-solving process in which the two parties in the dispute, or representatives of the two parties, meet face-to-face to work together, unassisted, to resolve the dispute.

▼ *Mediation* is a problem-solving process in which the two parties in the dispute, or representatives of the two parties, meet face-to-face to work together, assisted by a neutral third party, called the mediator, to resolve the dispute.

▼ *Consensus decision making* is a group problem solving process in which all of the parties in the dispute, or representatives of each party, meet to collaborate to resolve the dispute by crafting a plan of action that all parties can and will support and embrace. This process may or may not be facilitated by a neutral party.

CONFLICT STRATEGIES APPLIED IN SCHOOLS

Teachers, administrators, and other staff in schools charged with managing student behavior are all too aware of interpersonal and intergroup conflict. A considerable amount of these adults' responsibility to the school community concerns managing conflict. Indeed, to advise that schools not have in place methodologies to manage behavior arising from conflict would be unconscionable.

There are many possibilities for problem solving between people or groups of people. The use of arbitration as a problem-solving strategy is widely employed. Arbitration is the process whereby a party not involved directly in the conflict determines a solution to the conflict; the arbitrator rules, and the disputants are expected to comply with the ruling. This is the process that is characteristic of adult involvement in most conflicts between students in schools. However, conflict resolution programs, based on principled negotiation theory, differ from the prevalent practice in managing student conflict. Table 3 illustrates those differences.

Prevalent practice for managing conflict in schools involves arbitration, with the adult authority serving as arbitrator to settle the dispute for the parties. Conflict resolution involves bringing the parties of the dispute together, providing them the processes to resolve the dispute, and expecting them to do so, with or without involvement of others. The problem-solving strategies of conflict resolution are future directed. *The disputants craft and commit to a plan of action to behave differently from this point forward.*

Table 3. Prevalent Practice versus Conflict Resolution

PREVALENT PRACTICE	CONFLICT RESOLUTION
Relies on a third party to settle disputes	Directly involves the conflicting parties in both resolution process and outcome
Reactively offers services after the conflict occurs	Proactively offers skills and strategies to participants prior to their involvement in the conflict
Focuses on conflict after a school rule has been broken; often offers advice to ignore problem if it is thought not to be major or serious	Intervenes in conflicts and prevents their escalation into the broken-rule stage of violence
Uses arbitration almost exclusively to settle disputes	Maximizes the use of negotiation and mediation processes to resolve disputes
Requires adults to spend a disproportionate amount of time dealing with minor student conflicts	Uses teacher and virtually unlimited student resources to handle such conflicts and learn essential decision-making skills in the process
Relies on disciplinary codes that are ineffective in helping students reconcile interpersonal and intergroup differences	Focuses attention not on the disciplinary offense but on how to resolve the interpersonal and intergroup dimensions of a conflict

Importantly, not all disputes are suited to the problem-solving strategies of conflict resolution when those strategies are entrusted to students. There are instances where it may be appropriate for an adult arbitrator to be involved in the conflict resolution process. There are other instances where an adult authority may determine that the obvious issue of the dispute (for example, a fight between two students) is not appropriate for mediation or negotiation, even though the long-term relationship issues of the dispute might be suited to cooperative, collaborative problem solving. Cases will also exist in which the disputants will choose, for any number of reasons, not to participate in the problem-solving process. When any of these scenarios is present and the problem requires resolution, arbitration in some form is likely to be the most practical alternative. In brief, conflict resolution is impossible until all parties of the dispute agree to participate in the problem-solving process, and the process can continue only as long as all parties are willing to continue to work cooperatively toward resolution.

The problem-solving strategies of conflict resolution, based on principled negotiation theory, are consensual. The disputants must agree to participate and to work toward resolution. The concept of BATNA, or Best Alternative to a Negotiated Agreement (Fisher et al., 1991), is a prime determinant in deciding to participate in the problem-solving strategies of conflict resolution. The reason one negotiates is to produce something better than the results that could be obtained without negotiating. A person would likely choose not to participate in consensual problem solving if he or she believes doing so might be detrimental to the satisfaction of his or her needs—in other words, if the individual's belief is that the BATNA would be superior to a negotiated outcome. A person volunteers participation with the belief that doing so will enhance the opportunity to satisfy his or her needs—that is, if any of the conceived outcomes seems superior to his or her BATNA. The question "What might happen if you don't reach an agreement?" is useful in assessing the BATNA.

BATNA is in actuality the individual's perception of the possible outcomes from problem solving. An educational outcome for conflict resolution education is to help people assess their BATNAs creatively and accurately, to bring these perceptions closer to reality. An accurate BATNA protects the individuals from accepting agreements that are unfavorable and from rejecting agreements that would be in their long-term best interests. Becoming proficient in the principles of conflict resolution enables people to base assessment of the BATNA on understanding rather than fear and to approach situations with an "abundance mentality" rather than a "scarcity mentality." When this happens, people are more likely to choose to be directly involved in determining the resolution of problems that affect them. They will understand that their interests are more likely to be addressed when they inform others of and advocate for those interests.

The following situation illustrates how the BATNA is involved in the choice whether or not to problem solve: Sam and Terry have been best friends for several years. In the hallway just before school started today, Terry accused Sam of spreading rumors about Terry and another student. A loud argument ensued, and Sam shoved Terry into the lockers. At that very moment, a hall supervisor came around the corner and witnessed the shove. The supervisor sent Sam to the dean's office.

The dean assigned Sam to in-school suspension and also suggested that Sam and Terry request a mediation to try to work out their problem.

Sam has no choice but to serve the suspension. The decision whether to mediate (negotiate an agreement) will be a shared choice depending upon Sam's BATNA and Terry's BATNA—that is, what the best is they can expect if they do not deal directly with each other.

▼ Sam's BATNA: Terry will likely continue to think that Sam is spreading rumors and will remain angry at Sam for the shoving incident. Their friendship will be damaged.

▼ Terry's BATNA: Sam will likely be mad at Terry and blame Terry for causing the argument that resulted in Sam's suspension. Their friendship will be damaged.

If the mutual friendship is important to Sam and Terry, their BATNAs would suggest that a negotiated agreement is advisable since their best alternative to doing so is very likely a damaged relationship. Through mediation they can develop options to address relationship concerns—such as confidentiality and trust—and can thus continue as best friends. If the friendship is not important to one or both of them, or if they believe they can continue to coexist in the school without future problems, they will have little motivation to negotiate an agreement.

FOUR BASIC PRINCIPLES OF CONFLICT RESOLUTION

The four principles of conflict resolution outlined by Fisher et al. (1991) underlie the methodology for the peer mediation process in this book. These principles are universal to all conflict resolution strategies based on principled negotiation theory. In order for mediators to apply the steps of the mediation process effectively, they must fully understand these four principles.

Separate People from the Problem

The first principle, separating people from the problem, concerns people's strong emotions, differing perceptions, and difficulty communicating. When dealing with a problem, it is common for people to misunderstand one another, to get upset, and to take things personally. Every problem has both substantive issues and relationship issues. Unfortunately, the relationship of the parties tends to become involved in the substance of the problem. Fisher et al. (1991) assert that "before working on the substantive problem, the 'people problem' should be disentangled from it and dealt with separately. Figuratively if not literally, the participants should come to see themselves as working side by side, attacking the problem, not each other" (p. 21).

People problems fall into three categories: *perception, emotion,* and *communication.* These problems must be dealt with directly; they cannot be resolved indirectly with substantive concessions. Fisher et al. (1991) maintain, "Where perceptions are inaccurate, you can look for ways to educate. If emotions run high, you can find ways for each person involved to let off steam. Where misunderstanding exists, you can work to improve communication" (p. 22).

Perception

When dealing with problems of perception, it is important to remember that conflict does not lie in objective reality but in how people perceive that reality. As Fisher et al. (1991) point out, "Truth is simply one more argument—perhaps a good one, perhaps not—for dealing with the difference. The difference itself exists because it exists in [disputants'] thinking. Facts, even if established, may do nothing to solve the problem" (p. 29). Every conflict involves differing points of view; thus, every conflict involves differing notions of what is true, what is false, or the degree to which facts are important. Therefore, the "truth" and its importance are relative.

Emotion

When dealing with problems of emotion, it is important to remember that the parties may be more ready to fight it out than to work together cooperatively to solve the problem. As Fisher et al. (1991) state, "People often come to a negotiation realizing that the stakes are high and feeling threatened. Emotions on one side will generate emotions on the other. Fear may breed anger; and anger, fear. Emotions may quickly bring a negotiation to an impasse or an end" (p. 29). In conflict resolution the sharing of feelings and emotions is as important as the sharing of perceptions.

Communication

Given the diversity of background and values among individuals, poor communication is not surprising. Conflict resolution strategies are, simply put, processes of communication between disputing parties for the purpose of reaching a joint decision. As Fisher et al. (1991) claim, "Communication is never an easy thing even between people who have an enormous background of shared values and experience. . . . It is not surprising, then, to find poor communication between people who do not know each other well and who may feel hostile and suspicious of one another. Whatever you say, you should expect that the other side will almost always hear something different" (p. 32). There are four basic problems in communication:

▼ People may not talk to each other.

▼ Even if they do talk to each other, they may not be listening to each other.

▼ What one intends to communicate is almost never exactly what is communicated.

▼ People misunderstand or misinterpret what is communicated.

Techniques for dealing with the problems of perception, emotion, and communication are *foundation skills* for conflict resolution. These skills work because the behaviors of separating the relationship from the substantive problem changes people from adversaries in a personal confrontation to partners in a side-by-side search for a fair agreement, advantageous to each.

Focus on Interests, Not Positions

The second principle, focusing on interests, not positions, holds that the emphasis of conflict resolution should be not on the positions held by the people in dispute but on what the people really want—in other words, their interests. The objective of conflict resolution is to satisfy the underlying interests of the parties. Understanding the difference between positions and interests is crucial because interests, not positions, define the problem. Positions are something people decide they want; interests are what cause people to decide. Fisher et al. (1991) note that "compromising between positions is not likely to produce an agreement which will effectively take care of the human needs that led people to adopt those positions" (p. 57).

Reconciling interests rather than compromising between positions works because for every interest there are usually several possible satisfactory solutions. Furthermore, reconciling interests works because behind opposing positions lie more shared and compatible interests than conflicting ones. Thus, focusing on interests instead of positions makes it possible to develop solutions. Positions are usually concrete and clearly expressed, often as demands or suggested solutions. But the interests underlying the positions are less tangible and often are unexpressed. Asking questions to identify the interests of the parties in a conflict is a foundation skill of conflict resolution.

In almost every conflict there are multiple interests to consider. Only by talking about and acknowledging interests explicitly can people uncover mutual interests and resolve conflicting interests. In searching for the interests behind people's positions, it is prudent to look particularly for the basic psychological needs that motivate all people. If these basic needs are identified as shared or compatible interests, options can be developed that address these needs. Both shared and compatible interests can serve as building blocks for a wise agreement. Unless interests are identified, people in conflict will not be able to make a wise agreement. A temporary agreement may be reached, but such agreements typically do not last because the real interests have not been addressed. For lasting agreements, interests, not positions, must be the focus.

Invent Options for Mutual Gain

The third principle, inventing options for mutual gain, allows parties the opportunity to design options for solving the problem without the pressure of deciding. Before trying to reach agreement, the parties generate a wide range of possible options that advance shared interests and creatively reconcile differing interests. Fisher et al. (1991) say, "In most negotiations there are four major obstacles that inhibit the inventing of an abundance of options: (1) premature judgment; (2) searching for the single answer; (3) the assumptions of a fixed pie; and (4) thinking that 'solving their problem is their problem.' In order to overcome these constraints, you need to understand them" (p. 57).

The problem with premature judgment is that such judgment hinders the process of creating options by limiting imagination. When searching for the single answer, people see their job as narrowing the gap between positions, not broadening the options available. Looking from the outset for the single best answer impedes the wiser decision-making process in which people select from a large number of possible answers. When people make the assumption that resources are finite (in other words, a "fixed pie"), they see the situation as essentially either/or—one person or the other gets what is in dispute. If options are obvious, why bother to invent them? Thinking that solving the problem is the problem presents an obstacle to inventing options because each side's concern is only with its own immediate interests. This shortsighted self-concern leads people to develop only partisan positions, arguments, and solutions.

The foundation skill of *brainstorming* is used to separate the inventing from the deciding. Brainstorming is designed to produce possible ideas to solve the problem; the key ground rule is to postpone criticism and evaluation of those ideas. In order to broaden options, those in a dispute should think about the problem in different ways and use ideas to generate other ideas. Inventing options for mutual gain is done by developing notions that address the shared and compatible interests of the parties in dispute. The final decision on a solution is easier when there are options that appeal to the interests of both parties.

Use Objective Criteria

The fourth principle, using objective criteria, ensures that the agreement reflects some fair standard instead of the arbitrary will of either side. Using objective criteria means that neither party must give in to the other; rather, both parties can defer to a fair solution. Objective criteria are developed based on fair standards and fair procedures. Objective criteria are independent of will, legitimate, and practical. Theoretically, they can be applied to both sides. Fisher et al. (1991) use the example of the age-old way to divide a piece of cake between two children to illustrate the use of fair standards and procedures: One cuts and the other chooses. Neither complains about an unfair division. It is important to frame each issue as a joint search for objective criteria, to reason and be open to reason as to which standards are most appropriate and how they should be applied, and to yield only to principle, not pressure of will. Pressure of will can take the form of bribes, threats, manipulative appeals to trust, or simple refusal to budge.

One standard of justification does not exclude the existence of others. When what one side believes to be fair is not what the other believes to be fair, this does not automatically exclude fairness as a criterion, nor does it mean that one notion of fairness must be accepted over the other. It does require both parties to explain what the criterion means to them and to respond to reasons for applying another standard or for applying a standard differently. When people advance different standards, the key is to look for an objective basis for deciding between them, such as which standard has been used by the parties in the past or which standard is more widely applied. The principle response is to invite the parties to state their reasoning, to suggest objective criteria that apply, and to refuse to concede except on the basis of these principles. Plainly, a refusal to yield except in response to sound reasons is an easier position to defend—publicly and privately—than is a refusal to yield combined with a refusal to advance sound reasons. One who insists that problem solving be based on merits can bring others around to adopting that tactic once it becomes clear that doing so is the only way to advance substantive interests. The critical thinking skills of establishing criteria and evaluating possibilities based on criteria are the foundation for conflict resolution.

FOUNDATION SKILLS FOR CONFLICT RESOLUTION

In the problem-solving strategies of conflict resolution, certain attitudes, understandings, and skills are facilitative and/or essential. For problem solving in conflict situations to be effective, attitudes and understandings ultimately must be translated into behaviors—foundation skills. These foundation skills involve the following clusters of abilities.

Orientation abilities

Orientation abilities encompass the values, beliefs, attitudes, and propensities compatible with effective conflict resolution. They include the following:

▼ Nonviolence

▼ Compassion and empathy

▼ Fairness

▼ Trust

▼ Justice

▼ Tolerance

▼ Self-respect

▼ Respect for others

▼ Celebration of diversity

▼ Appreciation for controversy

These values, beliefs, attitudes, and propensities can be developed through teaching activities that promote cooperation and prejudice reduction.

Perception abilities

Perception abilities encompass the understanding that conflict does not lie in objective reality but in how people perceive that reality. Perception abilities include the following:

▼ Empathizing in order to see the situation as the other side sees it

▼ Self-evaluating to recognize personal fears and assumptions

▼ Suspending judgment and blame to facilitate a free exchange of views

▼ Reframing solutions to allow for face-saving and to preserve self-respect and self-image

These abilities enable one to develop self-awareness and to assess the limitations of one's own perceptions. They also enable one to work to understand others' points of view.

Emotion abilities

Emotion abilities encompass behaviors to manage anger, frustration, fear, and other emotions. These abilities include the following:

▼ Learning the language to make emotions explicit

▼ Expressing emotions in nonaggressive, noninflammatory ways

▼ Exercising self-control in order to control one's reaction to others' emotional outbursts

These abilities enable one to gain the self-confidence and self-control needed to confront and resolve the conflict. The basis for these behaviors is acknowledging that emotions—often strong ones—are present in conflict, that these emotions may not always be expressed, and that emotional responses by one party may trigger emotional responses from another party.

Communication abilities

Communication abilities encompass the behaviors of listening and speaking that allow for the effective exchange of facts and feelings. These abilities are as follows:

▼ Listening to understand

▼ Speaking to be understood

▼ Reframing emotionally charged statements into neutral, less emotional terms

These abilities include the skills of active listening, which allow one to attend to another person and that person's message, to summarize that message to check out what was heard and advise the other person of the message received, and to ask open-ended, nonleading questions to solicit additional information that might clarify the conflict. Also included are the skills of speaking to be understood rather than to debate or impress, speaking about yourself by describing the problem in terms of its impact upon you, speaking with clarity and concision to convey your purpose, and speaking in a style that makes it as easy as possible for the other party to hear. The skill of reframing, coupled with acknowledging strong emotions, is highly useful in conflict resolution.

31

Creative thinking abilities

Creative thinking abilities encompass behaviors that enable people to be innovative in problem definition and decision making. These abilities are as follows:

▼ Contemplating the problem from a variety of perspectives

▼ Approaching the problem-solving task as a mutual pursuit of possibilities

▼ Brainstorming to create, elaborate, and enhance a variety of options

Included is the skill of uncovering the interests of the parties involved in a conflict through questioning to identify what the parties want, as well as probing deeper by seeking to understand why they want what they want. The skill of problem definition involves stating the problem, and thus the problem-solving task, as a pursuit of options to satisfy the interests of each party. Flexibility in responding to situations and in accepting a variety of choices and potential solutions is an essential skill in decision making. The behavior is brainstorming—separating the process of generating ideas from the act of judging them. Also critical to success is the ability to elaborate potential solutions and to enhance and embellish existing solutions.

Critical thinking abilities

Critical thinking abilities encompass the behaviors of analyzing, hypothesizing, predicting, strategizing, comparing and contrasting, and evaluating. Included are the following:

▼ Recognizing and making explicit existing criteria

▼ Establishing objective criteria

▼ Applying criteria as the basis for choosing options

▼ Planning future behaviors

These skills are integral to the facilitation of the four principles of conflict resolution: separating people from the problem; focusing on interests, not positions; inventing options for mutual gain; and using objective criteria as the basis for decision making. When students and adults learn conflict resolution problem-solving strategies and the skills necessary to carry out these strategies, they are better able to resolve their own disputes and assist others in resolving disputes.

CHAPTER 4

DIVERSITY & CONFLICT RESOLUTION

We begin to examine the larger picture which reveals oppression as one of the roots of conflict and violence. If mediation only helps disputants to arrive at a solution that meets their needs, while not really addressing those more complex and controversial issues . . . are we not only missing an important opportunity, but also missing the boat?

—Cate Woolner
Rethinking Mediation: Living Peacefully in a Multicultural World

We live in an age of increasing youth violence. We also live in an increasingly diverse society. Violence and diversity are closely related. People and institutions often react to diversity with prejudice, resulting in discriminatory behaviors and actions. These reactions are of great concern because they contain the roots of conflict and violence. In its report "Violence and Youth: Psychology's Response," the American Psychological Association (1993) made a clear connection between the damaging effect of prejudice and discrimination on the self-confidence and self-esteem of those discriminated against. It saw prejudice and discrimination as laying the foundation for anger, discontent, and violence.

Indeed, many conflicts in schools are about diversity: conflicts based on differences in national origin, race, and ethnicity, but also on gender, sexual orientation, social class, or physical/mental abilities. Those conflicts usually are rooted in bias or prejudice, often reflecting inequality of privilege or status in relationships. Some of these conflicts also can be explained as differences in values, communication styles, and ideas about conflict. Students need to be aware that what one considers a value may, in reality, contradict equity policies of their school. Holding a value as an internal belief is each person's right, that of students included, but behavior based on a particular value may be perceived as racist or sexist or in some way a violation of the rights of others. Institutionally, such expressions cannot be allowed.

Schools usually represent a full spectrum of diversity. Diversity conflicts are complex and demand attention at many different levels. Teachers and students

The author of this chapter is Golie Jansen, Ph.D., Associate Professor of Social Work, Eastern Washington University, Cheney-Spokane. The authors kindly thank her for this contribution.

33

are not always able to identify conflict situations as rooted in a diversity issue and often feel inadequate to address diversity conflicts when they are identified. Conflict resolution programs are one response, as are equity or antiharassment policies. Conflict resolution programs and school policies are not enough to address bias and prejudice, however. A positive school climate must be created by focusing on bias awareness throughout the curriculum and within extracurricular activities. An environment that identifies, analyzes, and challenges prejudice is proactive in teaching tolerance and social justice. An environment that celebrates differences by honoring diverse talents and expressions truly prepares students for a world of diversity.

Specific questions to consider in fostering a positive school climate are as follows:

▼ What are the main type of conflicts involving diversity in our school?

▼ How are discrimination and conflicts rooted in prejudice, racism, or sexism addressed in our school?

▼ At what level are such discrimination and conflicts addressed (interpersonal, curriculum, student rights, and/or policies and procedures)?

▼ How are differences dealt with in our school (ignored, articulated, celebrated, inadvertently punished)?

▼ How are peace and understanding promoted in our school-community?

▼ How are social justice issues identified and discussed in our school-community?

▼ How is diversity honored in staff composition (administrators, teachers, other staff)?

DEFINING DIVERSITY

Diversity refers to cultural, social, and other identifiable differences among groups of people and between individuals. There are many different ways to categorize or describe diversity. In this chapter, diversity is explained in terms of cultural and social differences. *Cultural diversity* refers to differences in national origin, race, and ethnicity, whereas *social diversity* refers to differences in gender, sexual orientation, social class, or physical/mental abilities.

Cultural Diversity

Culture is the way of life of a given society or group. The commonality among people, a culture includes values, beliefs, customs, ways of thinking, material objects, and shared history. The most important aspects of a culture are its language, norms for behavior, and communication styles. Culture is the lens through which we view the world; it is the familiar, the norm. Culture is in continuous change and therefore is never free from conflict or opposition.

Cultural diversity usually refers to ethnic or racial diversity, including differences in national origin and religion. Cultural diversity, also termed *multiculturalism* or *pluralism*, is the historic legacy of the United States, despite the traditional view that the country is a "melting pot." The ethnic and cultural differences of distinct groups have always been part of the lives of people in North America and are not disappearing. The North American population will increasingly become more nonwhite. It is estimated that by the year 2000 in Canada and by the year 2020 in the United States, nearly half of each nation's school population will be students of color (Pallas, Natriello, & McDill, 1989).

Cultural diversity can be seen as both a challenge and an opportunity. The challenge for a society with different ethnic groups is to learn to live together without stereotypes and discrimination. The opportunity is to learn from one another and to integrate values and practices that are mutually enriching. It is important to note that cultural differences are not just differences in language, beliefs, or customs, but are deeply ingrained in systems of status and privilege. The result is subordination and marginalization, based primarily on skin color but also on ethnicity or national origin. Thus, cultural differences matter in how groups of people or individuals relate in the larger societal context. Many of these relationships over time have been characterized by practices of white, male, Eurocentric dominance, resulting in oppression of and discrimination toward other cultural groups.

Following are some terms used to discuss and understand cultural diversity: *Ethnic diversity* refers to group affiliation and identification of individuals, whether used broadly or for specific identification of national origin. For example, one can refer to oneself as having an African heritage, an Anglo-Saxon heritage, a Mexican heritage, or a Jewish heritage. More specifically, one can refer to oneself as a Polish American, Vietnamese American, German American, Chinese American, and so forth. Ethnic identification gives people a sense of belonging, a relationship to a cultural heritage, and refers both to people of European descent and people from other continents.

Diversity of color, also called *racial diversity*, relates to skin color, a recognizable, unchangeable characteristic observable to others. Historically, the term *race* has implied the superiority of white people and inferiority of people of color. Although many scientists now believe that racial classifications hold no scientific validity, racism still pervades policies and institutional practices. For census purposes and to prevent racial discrimination, in the 1970s the federal government created official categories by which people of color could identify themselves. Official government, employment, and education forms include categories such as African American, Asian American, Native American, Hispanic American, and European American. Although these categories serve a quantifying purpose and thus affect policies, they do not speak to personal identity and/or diversity within these categories. For instance, a third-generation Chinese American student may have very little in common with a first-generation Cambodian American student, yet they are both categorized as Asian Americans. As educators (and mediators) we must look beyond the categories for distinct stories of descent and personal history. Increasingly, concerns are voiced about the lack of a category for mixed-race people, one of the fastest growing groups among people of color.

Diversity of religion can be considered part of cultural diversity. Spirituality profoundly shapes people's beliefs and values. Such diversity speaks to what people hold sacred and gives inspiration for daily living. Religious convictions can bring out the best in people in terms of care, charity, unselfish deeds, and the willingness to forgive. Religious convictions also can incite highly charged conflicts over life-styles and life choices and are sometimes used to justify intolerance.

Social Diversity

As cultural diversity refers mainly to distinct differences between groups of people, *social diversity* refers to individual differences covering the spectrum of all ethnic and cultural groups. Historically, social differences are more than just differences—they reflect advantages in privilege and status. Being male, or middle class, or heterosexual, or without disabilities affords access to opportunities and fulfillments denied those who do not fall in these privileged categories.

Diversity of gender implies more than biological or anatomical differences between girls and boys, women and men. Although we are born females or males, socialization shapes us. From birth, girls and boys are raised with cultural expectations about behaviors and roles. Girls and boys mostly internalize these expectations, with the implication that maleness equals strength and aggression and femaleness equals weakness and submission. Experience shows that these understandings are stereotypes. Yet, still today, the result of this socialization is often that men are considered and consider themselves superior, whereas women are seen and experience themselves as inferior.

Heterosexuality is the accepted norm for loving another person and living as a couple in this culture. It is also considered morally right, yet plainly not everybody is heterosexual. The discussion of *diversity of sexual orientation* is controversial at best. The fact is in schools that gay and lesbian "bashing" is very prevalent and often ignored. Diversity training, with a focus on promoting understanding and acceptance, should include lesbian and gay people as subjects of bias and prejudice. Because this issue is highly politicized, each school must respond respectfully to its many constituencies and their reactions. It takes wisdom to decide how and where and with what support these discussions can take place in a school.

Diversity of social class is yet another area where differences exist. A sense of privilege and entitlement often accompanies those who come from wealthy and upper middle class backgrounds, whereas poverty and lack of resources have adverse effects on self-esteem and sense of well being. Regardless of differences in ethnic background, culture, or gender, poverty is accompanied by "injuries of class." A wide bridge exists between students who take material possessions or enrichment opportunities (sports, music, the performing arts) for granted and those who may come to school without breakfast, lack stylish clothing and shoes, and are unable to afford enrichment activities. Class differences are potentially as conflictual as cultural differences, yet they are inseparable because people of color are disproportionately poor.

Diversity of physical/mental abilities is increasingly an issue for schools. Currently, students with physical or mental disabilities are part of mainstream schooling. The learning environment therefore has an increasing number of learners who need different tools, attention, and understanding. Students with disabilities are often subjected to ridicule, verbal harassment, and exclusion. Actual physical violence toward these students is not uncommon. Not only teachers, but also fellow students, must appreciate and respect this type of diversity.

RESPONSES TO DIVERSITY

In a diverse society, the challenge is to develop tolerance and acceptance of others who are different. Fortunately, we see an increase in school and community violence prevention programs that focus on tolerance and acceptance by teaching antiracism and multicultural understanding. However, education is only part of the challenge. People of color experience differential access to jobs, housing, education, physical safety, and representation in leadership and government. So do women, the elderly, gays and lesbians, and people with disabilities. When one group assumes superiority over others by creating structures supportive of that superiority, inequality in interpersonal treatment and societal opportunities is the result. This is termed *oppression* or *discrimination*. Oppression divides and separates groups along lines of status and influence. Most of us—as members of different groups—have experienced both the feeling of being in control and the feeling of being controlled. Perceived differences of control and influence that serve to separate people into groups involve bias and prejudice. All of us have learned biases in the form of "isms": As part of dominant groups we are raised to participate in racism, sexism, heterosexism, and so on. Yet many of us are also victims of "isms" and learn to live with the message that we are inferior and with acts of mistreatment. When people believe that they are to be blamed for failure or negative events, they have internalized their oppression.

Negative Reactions to Diversity

Many expressions are used to describe negative reactions to diversity. Part of understanding diversity is to become familiar with these terms and to reflect on them in light of one's own position and behavior.

Bias and *prejudice* are attitudes (beliefs, opinions) expressed in unreasonable and unjustifiable negative judgments about groups or individuals. These judgments are preconceived ideas, not based on knowledge or facts. Bias and prejudice are learned, often early in life, through exposure to derogatory language: "nigger," "redneck," "fag," "wetback." Through verbal slurs children learn to reject the people who are the targets of these comments. Prejudice can be understood as affecting interpersonal relationships, but it also can be institutional, therefore affecting treatment of larger groups of people.

Stereotypes are fixed notions or ideas about a person or group. Statements reflecting the ideas that girls are not mechanical, black women are strong, or Asians are smart are all stereotypes. Stereotypes do not allow consideration of variety or individuality.

Oppression is institutionalized abuse of privilege by groups or individuals toward other groups or individuals, often referred to as minority populations. White people have personal and institutional privileges that exclude people of color from opportunities. Men have personal and institutional privileges that exclude women from opportunities and freedoms. Similarly, we can look at hetero-sexual privileges and privileges for people who live without disabilities. Thus, people who lack the status, privileges, and opportunities claimed by the dominant group are oppressed.

Internalized oppression is a response to long-time oppression when victims of oppression turn their anger, guilt, shame, and frustration not only upon themselves but also upon their family members and other people in their ethnic group. They are made to feel inferior and often act this out against one another or members of the dominant group. The phenomenon of internalized oppression helps explain much violence in our schools.

Discrimination is a form of oppression that occurs when people from dominant groups or institutions act on the basis of bias or prejudice. Individuals or groups are prejudged and negatively or illegally treated by those in positions of authority. Discrimination occurs based on skin color, country of origin, gender, sexual orientation, or economic or disability status. Discrimination prevents many individuals and groups from full and equal participation in U.S. society and therefore underlies group separation and hostility.

Ethnocentrism is the tendency to value the familiar and predictable beliefs and behaviors of one's own group as correct and natural. The norms of the familiar group are used as a frame of reference for judging other groups. Ethnocentrism is mostly an unconscious and unexamined response to ethnic and cultural differences. Ethnocentric beliefs and behaviors are considered universally true. This implies that those who do not have similar beliefs and behaviors are "wrong" and that "those people" should think and act like us. For students it may seem natural to agree automatically with or help someone from their own cultural group, even to favor that person. The effect may be hostility and exclusion.

Racism is authority plus prejudice: It involves the authority (power or capability to force or impel) to act on prejudiced beliefs. Racism results in behaviors and policies that exclude, subordinate, or ridicule people of color. Racial tensions in schools can be very strong and are perceived differently by students of color and white students.

Anti-Semitism is personal and systemic mistreatment of Jews by non-Jews. Although not always in the public eye, anti-Semitic verbal slurs and hate crimes against Jews are not a thing of the past.

Sexism is the attitude (beliefs, opinions) that men are superior. Treatment of women reflects this bias. Yet times are changing, especially in interpersonal codes of conduct. Comments or actions that are offensive to women but pass as jokes or teasing can no longer be defended as such. These acts can be termed *sexual harassment*. Sexual harassment is any unwelcome attention that focuses on a student's or employee's sex, rather than on his or her status as a student or employee. It often occurs when there is force, intimidation, and abuse of privilege or status involved. Sexual harassment is inappropriate and often illegal.

Heterosexism is the attitude (beliefs, opinions) that favors heterosexuality as the norm. It excludes and marginalizes homosexuals in all aspects of life. *Homophobia* is the irrational fear and hatred of those who love and sexually desire someone of the same sex. The effects of heterosexism and homophobia are gay bashing, rejection, threats of loss of friends or employment, and, even worse, beatings, rape, and sometimes murder.

Classism is the attitude (beliefs, opinions) based on the assumption that affluence or property entitles one to feel and act superior. Classism deals with privileges that the rich enjoy but that are denied to poor people—for example, political access, social and legal justice, and educational and job opportunities.

Positive Reactions to Diversity

Just as negative reactions to diversity exist, so do positive reactions. The following terms describe some of these more positive approaches.

Antiracism deals with the recognition of intentional and systemic discrimination, mainly against people of color. Antiracist education deals with correcting omissions of the contributions of people of color, analyzing distortions and discriminatory conditions, and promoting goals of equity.

Equity speaks to efforts to gain equality for those discriminated against. It seeks equality of opportunity and access. It also deals with the justice system to correct discriminatory laws. In schools, equity programs are designed to remedy the effects of past discrimination. Because many barriers are embedded in discriminatory policies and practices, equity programs focus on awareness and identification of barriers and on activities to remove them.

Multiculturalism is a term used in programs and movements that seek recognition of the intrinsic value and significance of various cultural and ethnic groups. Ultimately, multiculturalism involves equality of status and opportunity for those who do not have a European background. The multicultural movement focuses on accepting and appreciating diversity, becoming aware of and promoting diverse points of view, and developing pride in ethnocultural identities and heritage.

In summary, diversity awareness involves understanding all the "isms." It also involves unlearning internalized oppression and unlearning bias and prejudice. Thus, diversity awareness goes beyond understanding cultural differences to achieve the goals of antiracism, equity, and multiculturalism. Achieving these goals requires work against bias, prejudice, and oppression on personal, interpersonal, and institutional levels.

INFLUENCE OF DIVERSITY ON THE MEDIATION PROCESS

With regard to the underlying reasons for student conflict, Cate Woolner (1990) remarks:

> The incident that brought the students into mediation may have been name-calling, pushing, stealing or any of the usual precipitating events. But the underlying issues were bias or prejudice, expressed as racism, classism, sexism, homophobia and ethnocentrism. (p. 1)

The strengths of mediation are the built-in respect for differences, the practice of being nonjudgmental, and the promotion of a new way of communicating. The desired result of mediation is respect, relationship building, acceptance, and behavior change. Mediation uses differences to facilitate creative solutions without requiring disputants to give up their own beliefs and values. Diversity conflicts therefore create opportunities to challenge bias and oppression as well as to increase awareness and understanding of cultural and personal differences.

Diversity issues potentially affect every mediation. Both mediators and disputants reflect a "diversity status"—that is, the values of their own cultural or identity group (class, gender, sexual orientation, disability status, etc.). For instance, what issues are raised when an African American male mediates a conflict between two white female disputants? What are the issues when a migrant Mexican American female mediator mediates between a Pentecostal Russian immigrant student and a Catholic European American student? How well would an openly gay student be received as a mediator or be treated as a disputant?

Diversity Issues for Mediation Training

Training mediators involves more than training in the steps of the mediation process. It involves unlearning "isms" through active inclusion of antibias and antiprejudice training. It also involves learning about cultural differences in values and communication styles. Because people from diverse cultural backgrounds may define and approach conflict differently, another issue in mediation involves working toward a common understanding of conflict and what constitutes resolution.

To unlearn the "isms," prospective mediators must challenge their own culturally influenced perceptions and expectations, practice inclusiveness, and respect differences. Therefore, training for diversity awareness must facilitate self-understanding, understanding of others, and action for social justice.

Knowledge of self

Diversity awareness is a process. It starts with self-knowledge. It takes willingness to examine one's own cultural or ethnic assumptions and biases. When people appreciate their own ethnic or cultural background, they are more likely to be aware of and accept different cultural backgrounds. In addition, to be appreciative of differences in gender, sexual orientation, and class or ability, students must have an openness and willingness to look at what it means to be a woman or man, gay or straight, rich or poor, able-bodied or disabled. It also means examining one's beliefs and actions and how they may inadvertently hurt, oppress, or otherwise contribute to discrimination. Honest self-examination leads to a reduction in bias and prejudice.

Knowledge of others: Appreciating diversity

To develop diversity awareness, it is important to learn about the different life-styles, beliefs, and practices of those who are different from us. Knowledge, rather than preconceived ideas, reduces bias and prejudice. As part of the school curriculum or at home, reading books or watching movies or documentaries can help students understand those who are different. One of the best ways to learn about others—what they believe and value and how they see their experiences—is to be in close contact with them. Making friends and venturing out of one's own comfortable place or group into the world of "strangers" can enhance understanding.

Learning to see the world through the eyes of those we want to learn about can be a life-changing experience. The school or community group can help to bring students together for activities and projects that build positive relationships. Within the curriculum, schools can help students learn to explore similarities and differences between individuals and groups, to appreciate these differences, and to connect these findings to their daily lives.

Creating a peaceful and just world: Action for social justice

There is a slogan "If you want peace, work for justice!" It means peace requires relationships that are free of domination and oppression and situations where resources are equitable. In a school situation, faculty and students must be recruited to take responsibility and invited to oppose prejudiced or racist behavior in others, as well as to address inequities in opportunities. This represents an active stance, a commitment to creating a school that truly respects and celebrates diversity.

Differences in Cultural Values and Communication Styles

Training for peer mediators should involve teaching them to approach diversity conflicts in a flexible way. Mediators dealing with students of color should not assume that these students necessarily share the mediator's (or the other disputant's) values. Further, mediation training enables the mediator to approach each disputant as an individual rather than assuming that the disputant possesses certain values based on the individual's ethnic group. The same is true for students who come from other culturally and socially diverse backgrounds.

Cultural values

Every cultural, ethnic, or identity group in our society socializes children to hold a certain set of values and express a certain set of behaviors. These values have to do with how we think about ourselves and others and our place in the world. The goal of mediation is not to change values but to explore them and encourage understanding and respect.

Some values are expressed in verbal and nonverbal communications. Most values and behaviors can be seen on a continuum and generalized to cultural and personal traits (see Figure 1). As we interact with one another, we behave according to these values. Certain ethnic and cultural groups, as a whole, may fall on the extremes of this continuum, but individuals from these groups may vary considerably in the expression of these traits.

Conflicts arise when we expect others to conform to what is the norm for us—in other words, when we are ethnocentric. If we know where we fit on the continuum shown in Figure 1, we may be able to understand our own position better and therefore better understand others' positions. Such knowledge may also help mediators explain differing values and clarify how they affect behavior.

Communication styles

Each culture has different norms for verbal and nonverbal communication. The following discussion will address some differences in verbal and nonverbal communication that may affect mediation. The training activities in chapters 7 and 8 pose questions to help mediators discuss these points.

Differences in *verbal communication* play a role in each mediation. Expectations of gender, class, and ethnic background affect fluency of verbal communication. One special consideration applies to students who speak English as a second language. Depending on their fluency, students who are not used to communicating in English have a disadvantage over native English speakers. They may be considered less intelligent or less able to understand, or they may be viewed as

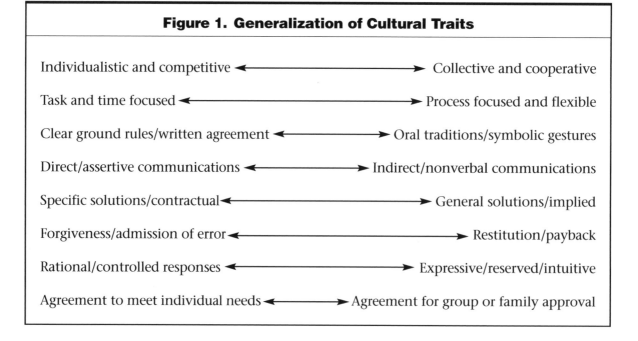

Figure 1. Generalization of Cultural Traits

Individualistic and competitive ←——————→ Collective and cooperative

Task and time focused ←——————→ Process focused and flexible

Clear ground rules/written agreement ←——————→ Oral traditions/symbolic gestures

Direct/assertive communications ←——————→ Indirect/nonverbal communications

Specific solutions/contractual ←——————→ General solutions/implied

Forgiveness/admission of error ←——————→ Restitution/payback

Rational/controlled responses ←——————→ Expressive/reserved/intuitive

Agreement to meet individual needs ←——————→ Agreement for group or family approval

being unable to contribute ideas. Conflict and misunderstanding may not be easy for these students to express because different languages may not have comparable words for certain feelings or observations and because translation of feelings sometimes falls short in terms of accuracy.

Differences in *nonverbal communication* also occur between cultures. In white cultures, making eye contact is a sign of paying attention and respect to the speaker. Not making eye contact is often interpreted as a lack of interest, defensiveness, or disrespect. In many nonwhite cultures, however, direct eye contact connotes disrespect. Avoiding eye contact is seen as respectful of the other person's right to privacy, whereas staring at another person is understood as wanting to gain control.

In white cultures, long silences often make people feel uncomfortable. Silence often is interpreted as being unfriendly, and the person who does not speak is seen as withdrawn and passive. In many nonwhite cultures, silence is respectful—it gives people time to think about what is said and can help maintain privacy. Therefore, silence is not experienced as uncomfortable.

In white cultures, shaking hands when closing on a deal or reaching a solution to a conflict confirms the agreement. In some nonwhite cultures, a taboo may exist against women's shaking hands with men, or this ritual may mean something different to one of the disputants. In addition, in white cultures, handshakes are firm, conveying self-assurance and trust. In other cultures, handshakes are more gentle—just a touch of hands rather than a strong grasp. A limp handshake may be interpreted as weak or frightened by people from white cultures, whereas a strong handshake may be interpreted as domineering by people from nonwhite cultures.

White cultures tend to be contractual worlds, worlds of written agreement. When things are written down, they are settled. Nonwhite cultures may rely on words as a binding agreement and find a written contract demeaning or expressing a lack of trust.

Other aspects of nonverbal communication, perceived differently by different groups, include emotional expression, personal space, and voice level. Some cultures value strong outward expression of feelings, whereas others teach self-containment. Whereas in white cultures people keep at an arm's length to maintain comfortable conversational space, other cultures permit closer proximity. In addition, in some cultures it is considered disrespectful and a sign of anger to raise one's voice, whereas in other cultures raising one's voice simply indicates animation and involvement in the conversation.

It is important not to assume that all cultures interpret nonverbal signals in the same way; doing so can lead to inaccurate judgments. It takes sensitivity, practice, and sometimes clarification to unravel the meaning of nonverbal communication.

Meaning of conflict

In white cultures, conflicts are dealt with rationally and directly. Resolving misunderstanding, admitting errors, and/or making up for mistreatment is the goal. When the goal is achieved, the conflict is seen as resolved. Individuals from nonwhite cultures sometimes prefer to avoid dealing directly with a conflict. In addition, conflicts may be seen not just as individual disputes but as involving the honor of the whole family, group, or gang. When disputants value group relationships and harmony, they may choose not to disclose hurt or mistreatment.

Guilt versus shame

In white cultures, people feel personally guilty when they engage in inappropriate or unacceptable behavior: They have violated their conscience. Discussing and resolving the conflict relieves these individuals from guilt. The relationship is restored.

In nonwhite cultures, inappropriate or unacceptable behavior may violate the honor of the family and bring shame not only to the offender but to the whole family. Willingness to mediate (in other words, to bring a conflict to the knowledge of a third person) therefore may not be a favorable option. If mediation takes place, solutions must include actions that satisfy the whole family.

How people perceive conflicts and what reactions conflicts evoke affect the mediation process and its outcome. Mediation will be more successful when mediators understand these aspects of diversity conflicts.

Special Concerns for Mediators

As discussed previously, diversity disputes involve, to a large extent, imbalance of privilege or advantage between disputants. Students of color and students belonging to other nonmajority groups generally have less social status or verbal skills and are disadvantaged when involved in a conflict with students who belong to the dominant group. Therefore, the mediator must pay particular attention to helping the less advantaged person get her or his needs met. This does not necessarily change a mediator's neutral stance or the equal respect the mediator gives to each disputant. It does mean that the mediator is flexible and exercises wise control to influence the process—specifically, with regard to trust building and use of time, when and what kind of interventions to make, the use of caucusing, and involvement of others.

Trust building

Trust building plays an important part in the success of mediation. The mediator should keep in mind that trust is promoted through positive experiences and information. When diversity conflicts involve a disputant who is somehow disadvantaged, is discriminated against, or experiences "underdog" status, the building of trust and respect is especially important. For instance, mediators may help negotiate disputes that involve gangs, "skinheads," or students belonging to strict religious groups. They may also work with disputants who belong to groups that have been invisible or silenced: students with certain disabilities, extreme loners, or gay or lesbian students who have just "come out." In such cases the process may take more time for one or both disputants to open up, get to the point, feel listened to, or trust that the process will work. Mediators should reinterpret resistance as a coping skill and part of the process of learning trust.

Mediators must also learn that hostility may not be directed at them personally but is instead part of a learned distrust for rules and agreements. Coming to a resolution may require more than one session.

Flexible interventions

In cases where there is inequality in perceived advantage, the mediator may need to be more directive in enhancing understanding. The following interventions may be helpful:

- ▼ Reminding parties that attacks or put-downs are counterproductive to resolution

- ▼ Actively clarifying misconceptions by providing information about possible cultural or other diversity issues

- ▼ Interrupting intimidating behavior and language

- ▼ Reframing statements to prevent disputants from losing face

- ▼ Encouraging disputants to challenge their assumptions

- ▼ Helping disputants confront statements and behaviors and not the other person

- ▼ Suggesting options for resolution

- ▼ Providing affirmation of the process

- ▼ Empowering each disputant to take control and responsibility

- ▼ Encouraging sharing of knowledge, expertise, and information

- ▼ Treating each disputant with equal respect and attention

Caucusing

Another procedure to enhance trust is caucusing, or meeting separately with each disputant. Caucusing reduces anxiety when inequality may be a barrier for resolution. The one-on-one forum is useful for explaining the process, providing an opportunity for disputants to ask questions, and discussing concerns in a nonthreatening atmosphere. Repeating caucusing during a mediation session may further increase respect for the process and assure the disputants that they are being heard.

Involvement of others

To promote understanding of the process or the differences that led to the conflict, the mediator may consider possible involvement of others. This may be especially important when a mediator identifies cultural or other barriers to solutions. The mediator can explore with each disputant whether he or she considers it desirable for others to be involved. Possible candidates include a friend, a non-school support person, or a family member.

Involvement of others may also be important in cases where the likelihood of nonresolution is high. For instance, when one of the disputants is expected by his or her family or peers to take revenge, involving those family members or peers may be necessary to establish a durable resolution.

In conclusion, diversity conflicts are complex because they involve bias and prejudice related to cultural and social differences as well as unequal distribution of assets, privileges, and opportunities. Conflict resolution programs are well suited to challenge inequities and to promote tolerance and acceptance through learning new ways to communicate. Mediators who face the complexity of diversity conflicts need training in the influence of diversity on the mediation process. This involves understanding the diversity status of both mediators and disputants, as well as being aware of different cultural values affecting communication styles and interpretation of conflicts. Understanding how diversity issues affect each mediation helps mediators address and confront bias and inequality.

CHAPTER 5

INTRODUCTION TO PEER MEDIATION

Peer mediation is a method for negotiating disputes and finding resolutions that combines the needs of the parties in conflict instead of compromising those needs. It is a way for students to deal with differences without coercion. Peer mediation works well to resolve conflict in schools because through it students gain power and learn responsibility. The more students become empowered to resolve their differences peacefully, the more responsibly they behave.

Peer mediation is voluntary. A student may request mediation when he or she is involved in a dispute, or a mediation between students may be requested by teachers, administrators, other school staff members, or parents. When both of the disputing parties agree to mediate, arrangements are made for an assigned mediator to meet with them.

ROLE OF THE PEER MEDIATOR

The mediation process is a step-by-step method that requires flexibility and spontaneity according to each situation. The peer mediator's role throughout the process is proactive—that is, the mediator is responsible for creating and maintaining an atmosphere that fosters cooperative, collaborative problem solving.

During a mediation session, the mediator follows a prescribed procedure. In doing so, the mediator custom tailors that procedure to fit each circumstance by deciding how to allocate time to a person or a particular issue and by determining what questions to ask in order to gather and use information. These decisions, within the framework of the mediation process, direct the flow of the mediation. It is the mediator's role to monitor the communication between disputants constantly and vigilantly to maintain a balanced exchange.

To build cooperation, the mediator works to achieve the following goals.

The peer mediator remains impartial.   The mediator must be neutral and objective and avoid taking sides. In addition, the mediator must be aware of his or her personal biases and work to keep them from distorting perceptions of people and situations.

The peer mediator listens with empathy. Effective communication skills are essential to mediation and influence each step of the process. Often the problem is clouded by issues in the relationship—emotions run high, unfounded inferences are treated as fact, and blaming focuses attention on past actions. Effective use of communication skills helps people acknowledge emotions and clarify perceptions, enabling them to better understand and work on the problem. The peer mediator uses the following active listening communication skills throughout the process:

▼ *Attending,* or using nonverbal behaviors to indicate that what the disputants are saying and feeling is of interest and has been understood. These nonverbal behaviors may include tone of voice, eye contact, facial expressions, posture, and gestures.

▼ *Summarizing,* or restating facts by repeating the most important points, organizing interests, and discarding extraneous information. In summarizing, the mediator also acknowledges emotions by explicating the feelings each person is experiencing.

▼ *Clarifying,* or using open-ended questions and statements to obtain more information in order to ensure understanding.

The peer mediator is respectful. The mediator is able to treat both parties with respect and understanding, and without prejudice. Being respectful means that the mediator understands a person's emotions and beliefs. A key to respect is knowing and accepting that we are all different.

The peer mediator is trustworthy. If students are to value the process, the mediator must build trust and confidence in the process. Disputants must be assured, through the actions of the mediator, that the mediation is not just another contrivance to tell them what to do—they will be allowed to author their own resolution to the problem. The mediator must also exercise the integrity to uphold confidentiality by keeping information from the mediation private. A mediator does not discuss the disputants or their problem with peers.

The peer mediator helps people work together. The mediator is responsible for the mediation process, not the solution to the problem. The solution to the problem is the responsibility of the disputants. When both parties cooperate, they are able to find their own solutions.

PREPARING FOR PEER MEDIATION

The proper physical arrangement is important to facilitate communication. Equality of equipment and positioning should be considered so that no party is at an auditory, visual, physical, or psychological disadvantage. With the proper preparations, the peer mediator demonstrates a sense of control and provides a secure climate in which the parties are able to work toward an agreement.

The ideal arrangement is for the disputants to sit facing each other across a table. The mediator sits at the head of the table between the parties and preferably nearest the exit. (Having the mediator sit nearest the exit subtly discourages either party from leaving the room.) When co-mediators are employed, it is best for them to sit side by side.

The mediator should prepare all necessary forms before the session begins and have ready any other materials that might be used—for example, pens, pencils, paper, easel pad.

Co-Mediators or Single Mediator

Mediation is a complex problem-solving process that must be tailored to each problem. Mediation is a comprehensive, interactive, often unpredictable affair. Mediators are required to facilitate a specific process but simultaneously must adapt that process, often in multiple ways, to enable the disputants to continue to cooperate to solve the problem. The mediator is required to pay close attention to maintain the essence of the process because the process guarantees that the principles of conflict resolution are addressed. Doing so requires the mediator's constant effort to evaluate the proceedings, make judgments about the most facilitative course of action, and act in a decisive manner—all this while also self-monitoring for allegiance to the process. For these and the following reasons, it is wise to consider using a co-mediation format in a school mediation program:

▼ Two trained mediators working together as a team provide mutual support and comfort. This may be especially valuable when programs are first initiated.

▼ Following a mediation, team members can provide each other with constructive feedback about ways to improve their mediation skills.

▼ Co-mediation is helpful in achieving a quality process because the mediators share responsibility for monitoring the mediation process and facilitating the specific problem solving.

▼ Forming co-mediation teams to match differing strengths in the two mediators provides for a potentially more successful mediation. Teams might be formed that combine a less experienced mediator and a more experienced mediator, thus providing an "on-the-job" learning opportunity. Teams pairing different genders, races, or cultures can show sensitivity and provide comfort to disputants.

In co-mediation, the team fulfills the same function as the single mediator. The team does not "divvy up" the disputants, one disputant for each mediator. It is most effective when the student co-mediators alternate being the leader for the steps in the process. In other words, one member of the team acts as facilitator of Steps 1, 3, and 5 while the other team member monitors the procedure and assists the teammate as needed. The mediators' responsibilities are reversed for Steps 2, 4, and 6.

Single mediators have been most successful at the secondary level. A well-trained and experienced single mediator can do an excellent job. Whether a single mediator or co-mediators are used, it is important that adult support during the mediation session be available to the mediators if needed.

The steps in the peer mediation process are as follows:

▼ Step 1: Agree to Mediate

▼ Step 2: Gather Points of View

▼ Step 3: Focus on Interests

▼ Step 4: Create Win-Win Options

▼ Step 5: Evaluate Options

▼ Step 6: Create an Agreement

Step 1: Agree to Mediate

An effective opening is very important in achieving a positive outcome in mediation. The opening sets the tone for the session and establishes that the peer mediator is in charge. The mediator begins the session by making introductions and welcoming the disputants to mediation. The mediator then makes a statement defining mediation. The opening statement defining mediation conveys the fact that the mediator's role is to help the disputants reach their own solution to the problem. Next, the mediator states the ground rules designed to facilitate the process:

▼ Mediators remain neutral; they do not take sides.

▼ Mediation is private.

▼ Take turns talking and listening.

▼ Cooperate to solve the problem.

Disputants are asked individually whether they agree to abide by these ground rules and to mediate. Mediation is an agreed-upon process, requiring consent by each party. The consent is to cooperate to solve the problem. Although rare, it is possible to cooperate and still not solve the problem. However, resolution can never take place without cooperation.

The ground rules, stated as positive behaviors, help structure a win-win climate by establishing the goal of reaching an agreement considerate of both parties. The mediator will likely need to restate the ground rules occasionally, reminding the disputants that they began the process with the desire to cooperate to reach a resolution and that the ground rules must be followed in order to do that. If at any point the disputants indicate a lack of desire to cooperate, the mediation ends. To reiterate, cooperation may not yield a solution, but no solution is possible in the absence of cooperation. In other words, willingness to cooperate is an enabling, necessary condition.

Step 2: Gather Points of View

The purpose of this step is to ascertain each disputant's point of view about the incident or situation and to allow the disputants to hear each other's points of view.

The peer mediator gathers information about points of view by first asking one disputant to tell what happened. The mediator then summarizes this disputant's point of view, checking to see if what was heard was what the disputant intended. The mediator next asks the other disputant to tell what happened. Again, the mediator summarizes the point of view expressed.

The mediator then asks each disputant in turn for additional comments about the conflict and continues to do so until all the important information has been stated. Each time a disputant offers a statement, the peer mediator summarizes what was heard before seeking a statement from the other disputant. In this exchange, the peer mediator is attempting to ensure that the information has been accurately heard and that each disputant is aware of major issues and the other's perceptions. As needed, the mediator seeks clarification by asking questions such as "What did you think when that happened?" "Explain more about that," and "What else happened?"

While gathering points of view, the mediator must validate the concerns and feelings of each disputant as well as clarify the history and sequence of events. When the mediator acknowledges the messages expressed and demonstrates an accurate perception of the problem, the disputants know they have been understood. This builds trust and encourages a constructive dialogue about the problem.

Step 3: Focus on Interests

In this most crucial step, the peer mediator helps the disputants identify their underlying interests. Often the disputants in a conflict are locked into their respective, rigid positions. The mediator asks them to look behind their opposing positions by asking, "What do you want, and why do you want that?" The *what* is the position; the *why* is the interest. At this point disputants discover that they share certain interests or that their interests, even if different, are compatible. By focusing on shared or compatible interests, the peer mediator helps the disputants fashion a resolution that preserves these commonalties. From this base of understanding and cooperation the disputants can seek fair ways to resolve their conflicting interests.

The peer mediator helps the disputants discover these common interests by asking such questions as "What do you really want?" "If you were in the other person's shoes, how would you feel? What would you think?" and "What might happen if you don't reach an agreement?"

During this questioning process, the mediator continues to practice active listening by summarizing the interests of each person. The mediator makes common interests explicit and formulates them as mutual goals. This is important because the disputants are likely still focusing on their differences. The mediator directs their attention to the commonalties with statements like "Both of you seem to agree that _____ ."

Underlying interests serve as the building blocks for the resolution. If they are not disclosed, there is little chance of reaching an agreement both sides can keep. The mediator does not move on to the next step until interests are identified. This is often the most challenging step in the process.

The peer mediator, as a result of the mediation training, understands that common interests are connected to the basic psychological needs for belonging, power, freedom, and fun. The mediator looks for basic needs to identify common interests. For example, students who appear very upset with each other may still want to be friends—or at least not be enemies if being enemies will continue to get them into trouble. Similarly, very few individuals would reject an opportunity to gain acknowledgment or respect from another person.

Step 4: Create Win-Win Options

Creating options involves *brainstorming*. This brainstorming step, designed to produce as many ideas as possible, helps individuals solve problems creatively—one idea usually stimulates another. Because evaluation hinders creativity, the process of generating options is separate from the processes of evaluating options and from creating an agreement.

At this stage, the disputants are not attempting to determine the best solution. Instead, they are inventing options upon which both sides can build and from which they can jointly choose in the next step of the process. A good agreement addresses the interests of both parties in the dispute, fairly resolves those issues in conflict, and has the potential to last. Such an agreement is more likely when a variety of options exist. Without brainstorming, disputants often are faced with choosing between two ideas: one that satisfies one disputant, the other that satisfies the other disputant.

To begin the brainstorming, the peer mediator explains that the purpose is to generate ideas and that it is helpful to follow specific rules to do so:

▼ Say any ideas that come to mind.

▼ Do not judge or discuss the ideas.

▼ Come up with as many ideas as possible.

▼ Try to think of unusual ideas.

The mediator asks the disputants to look for ideas that will address the interests of both. As necessary, the mediator helps the brainstorming process along by asking questions such as "What other possibilities can you think of?" and "In the future, what could you do differently?"

The mediator may need to remind the disputants of the common interests identified in Step 3 by saying, "You both agreed that you want *(common interest).*

What ideas would help that to happen?" The mediator also helps the disputants follow the brainstorming rules and not judge ideas, recording the ideas as the disputants generate them. Recording ideas in a way disputants may see them (on an easel pad, for example) can help stimulate other ideas and promote cooperative problem solving.

Step 5: Evaluate Options

In this step, the peer mediator asks the disputants to choose, from the list of options previously generated, the ideas or parts of ideas they think are fair and have the best possibility of working. The mediator circles the ideas each disputant suggests.

The disputants' task at this stage is to act as side-by-side problem solvers, evaluating and improving the circled options. The mediator may ask the following types of questions: "Is this option fair?" "Can you do it?" "Do you think it will work?" "What are the consequences of deciding to do this?" and "Does this option address the interests of everyone involved?"

Step 6: Create an Agreement

Once the disputants have discussed the various options, the peer mediator asks them together to make a plan of action deciding what they will do. When the disputants come to an agreement, the mediator helps them check to see whether it is sound—in other words, whether the agreement is balanced, specific, realistic, lasting, and fair. The mediator seeks clarification about the agreement and the plan to implement the agreement by asking each disputant to summarize the specifics of the plan: who, what, when, where, how. If the disputants do not accurately state the agreement, the mediator clarifies: "I thought I heard you agree to _____."

Following statement of the agreement, the peer mediator asks, "Is the problem solved?" Upon obtaining an affirmative response, the mediator finalizes the commitment. The commitment could be a handshake between the disputants, a written agreement, or both. In secondary school programs, a written agreement is recommended. It is prepared by the peer mediator on a standard agreement form. The form provides a brief, clear expression of the plan of action to which the students have agreed.

When the agreement is written, the mediator reads it aloud and asks if it expresses the intent of both students. The disputants and the mediator then sign the agreement. If problems arise after mediation, a well-written agreement can clarify issues and support the disputants' intentions at the time of mediation.

To close the session, the mediator shakes hands with both parties, thanks them for bringing their dispute to mediation, congratulates them for working to reach an agreement, and invites them to return to mediation if any problems develop in carrying out the agreement or if they have other conflicts, either between themselves or with others. The mediator may invite the disputants to shake hands with each other.

Caucusing, a private and independent meeting with each disputant, is rarely necessary in peer mediation. However, it can be a useful tool in situations where disputants are not communicating effectively and resolution appears doubtful.

Caucusing can be used at any point in the mediation process; it may be employed more than once or not used at all. The peer mediator decides whether or not a caucus is advisable. If a caucus is necessary, the mediator caucuses with each disputant independently. If a co-mediation is in process, the co-mediators meet as a team with each disputant. Before the mediation session is reconvened, the mediator(s) and disputant need a clear understanding regarding what information the disputant does and does not want revealed: All information disclosed during the caucus is confidential unless the disputant agrees that the information may be divulged.

The caucus might be used for the following specific purposes:

▼ To gain agreement to mediate when the parties seem reluctant to do so

▼ To allow for face-saving by disputants and to address different levels of understanding of the purpose of mediation

▼ To uncover information or clarify details that disputants may be willing to reveal only in private

▼ To move beyond an impasse

▼ To deal with issues of diversity or reduce tensions between disputants

▼ To explore options, especially consequences, that might not be obvious

▼ To help disputants understand the benefits of cooperating to reach an agreement—that is, to understand their BATNAs (Fisher et al., 1991; see chapter 3)

▼ To allow disputants time alone to think and reflect

▼ To allow disputants time to cool off

▼ To build trust in the peer mediator and/or the mediation process

DEALING WITH POTENTIAL PROBLEMS

A peer mediation program requires adult involvement and adult commitment. With consistent and supportive adult supervision, a peer mediation program will grow and improve as the mediators gain experience. Educators often anticipate problems with a peer mediation program, only to be surprised by not seeing those problems materialize or by discovering that the problems are not serious impediments. The common problems next described may arise, however. These can be viewed in the spirit of conflict resolution as opportunities for program growth.

Students misuse the process

One concern is that students will take advantage of peer mediation in a number of ways: Perhaps they will make up problems to get out of class. Perhaps they will not be truthful in the mediation. Perhaps they will create agreements just to end the mediation and then continue the dispute after the session is over.

Peer mediation is a very difficult process to abuse, however. If students are not committed to the process, this quickly becomes clear to the trained mediator during the session. Even if students begin with the intention of misusing peer mediation, they often discover that their interests are best served by trying to get what they want through the process. As for lying, students have no more reason to lie in mediation than they do in any disciplinary forum. In fact, because mediation is private, young people may be more likely to be honest, and student abuse of mediation is a minor problem (Cohen, 1995). Instead, experience has shown that students afford respect to the process, perhaps because it suggests that they are able to solve their own problems instead of being told what to do by an adult.

A student makes numerous requests for peer mediation

The student who repeatedly requests peer mediation could lack the social skills to interact appropriately with peers or could be using mediation to obtain individual attention. Although the student might profit from the mediation experience, mediation alone cannot address the student's underlying issues or serious lack of social skills. An adult involved in the program should assess the problem. Perhaps referring the student to a counselor or social worker for specific social-emotional counseling is appropriate. Perhaps the adult will decide that the student may participate in a specific, limited number of mediations.

More than two students request peer mediation

Mediation is a problem-solving process between two parties. Peer mediation works best when limited to the two students who have experienced the original problem. There may be times when small groups request peer mediation and times when one or both disputants will insist that others need to be involved. Generally, conducting a mediation between numerically unequal sides is not recommended. If such is the nature of the problem, it is best to conduct two or more separate mediations. Mediations involving more than four students, even if there is numerical balance for the opposing sides, are best handled by using the group problem solving format (see chapter 8). The adult coordinator is responsible for identifying the two students at the core of what appears to be a conflict between groups or for choosing a process other than mediation to problem solve.

Disputants hold to their positions

Peer mediators are trained to deal with this likelihood and can usually move disputants beyond arguing for their separate positions. Generally, the first 8 to 12 minutes of a mediation session will indicate whether a resolution can be

55

reached. When disputants appear unwilling to cooperate after this period of time, the mediator can exercise several options. The mediator might ask the participants to table the mediation until another time when they might be more prepared to cooperate, suggesting that until such time disputants agree to a truce. The mediator might choose to use caucusing. During separate caucuses, the mediator can ask each disputant if he or she still wishes to mediate and what might happen if the conflict is not resolved. As a last resort, the session can be terminated; the peer mediator would report to the adult supervisor that the mediation has not resulted in a resolution of the conflict.

Disputants violate ground rules

Disputants will very likely have strong feelings about the conflict, and those feelings may be expressed as anger or frustration. Such expression may occur as interruptions, name-calling, put-downs, threats, or other uncooperative behaviors. Mediators are trained to understand that strong emotions often are expressed in conflict situations and that the emotional response of one party may trigger a similar response in the other party. Mediators are trained to enforce the ground rules by reminding the disputants that they have previously agreed to follow those rules. If the reminders are too frequent or are ignored, a short break or caucusing might be necessary. It is important for disputants to state their feelings in an appropriate way, so as to allow others to understand those feelings. Additional ideas for understanding and dealing with anger are presented in chapter 8.

Tempers flare or emotions intensify

Educators are often concerned that students, alone but for the company of their peers, will become angry and begin fighting with each other during the mediation session. Although anything is possible, this has not generally been a problem. Fighting is unlikely in large part because numerous preventive measures are built into the process: cooling-off periods before mediations are held, rules about violence, choice of mediators who will be respected, and so on. In addition, there is usually an adult either in the room or right outside during the session. If anything, students usually become impressively calm, considered, and even respectful of each other during the course of most mediation sessions (Cohen, 1995). Verbal or physical threats are also unlikely but possible. Loud talk may occur. Mediators are trained to deal with these behaviors.

Agreement is not reached

Although rare, sometimes agreement will not be reached. Most programs report about an 85 to 90% rate in obtaining agreements (Cohen, 1995). It is important that peer mediators not feel they have failed if agreement is not reached. The agreement is the responsibility of the disputants. The mediators are responsible for the process designed to give the disputants the best chance to resolve their conflict. Even an attempted mediation can be a positive experience because the two people in the conflict will have communicated their thoughts and feelings about a problem. This in itself is a step toward mutual understanding and resolution. Further, mediators can advise the disputants that they are welcome to try mediation again at any time in the future.

The agreement is broken

Mediators are trained that it is better not to come up with an agreement than to let the parties create one that will not work. A broken agreement might mean that the mediation was incomplete because issues or interests existed that were not revealed or fully explored. Perhaps the parties are being affected by circumstances other than those anticipated when the agreement was made. Even agreements made in good faith are sometimes not finalized. Whatever the reason an agreement is not consummated, as long as the disputants are willing, the dispute can be brought back to mediation. A second mediation under these circumstances will usually produce a successful resolution. If for some reason agreements do break down, the school has all of its other resources available to handle the situation.

Privacy is violated

It is important that trust be established in the mediation process. Mediators are trained to maintain confidentiality by not talking about the mediation or the disputants with peers. However, issues may surface in a mediation session that mediators must not keep confidential. A peer mediator must report to an adult supervisor any evidence of or threats of physical harm from the disputants to self or others. Any evidence of illegal activity or weapons must also be reported. Rather than describe the mediation process as truly confidential, some would call the process private. An exception to privacy is made for any of the reasons just stated. Beyond these, the mediator keeps the proceedings private. The mediator decides with the disputants what will be said outside the session, if anything. It is often useful to suggest that it is acceptable for the disputants to tell others that an agreement has been reached and even to share what has been agreed upon, but not to discuss the details of the problem.

Two groups of students are in conflict

Many times two or more groups of students are in conflict. These groups could be formal clubs or organizations or informal cliques, even gangs. The mediation process described here is not appropriate for these disputes, but the similar process of group problem solving may be used to resolve multiparty disputes. Although time-intensive and dependent upon highly skilled facilitators, this process can be very effective. Group problem solving is presented as an advanced skill in chapter 8.

A student requests a mediation with a teacher

When a peer mediation program is established, it is not uncommon for a student to request a mediation with a teacher. Although generally the program is designed for peer-peer disputes, some teachers might welcome the opportunity to participate with a student, either at the student's or the teacher's request. If some adults find the process threatening or view participation as a loss of their authority, their views must be respected. As noted previously, mediation is a voluntary process; if one of the two parties is unwilling, a mediation cannot be conducted. If both parties agree, a co-mediation model involving one student and one staff mediator might be used for a student-adult mediation.

CHAPTER 6

PROGRAM ORGANIZATION & OPERATION

The design, implementation, and operation of a peer mediation program can be viewed as taking place in six developmental phases. Phase 1 involves creating and training of the conflict resolution program team, designating program coordinator(s), conducting a needs assessment, and building faculty consensus for program development. Phase 2 develops timelines for implementation, establishes an advisory committee, develops policies and procedures (including the role of mediation within the school discipline program), and identifies and develops funding sources. Phase 3 encompasses recruiting peer mediator applications and nominations, then selecting and training student mediators. Phase 4 focuses on educating a critical mass of the school population about conflict, conflict resolution, and the mediation process via workshops for staff, students, parents, and community. Phase 5 consists of developing and executing a promotional campaign. Phase 6 encompasses every aspect of program operation and maintenance: request for mediation, scheduling mediations and mediators, supervising mediators, recording mediation data, providing ongoing training and support, and evaluating the program. These six developmental phases, outlined in Table 4, can be readily adapted to serve the varying needs and interests of almost any school.

The remainder of this chapter describes these developmental phases in more detail and offers a number of sample forms useful in planning, implementing, and evaluating a peer mediation program. Necessary forms, presented as figures here, are reproduced for program use in Appendix A.

PHASE 1: DEVELOP PROGRAM TEAM
AND COMMITMENT TO PROGRAM

Create Program Team

A peer mediation program will succeed only if it is perceived to be need fulfilling by both staff and students. Formulating a leadership group comprised of administrators, classroom teachers, special educators, counselors, deans, social workers, and health educators who have an interest in developing a conflict resolution program within the school will provide the broad-based coalition necessary to build a need-fulfilling program. Additional choices for team membership include

Table 4. Phases in Developing and Establishing a Peer Mediation Program

Phase 1: Develop Program Team and Commitment to Program

▼ Create program team

▼ Train program team

▼ Designate program coordinator(s)

▼ Conduct needs assessment

▼ Build faculty consensus for program development

Phase 2: Design and Plan Program

▼ Develop implementation timeline

▼ Establish advisory committee

▼ Develop policies and procedures

▼ Identify and develop funding sources

Phase 3: Select and Train Mediators

▼ Conduct student orientation

▼ Select peer mediators

▼ Train peer mediators

▼ Recognize peer mediators

Phase 4: Educate a Critical Mass of the School Population

▼ Conduct staff inservice

▼ Conduct student workshops

▼ Provide family and community orientation

▼ Offer parent workshops

Phase 5: Develop and Execute Promotional Campaign

▼ Design and implement initial campaign

▼ Conduct ongoing promotional efforts

Phase 6: Operate and Maintain the Program

▼ Develop process for requesting mediation

▼ Schedule mediations and mediators

▼ Supervise mediation sessions

▼ Provide mediators with ongoing training and support

▼ Evaluate program

parents, students, and community members. The program team initiates the conflict resolution program and eventually will be charged with eliciting the support of the entire school staff for program development. Specifically, the program team's charge includes the following:

1. Designating program coordinators

2. Conducting a needs assessment

3. Building faculty consensus for program development and support

4. Developing policies and procedures

5. Determining the role of mediation within the school discipline program

6. Developing awareness of and support for the program among students, families, and community

7. Selecting and training peer mediators

Train Program Team

Once the program team has been formed, the next step is building their capacity to develop a quality peer mediation program. In order to become informed decision makers, effective implementers, and strong advocates for the program, program team members require training. In training program team members, it is beneficial to use the same model and resources used for training students and other staff. Because the program team will be responsible for the supervision and training of student mediators, they need training in both content areas (such as the principles of conflict resolution and mediation) and techniques or methods for mediation training.

Basic training typically ranges from 2 to 4 days, with approximately 6 contact hours per day. Such training covers the following content:

1. Understanding conflict

2. Principles of conflict resolution

3. Social and cultural diversity and conflict resolution

4. Mediation process and skills

5. Program organization and operation

6. Role of peer mediation in the school

7. Rationale for peer mediation

It is important for those who train students to have had actual mediation experience. Mediation is not something that can be learned by reading a book or following a step-by-step curriculum guide. Skilled mediators make a number of astute and consequential decisions during the course of the mediation process, based on their ability to apply the principles of conflict resolution. Unskilled mediators follow the six-step process without much discretion. Becoming a skilled mediator requires simulated and real mediation experiences with the guided feedback of skilled mediation trainers. Therefore, it is important for the team to be involved in mediation training and to continue to seek opportunities to increase their own skill level.

Designate Program Coordinator(s)

The effectiveness of the peer mediation program is strongly linked to the quality of the effort put forth by the program coordinator(s). The coordinator(s) are responsible for the ongoing organization and operation of the peer mediation program and, most importantly, must personify the conflict resolution principles they promote. Program coordinator(s) may be designated on the basis of interest, flexibility, commitment, and ability to lead both faculty and students. There are many approaches to coordinating peer mediation programs, ranging from an individual coordinator to various faculty combinations of co-coordinators. Some options to consider in designating peer mediation coordinator(s) include the following:

1. School social worker and school counselor co-coordinate.

2. Suspension room teacher and health education teacher co-coordinate.

3. Deans share coordination responsibilities.

4. Assistant principal coordinates with various teachers assigned to specific supervision times.

5. A peer mediation coordinator with no other assignments takes on the role.

Funding is typically the leading factor in deciding whether to employ a peer mediation coordinator or to designate the responsibilities to other faculty members within the school. Programs can function effectively whether people are employed for the sole purpose of program coordination or existing faculty integrate these responsibilities with their other professional duties.

Specific responsibilities of the program coordinator(s) are as follows:

1. Facilitating the program team in their efforts to design and plan the peer mediation program

2. Planning and conducting orientation sessions for faculty, students, families, and community

3. Coordinating the selection of peer mediators

4. Establishing and facilitating the advisory council

5. Coordinating training of students

6. Promoting the program

7. Receiving requests for mediation

8. Scheduling mediators and mediations

9. Arranging for supervision of mediators

10. Collecting mediation data

11. Providing for ongoing mediator training and support

12. Facilitating ongoing communication with the program team

13. Developing parent and community participation

14. Evaluating the program

Conduct Needs Assessment

To move beyond the individual efforts of staff members toward school-community support for a conflict resolution program, a needs assessment is helpful. Such an assessment can determine the specific nature of the need for conflict resolution in the school and identify the resources already available to the school to address those needs.

Support for any new school program depends to a large extent on (a) the degree to which the school staff see that the new program addresses current needs and/or (b) the degree to which the new program draws upon existing efforts, extending or embellishing the school mission. A well-designed needs assessment can elicit information relative to these two points.

General areas to assess in planning and designing a peer mediation program are detailed in Table 5. Some of these questions may not be applicable to a specific school, and not all are required of any school. In addition to general assessment in these areas, a more specific needs assessment can help gather information from potential program "consumers." A sample Conflict Resolution in Schools Needs Assessment is shown in Figure 2.

Build Faculty Consensus for Program Development

To begin building faculty consensus for peer mediation program development, the program team can share the results of the needs assessment, distribute written information regarding research results of peer mediation programs (see Appendix B), and involve staff in a strategy session to clarify beliefs, mission, and program goals. Showing *The Peer Mediation Video: Conflict Resolution in Schools* (Schrumpf & Crawford, 1992) to open this session provides the anticipatory set by presenting faculty with a vision of peer mediation. The program team may then use the following definitions and examples of belief statements, mission statement, and statement of program goals to help faculty develop a shared vision for conflict resolution education and to develop consensus regarding program development.

Belief statements

Belief statements are a comprehensive collection of statements expressing fundamental convictions and tenets. As related to conflict and conflict resolution,

Table 5. Sample Questions for Needs Assessment

1. To what extent are conflicts interfering with the teaching and learning processes within the school?

2. What percentage of these conflicts are attributable to:
   - ▼ The competitive atmosphere of the school or classroom
   - ▼ An intolerant atmosphere in the school or classroom
   - ▼ Poor communication
   - ▼ Inappropriate expression of emotions
   - ▼ Lack of conflict resolution skills
   - ▼ Adult misuse of power in the school or classroom

3. To what extent are diversity issues manifested as conflicts in the school-community?

4. To what extent is representation in decision making an issue manifested in the conflicts observed in the school?

5. What percentage of the conflicts arising in the school are:
   - ▼ Between students
   - ▼ Between teachers and students
   - ▼ Between teachers
   - ▼ Between students and school expectations, rules, or policies
   - ▼ Between teachers and administrators
   - ▼ Between school staff and parents
   - ▼ Between various other combinations specific to the school

6. What procedures are followed when conflicts disrupt the teaching-learning process?

7. Who administers which procedures?

8. Regarding the effectiveness of these procedures, what are the perceptions of students? Teachers? Administrators? Others?

9. What attitudes or behaviors exist that will facilitate implementation of a conflict resolution program in the school? Who exhibits these?

10. What attitudes or behaviors exist that will impede the implementation of a conflict resolution program in the school? Who exhibits these?

11. Which foundation skills for conflict resolution are now included in the school curriculum, when are they developed, who provides training in the skills, and which students receive training?

12. To what extent have staff members received training in conflict resolution?

13. What staff development opportunities in conflict resolution are available? What opportunities are desired?

14. What conflict resolution processes currently exist within the school? Within the school-community?

15. What community resources exist to assist the school in designing and implementing a conflict resolution program?

16. What present/future monetary resources are available to support program implementation?

Figure 2. Conflict Resolution in Schools Needs Assessment   **Page 1 of 3**

Answer each question by providing the response that most accurately reflects your personal view of your school.

1. I am a: ☐ student ☐ staff member ☐ parent ☐ other

2. Conflicts interfere with the teaching and learning process:

   ☐ Often ☐ Sometimes ☐ Rarely

3. Problems between people at this school are caused by:

a. expectation to be competitive	☐ Often	☐ Sometimes	☐ Rarely
b. intolerance between adults and students	☐ Often	☐ Sometimes	☐ Rarely
c. intolerance between students	☐ Often	☐ Sometimes	☐ Rarely
d. poor communication	☐ Often	☐ Sometimes	☐ Rarely
e. anger and/or frustration	☐ Often	☐ Sometimes	☐ Rarely
f. rumors	☐ Often	☐ Sometimes	☐ Rarely
g. problems brought to school from somewhere else	☐ Often	☐ Sometimes	☐ Rarely

4. Without exceeding 100% as the total, what percentage of the problems referred for disciplinary action are problems:

a. between students	_____ %
b. between student and classroom teachers	_____ %
c. between student and other staff members	_____ %
d. between student and school rules	_____ %
e. other: _____	_____ %

   Total 100%

5. Indicate the types and frequency of conflicts experienced by students in this school:

a. put-downs/insults/teasing	☐ Often	☐ Sometimes	☐ Rarely
b. threats	☐ Often	☐ Sometimes	☐ Rarely
c. intolerance of differences	☐ Often	☐ Sometimes	☐ Rarely
d. loss of property	☐ Often	☐ Sometimes	☐ Rarely
e. access to groups	☐ Often	☐ Sometimes	☐ Rarely
f. rumors	☐ Often	☐ Sometimes	☐ Rarely
g. physical fighting	☐ Often	☐ Sometimes	☐ Rarely
h. verbal fighting	☐ Often	☐ Sometimes	☐ Rarely
i. schoolwork	☐ Often	☐ Sometimes	☐ Rarely
j. other:_____	☐ Often	☐ Sometimes	☐ Rarely

Figure 2. Conflict Resolution in Schools Needs Assessment   **Page 2 of 3**

6. Indicate the effectiveness of each of the following actions in causing a student to change a problem behavior:

   a. time-out   ☐ Very effective   ☐ Somewhat effective   ☐ Not effective

   b. detention   ☐ Very effective   ☐ Somewhat effective   ☐ Not effective

   c. conference with an adult   ☐ Very effective   ☐ Somewhat effective   ☐ Not effective

   d. suspension   ☐ Very effective   ☐ Somewhat effective   ☐ Not effective

   e. contacting parent(s)   ☐ Very effective   ☐ Somewhat effective   ☐ Not effective

   f. expulsion   ☐ Very effective   ☐ Somewhat effective   ☐ Not effective

7. Without exceeding 100% as the total, what percentage of influence do the following groups have in the way the school operates?

   a. students   _____%

   b. teachers   _____%

   c. parents   _____%

   d. principals and school administrators   _____%

   e. superintendents and district administrators   _____%

   f. Board of Education   _____%

   g. other: _____   _____%

                                                                   Total 100%

8. In this school, I am generally:

   a. treated fairly

        ☐ Most of the time   ☐ About half the time   ☐ Not very often

   b. treated with respect

        ☐ Most of the time   ☐ About half the time   ☐ Not very often

   c. given equal opportunity

        ☐ Most of the time   ☐ About half the time   ☐ Not very often

   d. treated with compassion

        ☐ Most of the time   ☐ About half the time   ☐ Not very often

   e. accepted

        ☐ Most of the time   ☐ About half the time   ☐ Not very often

9. I am allowed to solve problems that affect me:

        ☐ Nearly always   ☐ Sometimes   ☐ Hardly ever

10. This school should do a better job teaching students to:

   a. tell other people how they feel ☐ Definitely yes ☐ Maybe ☐ Definitely no

   b. disagree without making ☐ Definitely yes ☐ Maybe ☐ Definitely no
   other people angry

   c. respect authority ☐ Definitely yes ☐ Maybe ☐ Definitely no

   d. control anger ☐ Definitely yes ☐ Maybe ☐ Definitely no

   e. ignore someone who is bothersome ☐ Definitely yes ☐ Maybe ☐ Definitely no

   f. solve problems with other students ☐ Definitely yes ☐ Maybe ☐ Definitely no

11. When I need help, I ask for it: ☐ Nearly always ☐ Sometimes ☐ Hardly ever

12. If I needed help, I think I could get it from:

   a. a parent ☐ Definitely yes ☐ Maybe ☐ Definitely no

   b. a brother or sister ☐ Definitely yes ☐ Maybe ☐ Definitely no

   c. another family member ☐ Definitely yes ☐ Maybe ☐ Definitely no

   d. a teacher ☐ Definitely yes ☐ Maybe ☐ Definitely no

   e. a counselor ☐ Definitely yes ☐ Maybe ☐ Definitely no

   f. another school staff member ☐ Definitely yes ☐ Maybe ☐ Definitely no

   g. another adult ☐ Definitely yes ☐ Maybe ☐ Definitely no

   h. another student ☐ Definitely yes ☐ Maybe ☐ Definitely no

13. I think this school has:

   ☐ more problems than most other schools

   ☐ about the same number of problems as most other schools

   ☐ fewer problems than most other schools

belief statements provide a basis for achieving consensus within the school-community regarding a conflict resolution program in the school. The beliefs are the basis for obtaining a commitment to a specific mission for such a program.

Belief statements are simply stated and easily understood. They establish moral and ethical priorities that guide all school policies and activities. As such, the statements must be supported by everyone in the group. Sample belief statements include the following:

▼ Conflict is a natural part of everyday life.

▼ Conflict is an opportunity to grow and learn.

▼ Neither avoidance nor violence are healthy responses to conflict.

▼ Through awareness of cultural differences, we grow to respect others and to cherish diversity.

▼ Adults provide powerful behavioral models for students; this is especially true in dealing with conflict.

▼ Students can learn to resolve many of their conflicts without adult involvement.

Providing a few examples from this list can help introduce the task; however, faculty should have the opportunity to brainstorm their own list of belief statements. Keep in mind that there are two phases to the brainstorming process: The first involves generating the list of beliefs; the second involves selecting from the list. It is important to separate these two parts of the process.

Mission statement

A mission statement is the broad expression of the purpose of a conflict resolution program for the school. It is the cornerstone upon which the entire plan for the program is built. Often expressed as a single, general statement, the mission expresses the primary focus of the program, emphasizes the distinctiveness of the program, and represents the commitment of resources to the program. The mission statement provides a means for focusing commitment to and conveying understanding of the program by all factions of the school-community. Following is a sample mission statement:

> The mission of the peer mediation program is to enable students to resolve conflicts peacefully, to promote mutual understanding of individuals and groups throughout the school, and to enhance the climate of the school by providing each person opportunities to learn that conflict is natural and that conflict offers opportunities when resolved through the problem-solving strategies of conflict resolution.

Faculty should be afforded the opportunity to develop their own mission statement, with the preceding mission statement being used only as an example to encourage discussion. One way of developing the mission statement is to organize small groups that represent the diversity of the total group. Each small group receives a list of the belief statements developed by the faculty and the sample mission statement. The goal of each small group is to generate a mission statement. The total group, working with the mission statements generated by the small groups, develops a consensus statement.

Statement of program goals

Goals for a conflict resolution program in the school are expressions of desired outcomes. The goals are manifestations of the mission, give direction to all implementation planning, guide the setting of priorities and the allocation of resources, and provide the framework for evaluating the program. Goals are aspirations and intentions. The mission frames the program's destination; the goals are the map for reaching that destination. Sample goals are as follows:

▼ To enable students to take responsibility for peacefully resolving disputes without the intervention of staff.

▼ To increase the ability of students to deal effectively with issues of cultural and social diversity.

▼ To prevent disputes from escalating into incidents requiring disciplinary action.

▼ To create a school climate characterized by cooperation and collaboration.

Faculty should develop statements of program goals, with a few of the preceding examples as guides. The previously agreed-upon beliefs and mission statement are the framework for establishing goals. A strategy for generating goals might be to organize into job-alike groups (e.g., administrators, support staff, core subject teachers, teachers of elective courses) and have each group come up with three or four goals. The total faculty would cluster, modify, and adapt these goals to build a consensus list.

After goal statements have been clarified, it is a good idea to poll faculty as to whether they support the development of a peer mediation program for the school. Faculty support is required for implementation. It is not required that each faculty member commit to direct involvement in the program, but nearly all must agree to support the program at least minimally. Minimal support means that each staff member believes providing a mediation service to students is acceptable and agrees to encourage students to use the service.

PHASE 2: DESIGN AND PLAN PROGRAM

Develop Implementation Timeline

Implementing a successful peer mediation program requires planning. After participating in the training outlined in Phase 1, the program team's next responsibility is developing a timeline for program execution. The Implementation

Timeline shown in Figure 3 has been designed to guide the program team through this crucial step in program development.

Establish Advisory Committee

The advisory committee, consisting of 10 to 12 members, has an important role in program development and support. In order to address the varied interests of the school-community, the committee should include parents, teachers, building administrators, district administrators, students, support staff, community representatives, and corporate sponsors. The overall responsibility of this committee is to provide consultation and recommendations regarding policy and program development to the program team and program coordinator(s). In addition, the advisory committee may help with program activities such as promotion, evaluation, training, orientation, and building financial support. The advisory committee will likely meet frequently during the initial stages of program development. As the program becomes more established, the committee may need to meet only quarterly. It is important to keep the advisory committee involved in ongoing program evaluation efforts and program design changes.

Develop Policies and Procedures

The program team collaborates with the advisory committee to determine policies and procedures for the mediation program. The following are major areas for consideration, with suggested questions to address.

Role within the school discipline program

Conflicts characterized as illegal acts and/or serious violations of the rules and policies of the school (fighting, property destruction, stealing, harassment, abuse, drug use or sale, weapons possession, etc.) generally should not be submitted for mediation. However, issues may be associated with these problems that are suitable for mediation—issues usually related to the disputants' need to continue to relate to one another. Mediation is not a procedure for initial response to a violent incident. Mediation is not a process for assigning blame or determining punishment. Mediation is best viewed as a process for planning for future acceptable behavior.

▼ What is the role of mediation, if any, when illegal acts or serious rule violations occur?

▼ What is the role of mediation when students are referred by a third party because of the need to plan a future acceptable behavior?

▼ May disputing students return to the class or activity when they have a mediated agreement? If not then, when?

Types of conflicts to mediate

If a dispute is referred to peer mediation and the disputants agree to the mediation process, the conflict is worth trying to mediate. When disputants are expected to or desire to have a continuing relationship, mediation provides a process for planning ways to relate in a manner satisfying to each disputant and acceptable

Figure 3. Implementation Timeline

PHASE 1: DEVELOP PROGRAM TEAM AND COMMITMENT TO PROGRAM

Create program team   _____

Train program team   _____

Designate program coordinator(s)   _____

Conduct needs assessment   _____

Build faculty consensus for program development _____

PHASE 2: DESIGN AND PLAN PROGRAM

Develop implementation timeline   _____

Establish advisory committee   _____

Develop policies and procedures   _____

Identify and develop funding sources   _____

PHASE 3: SELECT AND TRAIN MEDIATORS

Conduct student orientation   _____

Select peer mediators   _____

Train peer mediators   _____

Recognize peer mediators   _____

PHASE 4: EDUCATE A CRITICAL MASS OF THE SCHOOL POPULATION

Conduct staff inservice   _____

Conduct student workshops   _____

Provide family and community orientation   _____

Offer parent workshops   _____

PHASE 5: DEVELOP AND EXECUTE PROMOTIONAL CAMPAIGN

Design and implement initial campaign   _____

Conduct ongoing promotional efforts   _____

PHASE 6: OPERATE AND MAINTAIN THE PROGRAM

Develop process for requesting mediation   _____

Schedule mediations and mediators   _____

Supervise mediation sessions   _____

Provide mediators with ongoing training and support _____

Evaluate program   _____

to others. Typically, conflicts involving put-downs or teasing, rumors or gossip, access or possession, turn taking or fairness, harassment or extortion or bullying, physical and/or verbal aggression or fighting, invasions of privacy or turf, and academic work are candidates for mediation.

▼ Must the conflicts submitted to mediation be school based?

▼ May student-teacher disputes, or student-school rule/policy disputes, or teacher-teacher disputes be submitted to mediation?

Voluntary participation

In order for any conflict to be mediated, the disputants must voluntarily agree to participate in the mediation.

▼ Who will be responsible for obtaining this agreement from the disputants?

▼ How will this be done? When?

Privacy

Mediators are trained to keep the content of the mediation private. Generally, knowledge of illegal behavior or plans or threats to harm others or self are not covered under privacy restrictions.

▼ What are the limitations on privacy?

▼ What is the mediator's responsibility for reporting information not covered under privacy provisions?

▼ To whom is this knowledge to be reported? When and how?

Place of operation

Ideally, a specific location is established as a mediation center. The center provides a private space for the mediations to occur but is located so an adult is always easily accessible to the mediators. The privacy and adult availability concerns outweigh the concern for a single designated space. Thus, mediations may occur at different locations depending on the time of day, with each location providing privacy and access to an adult program coordinator. The center is equipped with a table and seating for the participants and mediators. An easel pad or chalkboard is useful.

▼ Where will the mediation center be located?

▼ Are there time limitations on the use of center space?

Hours of operation

The more accessible mediation is during the school day, the stronger the messages will be that mediation is endorsed by the school as a viable problem-solving process and that the school acknowledges students' problems as being important.

▼ When are program coordinators available to supervise mediations?

▼ May mediators be called out of classes to conduct mediations?

▼ Will disputants be excused from class to participate in mediations?

▼ If mediations are provided before or after school, will transportation be provided?

Request procedures

Peer Mediation Request forms should be readily available to students and staff (see Figure 4). Forms may be made available in classrooms, the school office, the offices of counselors and other support staff, and so on.

▼ Where may completed forms be deposited?

▼ How often will these depositories be checked?

▼ Once a mediation is requested, how soon will it be scheduled?

Identify and Develop Funding Sources

Funding for the development and ongoing support of a peer mediation program influences program design. Budgets for peer mediation programs can vary widely, as illustrated in Table 6. The decision to hire a program coordinator or to designate existing staff to coordinate the program is the major factor in program expense. The other area in which expense varies greatly relates to contracting professional trainers to conduct the peer mediation training. If a school chooses to contract with a professional trainer for such assistance, it is typically a one-time expense. Most program teams are able to assume this responsibility after working in collaboration with the professional trainer during the first year.

Even though money is an issue in implementing a peer mediation program, it is important to remember that having more money does not necessarily correlate with program success. An enthusiastic, well-informed program team and the involvement and education of the school community are factors more significant than money. An effective program can be designed within a limited budget.

Many schools have existing funds or grants for professional development, student leadership development, safe and drug-free schools, school improvement, drop-out prevention, and/or attendance improvement. These existing funds and grants often can be used for conflict resolution programs because the outcomes of conflict resolution programs closely align with these grant programs' priorities.

Community service organizations such as the Rotary Club, the Optimist Club, and the Urban League, as well as the business community, are other potential sources of support for peer mediation programs. This support may come in the form of in-kind services such as printing brochures and posters or donating lunch during training, or it may be in the form of cash grants. Businesses often fund projects that help prepare students to be effective members of the future work force. Teamwork and problem-solving ability are skills required to work effectively

73

Figure 4. Peer Mediation Request

Date _____

Names of students in conflict:

_____ Grade _____
_____ Grade _____
_____ Grade _____
_____ Grade _____

Where did the conflict occur? *(check one)*

☐ Bus   ☐ Outdoors
☐ Cafeteria   ☐ Gym/locker room
☐ Classroom   ☐ Bathroom
☐ Hallway
☐ Other *(specify)* _____

Briefly describe the problem:

_____
_____
_____
_____

Mediation requested by *(check one)*

☐ Student   ☐ Social worker
☐ Teacher   ☐ Dean/assistant principal
☐ Counselor   ☐ Principal
☐ Other *(specify)* _____

Signature of person requesting mediation _____

DO NOT WRITE BELOW THIS LINE
TO BE COMPLETED BY A PROGRAM COORDINATOR

What is the conflict about? *(check one)*

☐ Rumors   ☐ Fighting or hitting
☐ Harassment   ☐ Bias or prejudice
☐ Threats   ☐ Relationship
☐ Name-calling   ☐ Property loss or damage
☐ Other *(specify)* _____

Table 6. Sample Peer Mediation Program Budgets

SCHOOL A: UNDER $5,000

Program team training (7 people @ $400)	$ 2,800
Coordinator (faculty extracurricular pay)	1,000
Student training (conducted by program team)	
Materials (30 Student Manuals @ $12 each)	360
Food, T-shirts, certificates	400
Operating expenses	
Promotional materials (posters, brochures)	200
Forms and printing for ongoing training	200
TOTAL	**$ 4,960**

SCHOOL B: OVER $40,000

Program team training (7 people @ $400)	$ 2,800
Full-time coordinator salary	40,000
Student training (conducted by professional trainer in collaboration with program team)	
Trainer consultation fee (2 days)	2,500
Materials (30 Student Manuals @ $12 each)	360
Food, T-shirts, certificates	400
Operating expenses	
Promotional materials (posters, brochures)	200
Forms and printing for ongoing training	200
TOTAL	**$46,460**

in most companies today. Conflict resolution training certainly contributes to the development of these abilities. In addition, businesses benefit through tax deductions and improved public relations.

PHASE 3: SELECT AND TRAIN MEDIATORS

Conduct Student Orientation

Before selecting mediators, it essential to introduce peer mediation to the student body. Student orientation provides an overview of the program, generates student interest and support, describes the role of peer mediators, and helps recruit peer mediators through student nominations and applications.

Members of the program team may conduct the student orientation as an all-school assembly. Orientation can also be provided during grade-level assemblies or conducted throughout the day in separate classrooms. In any case, the program team introduces peer mediation by showing *The Peer Mediation Video* (Schrumpf & Crawford, 1992) or by having students familiar with the peer mediation process conduct a demonstration. Program team members then present a general overview of the peer mediation process, describe the role and responsibilities of peer mediators, and include time for questions. At the end of the orientation, Peer Mediator Application forms (Figure 5) and Peer Mediator Student Nomination forms (Figure 6) are distributed. Any interested student may apply or make nominations.

Select Peer Mediators

The group of mediators must represent the diversity of the student population in terms of race, gender, school achievement, behavior, extracurricular interests, group membership, and residential neighborhood. If only those with exemplary school behavior and high academic achievement are selected, many of the students will not see the program as representing their peer group and therefore will not choose to participate in mediation. Personal qualifications of student mediators include the following:

▼ Respect of peers

▼ Skill in communication

▼ Leadership ability

▼ Sense of responsibility

▼ Trustworthiness and fairness

▼ Empathy

Staff members may nominate peer mediators by completing the Peer Mediator Staff Nomination form (Figure 7). The most efficient way to gather staff nominations is to explain the criteria and distribute forms at a staff inservice meeting, described under discussion of Phase 4. Particular faculty—such as social workers,

76

Figure 5. Peer Mediator Application

Name _____ Grade _____

Address _____

1. I want to be a peer mediator because:

2. List your personal qualities that will help you be a good mediator.

If selected, as a peer mediator I agree to the following terms:

▼ To complete all required training sessions

▼ To serve as a mediator as scheduled

▼ To request mediation to resolve my own personal conflicts

▼ To make up class assignments missed during peer mediation training or duty

Signature _____ Date _____

Figure 6. Peer Mediator Student Nomination

I would like to nominate the following students to be peer mediators because I would respect and trust them to help me resolve a conflict:

1. _____

2. _____

3. _____

Signature _____ Date _____

Figure 7. Peer Mediator Staff Nomination

I would like to nominate the following students to be peer mediators because they show leadership potential within their group:

1. _____

2. _____

3. _____

Signature _____ Date _____

counselors, and disciplinarians—can be especially helpful in focusing their nominations to ensure a representative cross section of students.

As discussed, at the student orientation all students learn about the role of and expectations for peer mediators. Students then have the opportunity to apply or nominate other students for the program. The value of student input in the selection of mediators is twofold: First, students feel ownership of the program from the outset. Second, it is likely that peers will name some students who would not otherwise be identified. Students who are nominated by their peers or by faculty are encouraged to complete an application form if they have not done so prior to nomination.

Once application forms are complete, student mediators are selected. One of the more effective selection processes is a lottery. The advantage of selection by lottery is mainly that students typically perceive the lottery process as an opportunity and not a personal risk. More students will chance applying to become mediators if the selection criteria are random than if judges make the selection in a criterion-driven process. If the first experience a student has with the peer mediation program is one of rejection, the student may avoid participation in the mediation process. This rejection can potentially spread from individuals to groups of peers who refuse to participate in mediation.

In order for the lottery process to work appropriately, it must include a system to ensure proper representation of the diversity of the school. This system is a "controlled lottery," or actually several lotteries. For example:

1. To generate gender balance, separate the candidates into male and female groups and draw an equal number.

2. To reflect the school's racial composition, first draw from the minority pool the minimum number of candidates to guarantee a representative group.

3. Place all remaining minority candidates in the general pool and continue to draw until the total number of mediators is determined.

If desired, the pool may be separated by grade level or other desired criteria to ensure other types of diversity.

Selection may also be done by the program team or the program team in conjunction with the advisory committee. With these methods, the nomination and application forms are reviewed and evaluated. Prospective mediators may also be interviewed by the program team or program coordinator(s) before being finally selected.

Depending on the size of the school, it is recommended that between 20 and 40 students be selected to be peer mediators. The goal is to have enough mediators so that it will not be a burden for them to miss class and other school activities but not to have so many that trainees only infrequently mediate, thus reducing their opportunities to gain skill through practice. Also, the pool of mediators should be of a size so program coordinators can readily supervise and monitor skill development. Twenty to 40 mediators can handle several hundred mediation requests per school year.

After mediators have been selected, the principal may officially notify and congratulate them. The program coordinator(s) then notify the students' parents and obtain parental permission for their participation. A sample Parent Permission Letter is presented as Figure 8. Either before beginning training or at the first training session, mediators are expected to sign a Peer Mediator Contract (Figure 9), which spells out the terms of mediators' training and service.

Train Peer Mediators

The time for student training may vary from 2 to 4 days. The training design next described is based on a 2-day basic training program and a subsequent program of twice-monthly meetings for advanced training and support. Each program, basic or advanced, involves approximately 12 to 15 hours of training time. Basic training activities relate to the following areas:

▼ Understanding conflict

▼ Responses to conflict

▼ Origins of conflict

▼ Communication skills

▼ Role of the mediator

▼ Mediation process

Advanced training activities include these topics:

▼ Bias awareness

▼ Social/cultural diversity

▼ Advanced communication

▼ Dealing with anger

▼ Caucusing

▼ Negotiating

▼ Group problem solving

Detailed plans and preparation for basic training are provided along with the training schedule/agenda and lesson plans in chapter 7. Advanced lessons are detailed in chapter 8.

Recognize Peer Mediators

The program coordinator(s) may choose to distribute certificates as part of an award ceremony to which parents and school officials are invited. Certificates may also be presented at a ceremony during a school assembly as a way to announce the opening of the mediation program. A sample Peer Mediation Certificate appears as Figure 10.

Figure 8. Parent Permission Letter

Date_____

Dear_____:

It is my pleasure to inform you that _____ has been
selected to be trained to become a peer mediator. Peer mediators are students who, with adult
supervision, mediate conflicts between their peers.

Conflicts between students are a normal part of daily life. Conflicts that are most common in
school include name-calling, rumors, threats, and relationship or friendship issues. Mediation is
a conflict resolution process that provides students the opportunity to talk and effectively resolve
their conflicts. Peer mediators conduct the mediation process. They do not take sides or make
decisions for their peers in conflict. Peer mediators help the students in conflict listen to each
other's points of view, focus on the problem, and create their own solutions.

In mediation training, students learn communication, problem-solving, and critical thinking
skills and how to apply those skills in the six-step mediation process. Peer mediators participate
in both basic and advanced training. Advanced training sessions will be scheduled throughout
the school year during and after school. Basic training is scheduled for

Date(s)   _____

Time(s)   _____

Place   _____

Please give permission for_____ to participate
in the peer mediation program by signing the permission form below.

If you have any questions, please call me at _____.

Sincerely,

Please detach and return to_____ by _____.

I give my permission for _____ to participate
in peer mediation training to become a peer mediator.

Parent/guardian signature _____ Date _____

Figure 9. Peer Mediator Contract

As a peer mediator, I understand my role is to help students resolve conflict peacefully. As a peer mediator, I agree to the following terms.

1. To complete basic and advanced training sessions at the scheduled times

2. To maintain privacy for all mediations

3. To be a responsible peer mediator by conducting mediation sessions according to the process, completing all necessary forms, and promoting the program

4. To maintain satisfactory school conduct (this includes using mediation services for interpersonal conflicts)

5. To make up any class work missed during training or mediation sessions

6. To serve as a peer mediator for the year

Student signature _____ Date _____

Figure 10. Peer Mediation Certificate

Peer Mediation Certificate

This is to certify that

_____

**has successfully completed basic training
in peer mediation.**

_____

Date of completion

_____

Program sponsor

PHASE 4: EDUCATE A CRITICAL MASS
OF THE SCHOOL POPULATION

Conduct Staff Inservice

Staff inservice will require a minimum of 6 hours. This 6-hour workshop may be conducted in one session or divided into three 2-hour sessions. The purpose of the staff inservice is to develop among faculty and other school staff a common understanding of conflict and the mediation process, as well as to help them learn the principles of conflict resolution, ways to support the development of the program through curriculum integration and referral of conflicts to mediation, and ways to conduct the student workshops.

The agenda for staff inservice training includes the following topics:

▼ Understanding conflict

▼ Responses to conflict

▼ Origins of conflict

▼ Principles of conflict resolution

▼ Negotiation and mediation process

▼ Curriculum integration ideas

▼ Referral process

▼ Preparation for student workshops

Conduct Student Workshops

Student workshops require a minimum of 5 hours. The workshop may be conducted in one session or divided into shorter periods over a week. Program team members may work with other faculty to conduct these workshops. Workshop goals are for students to develop an understanding of conflict, peace, and peacemaking; to develop communication and negotiation skills; and to learn about peer mediation and ways to request peer mediation services.

The agenda for student workshops involves the following topics:

▼ Understanding conflict

▼ Responses to conflict

▼ Origins of conflict

▼ Peace and peacemaking

▼ Communication skills

▼ Negotiation skills

▼ Mediation process

▼ Request for peer mediation

Provide Family and Community Orientation

Parent and community involvement is a necessary and important part of program development. Often a parent group, community organization, service club, or the police department will form a partnership with the school to sponsor peer mediation. An evening and/or lunch meeting can provide these supporters with an overview of the program and an opportunity to discuss the benefits of peaceful problem solving. Parents and other community members often want to learn more about mediation after such an informational meeting. Offering an educational series for interested community members broadens program support and encourages volunteers who might help with the training and supervision of student mediators. Trained peer mediators can play an integral part in these orientation efforts.

Offer Parent Workshops

Workshops for parents interested in conflict resolution training support the potential for students to apply conflict resolution strategies in the home. A 4-hour workshop may be conducted in one session or divided into two 2-hour sessions. The purpose of the parent workshop is to help parents develop a common understanding of conflict, understand the principles of conflict resolution, and learn how to apply the principles of conflict resolution in the home. Peer mediators can assist in such training, and their participation may help ensure parental involvement.

The agenda for parent workshops covers the following subjects:

▼ Understanding conflict

▼ Responses to conflict

▼ Origins of conflict

▼ Principles of conflict resolution

▼ Conflict resolution strategies in the home

PHASE 5: DEVELOP AND EXECUTE PROMOTIONAL CAMPAIGN

Like many new ideas, peer mediation can be greeted with skepticism. Students may be reluctant to try the approach because it is new. Many students might think talking problems through is tantamount to backing down and losing face. Quality promotion among the student population is crucial to the success of the program.

Program promotion goals are as follows:

▼ To inform everyone in the school that peer mediation services are available

▼ To advance the benefits of conflict resolution and peer mediation

▼ To encourage students to request mediation as a normal process for resolving conflicts

▼ To inform everyone about the procedures for requesting mediation and the types of conflicts that can be mediated

Promotional campaigns may be planned by a committee of student mediators in conjunction with the program team and perhaps with the involvement of the advisory committee. Campaigns also may be developed through a school-business partnership. School faculty members, parents, community members, and students are all potential promoters of the mediation program.

Design and Implement Initial Campaign

This section offers a number of promotion ideas to help get the peer mediation program off to a good start. Appendix C provides a case example of an initial promotional program developed in Urbana, Illinois, by a group of students and a parent volunteer.

Demonstration presentations.   Groups of mediators may present either schoolwide or grade-level assemblies, or they may schedule visits to all classes or homerooms. Peer mediators are highly capable of conducting presentations that include mediation session simulations, information about the process of requesting mediation, and encouragement for seeking help in dealing with conflicts. These demonstrations may also be presented at administrative meetings, faculty meetings, school board meetings, and PTA or PTO meetings.

Program name.   Students mediators may brainstorm a name for the peer mediation program that gives it an identity with which youth connect. Some names that schools have used are Peace Corps, Common Ground, and RESOLVE.

Promotional items.   Students may create a graphic design including the program name, logo, and slogan. This design can be reproduced on a variety of items: bumper stickers, T-shirts, sweatshirts, caps, and the like. Sales of these items could become a fund-raising project for the mediation program. Mediators may want to select a day once a week to wear their mediation T-shirts or sweatshirts.

Poster campaign.   Covering the entire school with a series of 8 x 11–inch posters at regular intervals captures the attention of everyone in the school environ-ment. Posters with messages about mediation may be placed in strategic areas, such as cafeteria lines, vending machines, bathroom stalls, drinking fountains, lockers, classroom and office doors, ceilings, floors, hallways, phone booths, gyms, locker rooms, and the faculty lounge. Some sample poster messages follow:

▼ Think Peace–Mediate

▼ Talk It Out–Shift Happens

▼ Caution–Work It Out Zone

▼ Have You Made Peace Today?

▼ Got a Conflict? ME-D-8!

Other poster projects.   Art classes or clubs may develop conflict resolution murals and larger posters to display throughout the school and community.

Peer mediator business cards.   Generic peer mediation "business cards" can include information about mediation and how to request service. Mediators may distribute these cards to students throughout the school. A sample Peer Mediator Business Card is illustrated in Figure 11.

Brochures.   Students can help write and produce separate community and student brochures describing the peer mediation program. These brochures may be mailed to parents and community agencies along with a letter announcing the opening of the peer mediation program. Brochures may be distributed to students and faculty and become a part of the orientation information distributed to new students and faculty.

Conduct Ongoing Promotional Efforts

Many of the initial promotional activities must be revived periodically and continued throughout the life of the mediation program. In addition to the initial activities, the following activities can provide ongoing program support throughout each school year.

Promotional video.   Students may produce a video about conflict resolution and mediation as part of a television production course or community service learning project through the local community cable access channel.

Dramatic presentations.   Performing arts provides a medium for student musicians and actors to create rap songs, compositions, musicals, and other dramatic presentations about conflict resolution, mediation, citizenship, and violence prevention.

Figure 11. Peer Mediator Business Card

COMMON GROUND
Mediation Center

Peer Mediator
Washington Middle School

Got a conflict?
Request Mediation
Room 22

Peer mediation bulletin board. Pictures of student mediators may be displayed on a bulletin board along with information about the mediation program and mediation request forms.

School media exposure. Student newspapers, public address announcements, schoolwide television commercials, worldwide web pages, and parent newsletters are vehicles for promoting the mediation program. Regular features presenting the "conflict resolution tip of the week" or describing successfully resolved cases (without violating privacy) are quite effective.

Community media exposure. Community media—newspapers, television stations, and radio stations—are often interested in featuring peer mediation programs because of the human interest appeal and contribution to the community at large.

Poster committee. A student group can be responsible for the ongoing development of a poster campaign. (Posters must be changed periodically to be effective.)

PHASE 6: OPERATE AND MAINTAIN THE PROGRAM

Develop Process for Requesting Mediation

All members of the school community are encouraged to make referrals to peer mediation. Peer Mediation Request forms (see Figure 4) may be placed in display pocket folders in all classrooms, the main school office, offices of support staff, the peer mediation bulletin board, the mediation center, and any other location that provides easy access for students and faculty. Students or faculty may complete the form to request a mediation and deposit it in a drop box in the main office or the mediation center. A designated hallway locker may also serve as a central deposit location for mediation requests. The program coordinator(s) should gather requests from each location at least twice a day.

Schedule Mediations and Mediators

Mediations are scheduled as soon as possible after the request has been deposited. Disputants should not be required to wait more than 24 hours after they request mediation. Depending on the hours of operation determined by the program team, the peer mediation center may be open for mediations during school hours and before and after school. Some schools try to schedule mediations for disputants during homeroom, study hall, library periods, or during lunch in order to avoid missed class work. Because some conflicts seem to interfere with the disputing students' ability to engage productively in classroom activities, it is appropriate to schedule these disputes during class.

Two options for scheduling mediators are case-by-case assignment and period-team assignment. *Case-by-case assignment* allows coordinators to choose the mediators who are most appropriate for particular cases, taking into consideration issues of race, gender, and social diversity. With this process mediators co-mediate with a number of different peers, learning from each other and building on their respective experiences. With each new request, the coordinator selects and locates appropriate mediators. The *period-team assignment* method means teams of co-mediators are assigned to particular periods each day. Teams then mediate whatever cases are scheduled during their time slots. Although this process does not allow for flexibility in selecting the mediators for each case, it facilitates the scheduling process. Mediators report to the mediation center at their designated time, receive their cases, and mediate. With both options, it is helpful to assess the willingness of the mediators' teachers to release the mediators from class. Figure 12 presents a sample Peer Mediator Classroom Release.

Other considerations for the assignment of mediators include their relationship to the disputants, frequency of mediation experience, and the age or grade level of the mediators and the disputants. Mediators are required to withdraw from a case whenever they feel that their prior relationship with a disputant will interfere with their ability to conduct an effective mediation. It usually works best to assign mediators only to those cases in which they do not know the disputants. In situations where this is impractical, the mediators should carefully assess whether or not they can maintain impartiality when mediating the dispute. Disputants often speak more openly about their conflicts when they do not have an ongoing relationship with the mediator. Restraining biases, loyalty to friends, and perceptions of partiality are difficult challenges for student mediators when they have ongoing relationships with one or both parties.

It is important that mediators have frequent experience mediating. The confidence and skill of mediators increase with experience. Coordinators need to monitor the number of cases assigned to each mediator to ensure equal opportunity for growth and development.

Finally, mediators should be assigned to work with disputants their same age and grade level or younger. If the mediators are younger than the disputants, the process generally is not successful. If disputants are of different ages or grade levels, it is best to assign a co-mediation team that reflects each disputant's age or grade level.

Supervise Mediation Sessions

Coordinators may provide brief background information to peer mediators before the session begins. Because the mediators learn what they need to know about the dispute from the disputants during the session, this briefing need include only the information gathered from the Peer Mediation Request.

Passes designating the scheduled time of mediation can be delivered to the disputants in advance of the meeting. The students present these passes to the teacher during the period the mediation is assigned in order to leave the classroom. Disputants may also be summoned by the mediators and escorted to the mediation center.

When all parties are gathered together, the mediation session begins without the presence of an adult supervisor. Students are more likely to invest themselves in the process if adults are not present in the mediation room. However, a coordinator

Figure 12. Peer Mediator Classroom Release

Student _____ Grade _____

Teachers: There are times when a peer mediator might be asked to conduct a mediation during class. The student will be released from class only with your permission. Please indicate on this form if you approve an occasional release for this student.

Period	Subject	Room Number	Approval (Y/N)	Teacher Signature
1				
2				
3				
4				
5				
6				
7				
8				
9				

or another trained adult must remain in the area in case the mediators need assistance. After about 12 to 15 minutes, the supervisor may check with the mediators to be sure that everything is going as expected.

During the session, mediators use the Brainstorming Worksheet (Figure 13) to help disputants generate options to solve the problem. If the mediation is successful, mediators have the disputants sign the Peer Mediation Agreement (Figure 14). If they have not reached an agreement, the mediators consult with the adult supervisor prior to closing the session.

At the end of the mediation session, each disputant separately completes a copy of the Post-Mediation Session Assessment (Figure 15). Together as a team, the mediators complete the Peer Mediator Self-Evaluation (Figure 16). After the disputants leave the mediation room, the coordinator or supervising adult uses these forms as a focus for discussion with the mediators. This debriefing is designed to help mediators assess what went well during the session and to problem-solve about the parts of the process that challenged them.

Provide Mediators with Ongoing Training and Support

It is recommended that peer mediators meet regularly as a group with the program coordinator(s). Ideally, meetings are held twice monthly for about 2 hours each. A portion of that time should be used for the peer mediators to share experiences and take turns presenting cases that illustrate particular challenges and issues. Coordinators caution about privacy concerns for this exchange. The remaining time may be used to extend the peer mediators' training. This training may involve a review of aspects of the basic training (chapter 7) and/or advanced training (chapter 8).

Evaluate Program

Evaluation provides the information needed to plan for continuous improvement in program quality. In addition, evaluation can build substantive evidence of program efficacy. Evaluations of peer mediation programs may be uncomplicated designs that program coordinators assimilate into their responsibilities, or they may be more complex experimental designs conducted by researchers. Because schools typically do not have the financial or human resources to conduct an elaborate program evaluation, a simple plan for program evaluation is described here.

With the assistance of student mediators, the program coordinator(s) monitor the number of mediations, length of mediation sessions, types of conflicts, source of requests, location where conflicts materialized, attributes of disputants, outcomes of mediations, and durability of agreements. The Peer Mediation Record (Figure 17) provides an efficient form for merging information from the Peer Mediation Request and Peer Mediation Agreement.

The primary goal of the mediation program is to bring about changes in students' and educators' attitudes and behavior concerning conflict and approaches to resolution. In addition to monitoring the program, the program coordinator(s) may conduct pre-assessments and post-assessments to determine whether or not changes are taking place. The Pre-Program Student Assessment, Pre-Program Staff Assessment, Post-Program Student Assessment, and Post-Program Staff Assessment instruments are designed to assess the impact of the peer mediation program. (Copies of all these instruments appear in Appendix A.) The pre-program assessments should be completed by all staff and students during the same period of time that the needs assessment is being conducted (during Phase 1 of program development). The post-program assessments should be conducted at least 6 months after the mediation program has been in place. For staff, forms should be distributed during a staff meeting. It will take staff approximately 5 minutes to complete each form. For students, forms should be distributed, completed, and collected during a class period where every student in the school will be present. It will take students approximately 10 minutes to complete each form.

Figure 13. Brainstorming Worksheet

OPTIONS LIST

▼ What are some possible options that address both of your interests?

▼ What other possibilities can you think of?

1. _____

2. _____

3. _____

4. _____

5. _____

6. _____

7. _____

8. _____

9. _____

10. _____

Figure 14. Peer Mediation Agreement

Date_____

We voluntarily participated in a mediation. We have reached an agreement that we believe is fair and that solves the problem between us. In the future if we have problems that we cannot resolve on our own, we agree to come back to mediation.

Name _____   Name _____

_____   _____

_____   _____

_____   _____

_____   _____

_____   _____

_____   _____

_____   _____

_____   _____

_____   _____

_____   _____

Signature _____   Signature _____

Mediator signature _____

Mediator signature _____

Figure 15. Post-Mediation Session Assessment

Name _____ Date _____

Please check the boxes that represent your honest thoughts and feelings.

1. I am a: ☐ Student ☐ Teacher ☐ Administrator ☐ Parent ☐ Counselor

   ☐ Other _____

2. Have you ever participated in a mediation before? ☐ Yes ☐ No

   If yes, how many times? _____

3. Do you think that the mediators:

   Listened to you? ☐ Yes ☐ No

   Understood your interests? ☐ Yes ☐ No

   Acted fairly? ☐ Yes ☐ No

4. Describe your relationship with the other person before this conflict occurred. *(check as many as you like)*

   ☐ Friend ☐ Acquaintance ☐ Stranger

   ☐ Relative ☐ Boyfriend/girlfriend ☐ Other

5. What were your feelings about the other person when you came into the mediation session?

6. How do you feel about the other person now?

7. If you reached an agreement, are you satisfied with your agreement? ☐ Yes ☐ No

8. If you did not reach an agreement, what are your alternatives for dealing with this problem? What will you do next?

Figure 16. Peer Mediator Self-Evaluation   **Page 1 of 2**

Date _____

Mediator _____

Mediator _____

Place a check mark (✓) by each step where you did quality work. Place an asterisk (*) by each step where you think the quality could improve. Co-mediators complete this form as a team.

STEP 1: AGREE TO MEDIATE

☐ Welcomed both people and introduced yourself as the mediator.

☐ Explained the mediation process.

☐ Explained ground rules.

☐ Asked each person: "Are you willing to follow the rules?"

STEP 2: GATHER POINTS OF VIEW

☐ Asked each person to tell what happened.

☐ Listened, summarized, clarified.

STEP 3: FOCUS ON INTERESTS

☐ Found real interests.

☐ Listened, summarized, clarified.

☐ Summarized interests before going to the next step.

STEP 4: CREATE WIN-WIN OPTIONS

☐ Explained brainstorming rules.

☐ Asked for ideas that address the interests of both parties.

STEP 5: EVALUATE OPTIONS

☐ Asked parties to combine options or parts of options.

☐ For each option, asked:

    Is this option fair?

    Can you do it?

    Do you think it will work?

STEP 6: CREATE AN AGREEMENT

☐ Asked disputants to make a plan of action: Who, what, when, where, how?

☐ Wrote the plan.

☐ Asked each person to read the plan and sign the agreement.

☐ Closed the session with a handshake.

OTHER

☐ Remained neutral—did not take sides.

☐ Avoided making suggestions to solve the problem.

☐ If parties did not reach an agreement, knew what to say to end the session.

☐ Worked together with co-mediator.

☐ Gave each party a turn to talk without interruption.

Answer the following questions.

1. What did you do well?

2. If you could do this mediation again, what might you do differently?

3. Were certain steps more difficult for you than others? If so, what could you do to strengthen these steps?

4. Do you have any other concerns or questions?

Staff supervisor_____ Date _____

Comments:

Figure 17. Peer Mediation Record

Month_____ Year_____ Page_____ of _____

Mediation Case Number	Date	Grade	Sex (M/F)	Race	Location	Requested By	Type	Time	Signed (Y/N)	Kept (Y/N)

KEY

Location
B = Bus
C = Cafeteria
R = Classroom
H = Hallway
G = Gym/locker room
D = Outdoors
B = Bathroom
O = Other

Requested By
S = Student
T = Teacher
C = Counselor
W= Social worker
D = Dean/assistant principal
P = Principal
O = Other

Type
R = Rumors
H = Harassment
T = Threats
N = Name-calling
F = Fighting or hitting
B = Bias or prejudice
RL = Relationship
P = Property loss or damage
O = Other

Time: To the nearest 5 minutes.

Signed: Was agreement signed?

Kept: Was agreement still in force at 1-month follow-up interview with selected disputants?

CHAPTER 7

BASIC TRAINING

Basic training for peer mediators consists of 16 core training activities to orient students to the program, provide foundation skills for conflict resolution, develop understanding of the principles of conflict resolution, and offer practice to master the basic steps of the mediation process. Basic training requires a period of time roughly the equivalent of 2 full days (12 to 15 contact hours) and will equip students to conduct most of the mediations that will be requested in a school peer mediation program.

Training Activities and Agenda

Basic training activities range in time required from 15 to 90 minutes. (Activity 15 has two parts. The first part requires 90 minutes; for the second part, 45 minutes are recommended.) The suggested time for each activity is a general guideline to follow in order to provide all of the activities within 12 to 15 contact hours. Some groups may need more time for some activities and less for others.

In the activities, instructions are given to present corresponding segments of the Student Manual. Trainers are encouraged to vary the presentations, mixing reading aloud by an adult or student, reading silently, discussing in cooperative learning groups, and so forth. For the trainer's convenience, the information and worksheets from the Student Manual have been reproduced in this chapter (and chapter 8) as shaded text.

Table 7 presents a sample agenda for a 2-day training program. This 2-day training schedule is efficient but intense, even overwhelming, for some groups of trainees. It may be better for peer mediators if training can be offered during four half-day sessions.

Staffing

The basic training program can be delivered by one or two trainers. These individuals should be experienced in conflict resolution, communication, and mediation. The trainer(s) will need assistance from other adults in conducting the training activities—advisory committee members, other members of the school staff, parent volunteers, and so forth. Previously trained peer mediators can

Table 7. Sample 2-Day Training Agenda

DAY 1   **Morning**

8:00	Boundary breaker	
8:15	Activity 1	Welcome and Overview
8:30	Activity 2	Introduction to Peer Mediation
8:45	Activity 3	Understanding Conflict
9:25	*Break*	
9:35	Activity 4	Origins of Conflict
10:25	Activity 5	Understanding Peace and Peacemaking
11:10–11:40	*Lunch*	

Afternoon

11:40	Activity 6	Communication Skills
12:25	Activity 7	Qualities and Role of the Peer Mediator
12:55	Activity 8	Overview of the Peer Mediation Process
1:25	*Break*	
1:35	Activity 9	Step 1: Agree to Mediate
1:50	Activity 10	Step 2: Gather Points of View
2:20	Activity 11	Step 3: Focus on Interests (Part 1)
2:50	Closure	

DAY 2   **Morning**

8:00	Boundary breaker	
8:15	Review Day 1	
8:30	Activity 11	Step 3: Focus on Interests (Part 2)
9:30	Activity 12	Step 4: Create Win-Win Options
10:00	Activity 13	Step 5: Evaluate Options
10:30	*Break*	
10:40	Activity 14	Step 6: Create an Agreement
11:10–11:40	*Lunch*	

Afternoon

11:40	Activity 15	Co-Mediation Practice
1:25	*Break*	
1:35	Activity 16	Support for Peer Mediation and Peer Mediators
2:30	Closure	

also serve as assistants. A ratio of one adult (or previously trained peer mediator) to three or four students is ideal. Maintaining this ratio is very important while prospective peer mediators are learning the mediation process.

Training for peer mediators can be successful with anywhere from 15 to 40 students. Because many of the training activities involve simulated mediations, selecting a number of students that is both a multiple of two and a multiple of three (for example, 18, 24, 30, 36) allows practice groups to be conveniently formed.

Training Environment

The ideal environment for training is a large room with movable furniture—chairs and small round or square tables—with students clustered in groups of 3 or 6 at each table. If possible, the furniture should be arranged in a semicircle, allowing the participants to make visual contact with the trainer(s) and with one another. The room should be large enough to avoid distractions when the prospective peer mediators practice mediation simulations in small groups. Consideration might be given to finding a training location off school grounds. Leaving school may make the experience special and exciting for the students, and it will remove them from the distractions of school and other peers, thus freeing them to focus their attention on the training.

Training Materials

Materials and supplies needed for the training include the following:

1. A Student Manual for each student participant

2. An easel pad and marker or chalkboard and chalk

3. Newsprint and markers

4. Pencils

5. Masking tape

6. Name tags

7. Photocopies of selected forms and simulations as specified in the training activities

The Peer Mediation Video: Conflict Resolution in Schools (Schrumpf & Crawford, 1992) can greatly enhance training, although it is not required. If the videotape program will be used, a videocassette recorder and monitor will also be needed. *The Peer Mediation Video* is available from Research Press at the address given on the title page of this Program Guide.

Tips for Successful Training

Successful training requires a climate that encourages participants to take risks, share, and become actively involved. The training atmosphere must be cooperative and supportive; all students must be directly involved in the activities and in practicing the mediation process. The following guidelines are offered to help the trainers establish such an environment:

1. Present an overview of the entire training agenda to the students in the beginning. (A sample overview statement appears in Activity 1.)

2. State expectations for behavior and participation. (A statement of expectations also appears in Activity 1.)

3. Use boundary breakers and closure activities like those described in Appendix D at the beginning and end of each training segment. These activities promote collaboration and collegiality and are well worth the time spent in order to help the group bond.

4. Invite trainers and training assistants to participate in the activities and share their experiences with student trainees. The thoughts and feelings of adult participants are important and valuable.

5. Model good communication skills by actively listening—attending to, summarizing, and clarifying student responses.

6. Ask students to self-evaluate and provide one another with feedback instead of always having an adult judge the quality of students' performance, especially in the simulation activities.

7. Encourage students who resist or who express discomfort with a topic or exercise to participate. Strategies to encourage participation include providing individual attention or coaching, offering to model the behavior for the student, and suggesting that the student talk about someone he or she knows instead of revealing personal information.

8. Be enthusiastic and friendly. Smile often and be accepting, even when challenged. Look for and acknowledge effective behaviors. Your positive energy will set the tone for the group.

ACTIVITY 1

WELCOME AND OVERVIEW

PURPOSE

Students will receive an orientation to peer mediation and learn the goals and ground rules for peer mediation training.

TIME

15 minutes

MATERIALS

Student Manual (pages 3–5)

PROCEDURE

1. Welcome students to peer mediation training. Present the following section from the Student Manual.

Congratulations!

You are here because you have chosen to learn to be a peer mediator. Each of you has your own reasons for making that important choice.

Peer mediators possess qualities that contribute to their ability to help others:

▼ They have good judgment.

▼ They are respected by peers.

▼ They are someone other students can talk to and trust.

Each of you represents one or more of the various groups that make up our school. Our school has a variety of people, personalities, cultures, and ethnic groups. It is important that peer mediators represent this full spectrum of the student population, so during this training, please speak from your personal experience and for the peers you represent.

During this training, you will build upon your positive qualities and abilities. You will learn how to help others who are experiencing conflict to work together to resolve their problem.

This process of conflict resolution is called **mediation,**
and you will learn to be a **peer mediator**.

WHAT YOU WILL LEARN

During training, you will be actively involved in learning a great deal about the mediation process. Together we will investigate the following major topics:

▼ What mediation is

▼ Understanding conflict—nature of, origins of, and responses to conflict

▼ Principles of conflict resolution and peacemaking

▼ Communication skills

▼ The six-step mediation process

▼ Mediation practice

▼ How the peer mediation program will operate

At the end of training you will be a **peer mediator**.

GROUND RULES FOR TRAINING

You are here to learn to be peer mediators, and the expectation is that you will each be successful. Mediation is a powerful process, but it requires a high level of skill to use effectively. It also requires that each person learn to use the process in a way that fits his or her own personality. The training will be experiential, which means you will learn by doing. You will be trained to be true to a specific process, but you will also be asked to practice the process so you can make it work for you personally. Some of the adults here have used mediation, but there are no absolute "experts." We learn more about mediation each time we use the process, see others use it, or provide training.

During this training we are all here to learn and help others learn. You will be asked to try some things that may be new and strange to you. It is important that we all feel free to try these new things and that we help one another.

Let's all agree that we will not put anyone down or ridicule anyone's effort, but that we will encourage and help one another. We expect this to be hard work, but it will also be fun. We will all laugh because some of what happens will be funny, and we need to laugh. When you are finished with the training you will have skills few others have—you will be able to serve others as a **peacemaker**. So, during the training:

▼ Show respect for others.

▼ Be a good listener.

▼ Honor differences. Remember, we each represent different groups as well as our own different experiences.

▼ Cooperate and help one another.

2. Ask, "Are there any questions about why you are here or about the training you are about to experience?" Discuss.

INTRODUCTION TO PEER MEDIATION

PURPOSE

Students will learn the definition of mediation and examine the beliefs underlying peer mediation.

TIME

15 minutes

MATERIALS

Student Manual (page 6)

Index cards (one per student)

PROCEDURE

1. Explain that peer mediation seeks to give responsibility, control, and opportunity to the people who can best solve their problems—the people themselves.

2. Present and discuss the following section from the Student Manual.

WHAT IS MEDIATION?

Mediation is a communication process in which the people with the problem work together, with the assistance of a neutral third party, cooperating to resolve their conflict peaceably.

The **mediator** is the neutral third party. When students serve as mediators to assist other students, they are called **peer mediators**.

Mediation is an approach to resolve conflict in which the **disputants**—the people who disagree—have a chance to sit face-to-face and talk, uninterrupted, so each **point of view** is heard. After the problem is identified, the disputants create options for mutual gain and choose a **win-win** solution. They then finalize an **agreement** to behave in some way from that point forward.

PEER MEDIATION: BELIEFS

It takes cooperation and understanding to resolve conflicts. Peer mediation is based on the belief that in order to resolve conflicts constructively, those with the conflict must be willing to do as follows:

▼ Stay calm and control their anger, frustration, or other strong feelings.

▼ Focus on the problem and not blame the other person.

▼ Accurately state their feelings and wants.

▼ Respect and work to understand different points of view.

▼ Cooperate and create solutions that meet the needs of everyone involved.

The mediator helps the disputants behave in these constructive ways.

3. Tell the peer mediators that stating the definition of mediation is something that they will be expected to do each time they begin a mediation session. Therefore, they will need to be able to state the definition in their own words from memory.

4. Have students write a definition in their own words on an index card. (Training assistants should check each definition for completeness.)

5. Tell students to memorize their own definition of mediation before the next day of training.

UNDERSTANDING CONFLICT

PURPOSE

Students will learn that conflict is a natural part of life and happens every day, that conflict can be a force for growth and change, and that responses to conflict will determine whether it is a positive or negative force.

TIME

40 minutes

MATERIALS

Student Manual (pages 7–12)

Easel pad or chalkboard

Markers

Newsprint

Masking tape

PROCEDURE

1. Tell students that this activity will help them think and learn about conflict. Add that we all have various ideas and images of conflict—where it happens and how we respond to it.

2. Ask students to refer to the Defining Conflict Worksheet on page 7 of their Student Manuals.

DEFINING CONFLICT WORKSHEET

PART 1

Conflict	Conflict

Conflict	Conflict

PART 2

Conflict	Conflict

3. Read the word *conflict* and ask students to write or draw the first word, symbol, or phrase that comes to mind in Part 1 of the Defining Conflict Worksheet. Read the word *conflict* three more times, each time asking the students to write or draw another word, symbol, or phrase.

4. Instruct students to compare their responses with the responses of others in their group. Start with one group and ask them to share any common responses. Record these on an easel pad or chalkboard. Move to the next group and record any responses different from those already on the easel pad or chalkboard. Continue the process for each group. Typical responses include *fight, hassle, argument, war, hate, compromise, battle, harassment, yell, hit, controversy,* and *disagreement.*

5. Instruct students to look at the list on the easel pad or chalkboard and ask which items represent negative images and which represent positive images. Mark those that most believe are negative with a minus (–) and those that most believe are positive with a plus (+).

6. Explain that most of our ideas about conflict are negative because most of us have negative responses to conflict. This is true for most students and most adults. However, conflict can also be seen as an opportunity to learn and grow.

7. Instruct students to record a positive word, symbol, or phrase in each of the remaining two boxes in Part 2 of their Defining Conflict Worksheet. Ask students to share with the larger group some of their positive responses to conflict.

8. Instruct students to refer to the Conflict Happens Worksheet on page 8 of the Student Manual and describe two or three conflicts for each of the settings named. The examples they describe may be either conflicts in which they themselves have been involved or ones they know others have experienced.

CONFLICT HAPPENS WORKSHEET

Record two or three examples of conflicts you have experienced or know that others have experienced for each of the following settings.

HOME (with parents or other adults)

HOME (with brothers, sisters, other kids)

AT SCHOOL (with peers)

AT SCHOOL (with teachers, other adults)

AT SCHOOL (with rules, expectations)

IN THE NEWS

9. Divide students into six groups of equal number and give each group a marker and a large sheet of newsprint. Assign each group a different setting; tell them to list on the newsprint a number of conflict situations. They may use the ideas they recorded on their individual worksheets as well as brainstorm other possibilities.

10. After 5 minutes, ask groups to share their lists. Post the lists about the room so they can be referred to as examples throughout the training. Point out how these and other conflicts are examples of challenges from which we can learn and that they test our communication and problem-solving skills.

11. Present the following section of the Student Manual.

STATEMENTS ABOUT CONFLICT

Most of us have negative ideas about conflict, and these negative ideas often create barriers to our willingness or ability to deal with conflict. People live, work, and play together. To do so, people must understand the following ideas about conflict:

▼ Conflict is a part of everyday life.

▼ Conflict can be handled in positive or negative ways.

▼ Conflict can have either creative or destructive results.

▼ Conflict can be a positive force for personal growth and social change.

Therefore . . .

▼ Conflict will happen; violence does not have to happen.

▼ It is not our choice whether or not to have conflict.

▼ It is our choice how to act when we do have conflict.

12. Next instruct students to refer to the Responses to Conflict Worksheet on page 10 of the Student Manual. Tell them that we all have conflicts, but that each of us responds to conflict in a different way. Explain how to fill out the worksheet in the following way:

Think about conflicts you have had with peers or adults. How did you respond? This worksheet lists several typical responses people have to conflict. Is the first response, "Yell back or threaten the person," something you do often? If so, put a check mark in that column. Or is that a behavior you use sometimes or would never use? You should have a check mark in one of the three columns after each response indicating what is mostly true about how you respond.

RESPONSES TO CONFLICT WORKSHEET

Put a check mark (✓) in the boxes that show the responses that are most typical for you when you are in conflict with another person.

	Often	Sometimes	Never
Yell back or threaten the person	❑	❑	❑
Avoid or ignore the person	❑	❑	❑
Change the subject	❑	❑	❑
Try to understand the other side	❑	❑	❑
Complain to an adult	❑	❑	❑
Call the other person names	❑	❑	❑
Let the person have his or her way	❑	❑	❑
Try to reach a compromise	❑	❑	❑
Let an adult decide who is right	❑	❑	❑
Talk to find ways to agree	❑	❑	❑
Apologize	❑	❑	❑
Hit or push back	❑	❑	❑
Cry	❑	❑	❑
Make it into a joke	❑	❑	❑
Pretend my feelings are not hurt	❑	❑	❑

13. Poll the group by asking, for each possible response, for a show of hands: Who checked *often*? Who checked *never*?

14. Tell students that responses will either escalate (increase) or deescalate (decrease) a conflict. Ask students to indicate with thumbs up or thumbs down whether they think each of the possible responses would increase the conflict (thumbs up) or decrease the conflict (thumbs down).

15. Present the following section of the Student Manual.

RESPONSES TO CONFLICT

Responses to conflict generally fall into one of three categories: soft responses, hard responses, or principled responses.

Soft Responses

Sometimes we respond to conflict in soft ways. Have you ever:

▼ Ignored a conflict, hoping it would go away?

▼ Denied that a conflict mattered to you?

▼ Withdrawn from a situation and not shared what you felt?

▼ Given in just to be nice?

Soft responses to conflict involve **avoidance**. People avoid conflict by withdrawing from the situation, ignoring the problem, or denying their feelings. Avoiding conflict may help in the short run—for instance, it might help someone keep from losing his or her temper. However, avoidance usually causes self-doubt and makes a person feel anxious about the future. In addition, because the conflict is never brought up, it can never be resolved.

Hard Responses

Sometimes we respond to conflict in hard ways. Have you ever:

▼ Threatened another person?

▼ Shoved or pushed someone out of frustration?

▼ Yelled words you really didn't mean?

▼ Hit someone or destroyed something out of anger?

Hard responses to conflict involve **confrontation**. Confrontation in response to conflict means a person expresses anger, verbal or physical threats, or aggression. It may also mean the person resorts to bribery or to punishments like withholding money, favors, or affection. These actions show a **win-lose** attitude toward conflict, or the attitude that one person must win and the other person must lose in a conflict. This attitude prevents cooperation and keeps people from reaching a mutually satisfying solution.

114

Principled Responses

A third type of response to conflict is a principled response. Have you ever:

▼ Listened with the intent to understand the other person's point of view?

▼ Cooperated with someone else without giving in?

▼ Shown respect for differences between you and another person?

▼ Looked for ways to resolve a problem that helped everyone involved?

A principled response to conflict involves **communication**. Communicating means participating in a common understanding, not necessarily agreeing. In order for people to cooperate, they must first communicate. People in conflict who seek first to understand the other person's side, then be understood, produce **win-win** solutions.

A principled response to conflict means both people get
their needs met, and no one loses.

16. List and briefly discuss possible outcomes if conflict is unresolved or resolved. Some likely outcomes if conflict is unresolved are:

▼ Threats and blame continue.

▼ Feelings are hurt, relationships are damaged.

▼ Self-interest results, positions harden.

▼ Emotions increase, tempers get out of hand.

▼ Sides are drawn, other people get involved.

▼ People do not get what they want and need.

▼ Violence can result.

Some likely outcomes if people work together toward resolution are:

▼ Better ideas are produced to solve the problem.

▼ Relationships and communication are improved.

▼ Views are clarified, problems are dealt with.

▼ People listen to and respect each other.

▼ There is cooperation.

▼ People get what they want and need.

▼ Fairness and peace are achieved.

If time allows, instead of discussing these lists you may choose to have students work in four to six small groups to generate their own possible outcomes if conflict is unresolved or resolved. Give each group a sheet of newsprint and marker. Instruct half of the groups to make a list of what might happen if a conflict is resolved; instruct the other half to make a list of what might happen if a conflict is not resolved. Allow about 10 minutes, then ask each group to share their responses. Post the sheets.

ACTIVITY 4

ORIGINS OF CONFLICT

PURPOSE

Students will learn that the origins of conflict are basic psychological needs, that conflicts often involve limited resources and/or different values, and that issues of social and cultural diversity often are enmeshed in values.

TIME

50 minutes

MATERIALS

Student Manual (pages 13–18)

PROCEDURE

1. Present the following section of the Student Manual.

BASIC NEEDS

Understanding how to resolve a conflict begins with identifying the origin of the conflict. Most every dispute between people involves the attempt to meet certain **basic needs** for belonging, power, freedom, or fun.

▼ Our **BELONGING** need is met by developing and maintaining relationships with others where we have the opportunity to love, share, and cooperate.

▼ Our **POWER** need is met by achieving, accomplishing, and being recognized and respected.

▼ Our **FREEDOM** need is met by making choices in our lives.

▼ Our **FUN** need is met by laughing and playing.

We might think that people or situations cause us to act a certain way, but this belief is not true. We act the way we do because we are trying to meet our basic needs. Here are some examples:

Suppose you are upset because your friend is going to a party and you were not invited. You might get into a conflict with the friend because you are not getting your need for belonging met.

Suppose you are in conflict with a parent about the chores you must do around the house. This conflict might be the result of your need to have the freedom to make your own choices about how to spend your time.

You may be mad at the coach because you think you deserve more playing time, and her decision not to let you play is frustrating your power need—you think she doesn't recognize your ability and not playing deprives you of the chance to gain respect from your teammates and the fans.

2. Instruct students to refer to the Basic Needs Worksheet on page 14 of the Student Manual. Tell students to list, in the boxes provided, at least two things they personally do to satisfy each of the basic needs. Allow 5 minutes.

BASIC NEEDS WORKSHEET

BELONGING

POWER

FREEDOM

FUN

3. Instruct students to share their responses with the other students in their small group. Process the experience by asking the small groups to tell the larger group some of the similarities and differences they noticed in their group during the sharing.

4. Discuss the ideas presented at the bottom of the Basic Needs Worksheet. Stress the idea that, although we all have the same basic needs, we choose different ways to satisfy those needs, thus creating conflict. Explain that we are making choices constantly to satisfy our needs. Whatever choice we make is always the one we think will best satisfy us. However, one person's choice

is not always viewed by another as a good choice. For example, you may view the student who pesters you regularly as a nuisance, but that student may be doing the best he or she knows how to do to get your attention so the two of you can relate. It may be very irritating to you when another student puts you down continually, but that student may just be trying to get your recognition.

We are all born with the same four basic needs. However, the things we each choose in order to meet those needs may be different from what others choose. These different choices may cause a conflict, either because two people are trying to satisfy the same need in two different ways or because they are each trying to satisfy a different basic need.

5. Tell students that conflicts often appear to be about something other than these basic needs. Present the following section of the Student Manual; have students volunteer examples of conflicts they have experienced involving limited resources.

LIMITED RESOURCES

When **resources** are limited, conflicts may result. Conflicts that involve limited resources are about time, money, property, or some combination of these things. For example, two classmates might be having a conflict over property when they are arguing about who will get to use a certain book they both want for a report.

Think of examples of conflicts you have experienced involving limited resources:

▼ A conflict about **money**

▼ A conflict about personal/school **property**

▼ A conflict about **time**

6. Present the following ideas from the Student Manual to summarize how limited resources are involved in conflicts.

We each want money or property or time because we see these as things that allow us to satisfy our basic needs. If we have money, we can afford to do more (freedom, fun, belonging). We can buy things like great clothes, sports equipment, or audio-video products to gain recognition (power). When we have plenty of time, we can do our work (power) and also hang out with our friends (fun, belonging, freedom).

Resources are **wants** that we choose to satisfy our basic needs. The two students arguing over the book they both want for a report are likely each attempting to satisfy their power need: If they can write a quality report they will feel they have accomplished or achieved and they will likely be recognized by the teacher and perhaps others for doing so.

Unmet basic needs are at the heart of conflicts over limited resources.
If the parties can communicate, they can develop a plan to cooperate
and share the limited resource.

7. Explain that some conflicts appear to be because the people involved are very different. These conflicts involve different values. Instruct students to complete the Cultural and Social Diversity Worksheet on page 16 of the Student Manual.

CULTURAL AND SOCIAL DIVERSITY WORKSHEET

Each of us has received a variety of gifts, making each of us unique. You probably like some gifts more than you like other gifts. You may even wish you could exchange some of your gifts: Some you can change, but many you cannot. Check the categories or fill in the blanks for those items that are most nearly true about you.

Gift of Race/Ethnicity
- ❏ African American
- ❏ Asian American
- ❏ European American
- ❏ Hispanic American
- ❏ Native American
- ❏ Other _____

Gift of Ability
- ❏ Artistic
- ❏ Leadership
- ❏ Mathematical
- ❏ Mechanical
- ❏ Musical
- ❏ Physical
- ❏ Verbal
- ❏ Other _____

Gift of Culture
Family practices in:
- ❏ Dress
- ❏ Food
- ❏ Holidays
- ❏ Language
- ❏ Other _____

Gift of Gender
- ❏ Female
- ❏ Male

8. Ask students to use their completed Cultural and Social Diversity Worksheets to help them think of a time they felt judged, teased, or discriminated against because of one or more of the gifts they have received. Have them share these experiences in their small groups. Allow three or four volunteers to share their experiences with the larger group.

9. Tell students that values may be expressed as racism, sexism, classism, ageism, and so forth; therefore, conflicts about different values may be the result of prejudice and discrimination. Conflicts involving prejudice and discrimination are very difficult to resolve. Often fear, anger, and/or mistrust are prevalent in these conflicts.

10. Present the following ideas from the Student Manual to summarize how different values are involved in conflict.

Different Values

We all have different **values**. Values are the beliefs, convictions, priorities, and rules we follow. Differences in values may result in conflicts.

Conflicts involving values tend to be difficult to resolve because when people's values are different, they often perceive the dispute as a personal attack. When a person feels attacked, he or she often either withdraws or attacks—and neither of these reactions will likely de-escalate the conflict. For example, a student who values honesty in her friends will probably be very upset and angry if she learns that a friend has lied to her.

Our values are very much influenced by who we are and by our social environment. Our gender, our race, our social status, our ethnic group, our culture, and our abilities are differences that all play a part in forming our values. These differences are referred to as **cultural diversity** and **social diversity.** They also include diversity of religion, national origin, age, sexual orientation, and so on.

Values are wants that we use to guide our actions because we believe that they show us the best way to satisfy our needs. We may believe this because of our gifts or because we think our gifts are better than or not as good as another's gifts.

Unmet basic needs are at the heart of conflicts over different values.

The student who is angry because her friend lied to her is attempting to satisfy her belonging need, but she finds it difficult to share and cooperate with someone who is dishonest. Her friend may also be attempting to satisfy her belonging need, but she fears that if she is honest with her friend the truth will hurt her friend's feelings and the friend will become angry and choose to avoid her.

Resolving conflicts involving differing values does not mean the disputants have to change or align their values. They may need to agree to disagree, respectfully. Often a mutual acknowledgment that they see things differently is the first step toward a resolution.

When values are expressed as a behavior that limits another's basic rights, that behavior is inappropriate, and the rules of the school should prohibit it. A peer mediation may help the individuals in dispute plan a different, more acceptable behavior.

11. Direct students to the Conflict Diagram on page 18 of the Student Manual. Summarize that the basic psychological needs are at the core of conflicts and that the resolution of many conflicts will require that the disputants look beneath the limited resources or different values that appear to frame the conflict. The mediator helps the disputants use principled responses instead of soft or hard responses.

CONFLICT DIAGRAM

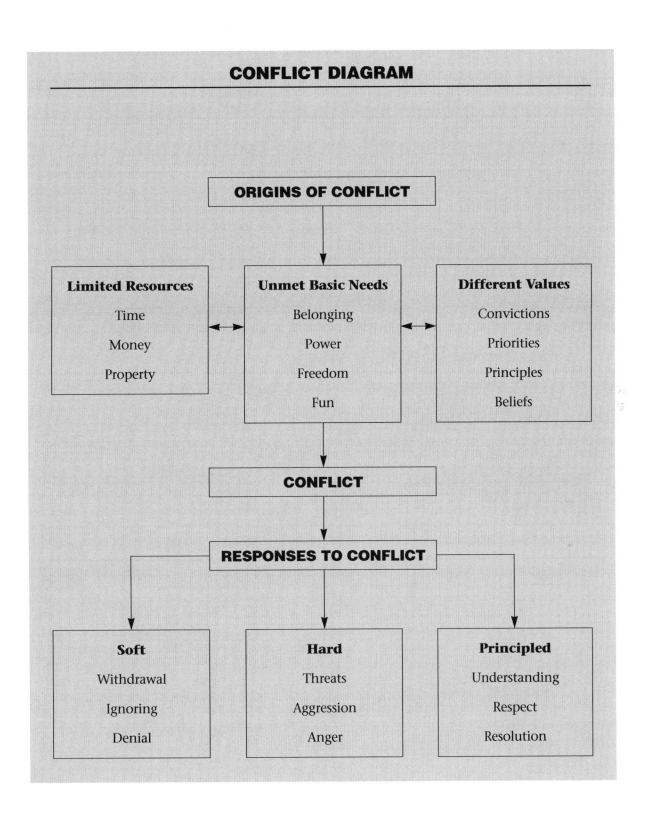

ORIGINS OF CONFLICT

Limited Resources

Time

Money

Property

Unmet Basic Needs

Belonging

Power

Freedom

Fun

Different Values

Convictions

Priorities

Principles

Beliefs

CONFLICT

RESPONSES TO CONFLICT

Soft

Withdrawal

Ignoring

Denial

Hard

Threats

Aggression

Anger

Principled

Understanding

Respect

Resolution

UNDERSTANDING PEACE AND PEACEMAKING

PURPOSE

Students will understand peace as a behavior and learn that the four principles of conflict resolution are the behaviors of peacemaking.

TIME

45 minutes

MATERIALS

Student Manual (pages 19–22)

Negotiation Simulation 1 (from Appendix E)

Easel pad or chalkboard

PROCEDURE

1. Explain that peace means different things to different people. Peace is a concept that some people, including some students, do not easily identify with. Present the following definitions from the Student Manual.

PEACE IS . . .

 is that state when every person is able to survive and thrive without being hampered by conflict, prejudice, hatred, or injustice.

PEACE is that state when each individual fully exercises his or her responsibilities to ensure that all individuals fully enjoy all rights.

PÉACÉ is a process of responding to diversity and conflict with tolerance, imagination, and flexibility; war is a product of our intent to stamp out diversity and conflict when we give up on the process of peace. George E. Lyon

PEACE *is balance and harmony.*

2. Ask students how they might define *peace*.

3. Explain that it is useful to think of peace as an action and that each person can choose to act in ways that promote peace. Actions that promote peace are called *peacemaking behaviors*, and each of us makes peace, moment by moment.

4. Present the following material from the Student Manual.

Peacemaking is honoring yourself, honoring others, and honoring the environment. Peer mediators are peacemakers who also have the skills to help others make peace.

---

5. Instruct students to work cooperatively in their small groups to complete the Peace or Violence Worksheet on page 20 of the Student Manual. Allow about 5 minutes.

PEACE OR VIOLENCE WORKSHEET

1. What are some peacemaking behaviors students exhibit in your school?

2. What are some peacebreaking behaviors students exhibit in your school?

3. Is your world becoming more peaceful or more violent? Why?

4. What are some results of violence? On a person? On a school? On a community?

5. Why do you think your peers might choose to mediate a dispute?

6. Why do you think your peers might choose not to mediate a dispute?

When conflicts remain unresolved, violence may result.

6. To process the experience, ask each group to share some of their responses with the whole group. (It helps to ask a different small group to go first for each item on the worksheet, then ask if any of the other groups have something unique to add.) Some typical student responses as to why mediation might or might not be chosen include the following:

   ▼ There is pressure from others to fight.

   ▼ They don't want to fight.

   ▼ Other people are involved.

   ▼ They want to save face.

   ▼ They want to win.

   ▼ They are afraid they will lose.

   ▼ They don't know about mediation.

   ▼ They are afraid of the other person.

7. Form pairs; instruct each student to sit facing his or her partner. Explain that each pair will participate in a simulation and that each member of the pair will be assigned a role to play. The situation involves two students in conflict who have consented to sit down and talk with each other. Explain that each member of the pair will be provided with specific information about the conflict:

   You will receive a page assigning you to be either Student A or Student B. This page will provide you with a description of the situation, a statement of your point of view, and background information to help you understand who you are and what you want. Your page and your partner's page will have different information. Read your page, and when you and your partner are ready, begin talking to each other. DO NOT READ YOUR PAGE TO YOUR PARTNER!

8. Distribute Negotiation Simulation 1. Give the Role-Play Instructions for Disputant A to one member of the pair; the other member receives the instructions for Disputant B. Allow the negotiation to proceed for 5 to 8 minutes. Process the experience by asking for a show of hands:

   ▼ Do you think you and your partner were making progress toward solving the problem between you?

   ▼ Do you think you and your partner were making no real progress toward a solution or even making the problem worse?

9. Instruct students to try to forget about the specific problem between the two people in the simulation and to focus on the behaviors that occurred between them as they talked about the problem. Ask pairs who thought they were not making progress or were making the problem worse to tell how they were behaving toward each other. Record student responses on the easel pad or chalkboard. Next elicit and record how pairs who thought they were making progress were behaving toward each other. Compare the two lists.

10. Explain that when people are in conflict they often are unable to resolve the conflict and may make the problem worse because of the behaviors they choose. Behaviors that are helpful in resolving conflicts are those that support the principles of conflict resolution. Present the following section of the Student Manual.

PRINCIPLES OF CONFLICT RESOLUTION

The process of mediation is based on four principles of conflict resolution. **Peacemaking behaviors** are based on these principles because they allow disputants to reach agreements that honor themselves, the other person and, often, others around them, too. The agreement may also involve honoring the environment.

Principle 1: Separate the People from the Problem

This principle concerns behaviors in three areas:

▼ **Perceptions:** Each person in a conflict will view the conflict differently. For resolution it is important that each understand how the other views the problem.

▼ **Emotions:** People in conflict often have strong feelings about each other or about the problem. The expression of those feelings is important in gaining a full understanding of the problem. Because the expression of strong emotions by one person may provoke an equally strong expression from the other, it is important that while one person expresses emotions, the other listen and refrain from reacting.

▼ **Communication:** Conflict resolution requires that each of the individuals in the conflict talk about the conflict and listen to the other.

Principle 2: Focus on Interests, Not on Positions

This principle recognizes that individuals in conflict have different ideas about what should happen and that each has reasons to support his or her ideas.

▼ **Position:** What the disputant wants; may be expressed as a proposed solution or as a demand.

▼ **Interest:** A reason why the disputant wants what he or she wants or why the disputant thinks a particular solution will solve the problem.

Generally, each position is supported by several interests. When disputants focus discussion on positions, rarely are they able to reach a satisfactory agreement. But if they focus discussion on interests, they very often can find a resolution that satisfies both of their interests.

Principle 3: Invent Options for Mutual Gain

This principle recognizes that it is better for disputants to try to think of ideas that allow each person to gain than to argue over who will win and who will lose or simply to work on a compromise. The process used is **brainstorming**. Brainstorming is generating ideas without deciding.

Principle 4: Use Objective Criteria

This principle recognizes that applying standards allows disputants to accept an agreement. If each person thinks an idea is fair, he or she will likely commit to and keep the agreement.

Peer mediators help disputants behave according to these principles
of conflict resolution.

Many students believe the world is becoming more violent, have personally experienced violence, and feel there is little they can do about violence. The intent of mediation training is for the students to begin to see that conflict resolution—specifically, mediation— is an alternative to violence. This is an appropriate time to point out that mediation is not intended as a way to deal with a violent incident. Rather, it is a strategy to help people choose peacemaking behaviors that will solve a problem before violence occurs.

COMMUNICATION SKILLS

PURPOSE

Students will acquire the skills of active listening and learn about effective communication.

TIME

45 minutes

MATERIALS

Student Manual (pages 23–27)

Six labels, each prepared before the activity with one of the following phrases: *interrupt me, give me advice, make fun of me, criticize me, distract me,* and *tell me your problems*

PROCEDURE

1. Tell students that effective communication is the basis for cooperative, collaborative problem solving. In fact, conflict often arises because of problems in communication. Communication may be a problem because:

   ▼ People in conflict may not be talking to each other.

   ▼ They may not listen to each other when they do talk.

   ▼ They may talk in ways that make it difficult for the other person to receive the message.

   ▼ They may misunderstand or misinterpret was is said.

   Mediators need to learn effective communication skills and strategies to help disputants communicate with each other. It is by communicating that the disputants apply the principles of conflict resolution.

2. Obtain six student volunteers and seat them in a circle of six chairs. Place one of the prepared labels on each student's forehead without allowing the student to see what is on the label. Tell the volunteers that they will be asked to perform a task and during the performance of that task they should respond to others in the group according to the label on that person's forehead. Tell the group that they are a committee responsible for planning the next school dance. They must decide such things as place, music, theme, decorations, clean-up, refreshments, ticket prices, and so on. Select the student labeled *give me advice* as the committee chair. Allow 4 to 5 minutes.

3. Process the exercise by asking the volunteers how well they think they communicated as a group. Before allowing the volunteers to see their own labels, ask each one individually to say what he or she thinks is on the label and to tell how he or she felt about people's communication based on that label. Discuss the idea that the labels represent typical behaviors people often use in communication and that these behaviors interfere with clear communication.

4. Present the following section of the Student Manual.

WHAT IS COMMUNICATION?

Communication occurs when a listener hears and understands a speaker's essential thoughts and feelings. Often, conflicts continue because of poor communication between people.

COMMUNICATION PITFALLS

A peer mediator facilitates communication between disputants. Following are some ways that the peer mediator can shut down, rather than facilitate, communication:

DON'T

Interrupt

Offer advice

Judge

Ridicule

Criticize

Distract

Bring up your own experience

Be sure to avoid these common pitfalls.

---

5. Tell students that they are going to practice communication between two individuals. Ask students to find a partner and sit facing the partner. Ask one member of the pair to agree to be known as Student A, the other as Student B, for the purpose of getting directions for the practice activity. Instruct Student A as follows: "You have 1 minute to tell Student B your idea of a perfect Saturday night." Instruct Student B as follows: "Your job is to encourage Student A to talk, but you may not speak." Allow 1 minute for Student A to talk. Call time and ask:

   ▼ Student A, did you think Student B was listening to you?

   ▼ Student B, did 1 minute seem like a long time just to listen?

   Reverse roles, asking Student B to talk on the same topic for 1 minute and Student A to provide encouragement without talking. Call time and ask the same questions as before.

6. Process the activity by using the following questions:

   ▼ Was it difficult to listen without interrupting?

   ▼ Did you want to question the speaker?

   ▼ What did your partner do that made you think he or she was listening and interested in what you had to say?

7. Present the following section of the Student Manual.

ACTIVE LISTENING

In order to help disputants communicate, the peer mediator uses the following specific communication skills:

▼ Attending

▼ Summarizing

▼ Clarifying

Altogether, these skills are called **active listening**. This name signifies that listening requires one to be active and diligent, not passive.

Attending

Attending means using nonverbal behaviors to show you hear, that you are interested, and that you wish to understand. These nonverbal behaviors include such things as eye contact, facial expressions, gestures, and posture. Also included are very brief verbal utterances like "Hum!" "Uhm," "Uh-huh!" "OK!" "Wow!" and so forth. Generally, if you are leaning forward, smiling, nodding your head, and ignoring outside distractions, you are attending.

It is important for the peer mediator to attend to the disputant when he or she is speaking and to attend equally to each disputant during the mediation.

8. Ask the group, "How do you think you will feel if when you are mediating a conflict a disputant has a hard time looking at you? How will you interpret that behavior?" Tell students that different cultures have different norms for nonverbal behaviors in communication. For example, eye contact may be a way to show respect in one culture yet be seen as a sign of disrespect in another. Smiling is a way to show agreement in some cultures but is something you are expected to do in other cultures even when you disagree. Posture and conversational distance may be a personal preference. Some individuals are comfortable when you are close to them; others feel you are violating their personal space. Thus, there are no absolutely correct ways to attend. Ignoring distractions is always important. Aside from that, you should do what you think is appropriate and try to judge the effect of your behavior on the other person. If the person talks freely, he or she is probably seeing you as encouraging; if the person seems uncomfortable, you should try other behaviors.

9. Present the following section of the Student Manual.

Summarizing

Summarizing means you do two things: You restate facts by repeating the most important points, organizing interests, and discarding extra information. Also, you reflect feelings about the conflict. It is very important when summarizing to recognize feelings in the situation as well as facts.

10. To practice summarizing facts and feelings, have the students again face their partners: Student A talks uninterrupted for 1 minute about a recent conflict while Student B demonstrates attending behaviors. After the minute is up, Student B summarizes facts and reflects feelings. The partners then switch roles.

11. Process the exercise by discussing the following questions:

   ▼ Was it difficult to summarize both facts and feelings accurately? Why or why not?

   ▼ Did the listener accurately summarize the information?

   ▼ How did the listener show understanding of your feelings?

12. Present the following section of the Student Manual.

Clarifying

Clarifying means using open-ended questions or statements to get additional information and to make sure you understand. Some examples of open-ended questions include:

▼ How did you feel when that happened? *(question)*

▼ Do you have anything to add? *(question)*

▼ Tell me what happened next in the situation. *(statement)*

▼ What do you think is keeping you from reaching an agreement about this problem? *(question)*

Open-ended questions can be answered in many different ways and help keep people talking. The answer to a closed question provides little information and is often simply yes or no. Closed questions and statements such as the following tend to discourage people from further discussion:

▼ Did you feel angry when that happened?
(yes-or-no question)

▼ You've been fighting for a long time.
(no response needed)

▼ Do you think you can reach an agreement about this problem?
(yes-or-no question)

13. To practice clarifying, have students face their partners again: Student A talks on the topic of a recent conflict. Student B actively listens, summarizes, and clarifies, repeating this active listening cycle until the conflict is clearly defined and understood. Allow about 2 minutes, then have the partners switch roles.

14. To process the activity, discuss the following questions:

   ▼ What was the most difficult thing about clarifying?

   ▼ Did the listener summarize after each statement and use open-ended questions or statements to get additional information?

   ▼ Do you think the listener clearly understood the conflict?

15. As a summary, present the following section of the Student Manual.

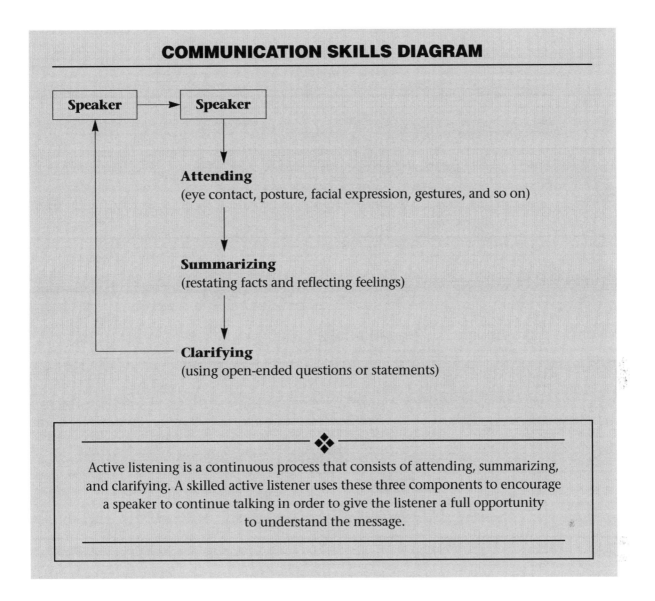

COMMUNICATION SKILLS DIAGRAM

Speaker → **Speaker**

Attending
(eye contact, posture, facial expression, gestures, and so on)

Summarizing
(restating facts and reflecting feelings)

Clarifying
(using open-ended questions or statements)

Active listening is a continuous process that consists of attending, summarizing, and clarifying. A skilled active listener uses these three components to encourage a speaker to continue talking in order to give the listener a full opportunity to understand the message.

Optional Activity 1

The following activity is recommended for basic training if time allows. If time is not available in basic training, this makes a good follow-up activity.

1. Instruct students to complete the Talk about a Conflict Worksheet on page 26 of the Student Manual. This worksheet helps students analyze a conflict.

2. Instruct students to find a partner different from the one in the main activity and again sit face to face. Tell them that they will each have 3 to 5 minutes to tell their partner about the conflict they described in their Talk about a Conflict Worksheet. The partner is to practice active listening (just as a mediator might). After 3 to 5 minutes, call time and tell the partners to switch roles.

3. Discuss the experience in the larger group.

TALK ABOUT A CONFLICT WORKSHEET

Think about a conflict you have had recently and complete this worksheet.

1. What happened? Who is involved?

2. How do you feel about the situation?

3. How do you think the other person feels?

4. What do you want? What are some of your reasons?

5. What do you think the other person wants? Why?

6. How have you responded to the conflict? *(soft, hard, principled response)*

7. How has the other person responded? *(soft, hard, principled response)*

Optional Activity 2

This activity can be conducted as a follow-up or as homework.

1. Instruct students to complete the Effective Communication Worksheet on page 27 in the Student Manual.

2. Invite them to comment briefly on how they feel about their new communication skills.

EFFECTIVE COMMUNICATION WORKSHEET

Use this checklist to evaluate your communication behaviors. Put a check mark (✓) in the box that shows the degree to which you use each of the behaviors listed.

	Often	Sometimes	Never
1. Do you make eye contact?	❏	❏	❏
2. Do you watch the person's body posture and facial expressions?	❏	❏	❏
3. Do you empathize and try to understand feelings, thoughts, and actions?	❏	❏	❏
4. Do you keep from interrupting and let the person finish, even when you think you already know what the person means?	❏	❏	❏
5. Do you ask questions to clarify information?	❏	❏	❏
6. Do you nod your head or use gestures to show interest?	❏	❏	❏
7. Do you listen, even if you do not like the person who is talking or agree with what the person is saying?	❏	❏	❏
8. Do you ignore outside distractions?	❏	❏	❏
9. Do you listen for and remember important points?	❏	❏	❏
10. Do you suspend judgment about what is said—do you remain neutral?	❏	❏	❏

QUALITIES AND ROLE OF THE PEER MEDIATOR

PURPOSE

Students will become aware of the qualities of an effective peer mediator and understand the mediator's role in the process.

TIME

30 minutes

MATERIALS

Student Manual (pages 28–29)

Yardstick

A pair of cowboy boots

A pair of ballet slippers

A 6-foot length of rope

PROCEDURE

1. Tell students that peer mediators have personal qualities that contribute to their ability to learn the mediation process and to help others. Instruct students to refer to the Statements about Me Worksheet on page 28 in the Student Manual; explain that this worksheet is designed to help them understand the personal qualities that can help them become effective peer mediators. Allow 5 minutes for students to complete the worksheet.

STATEMENTS ABOUT ME WORKSHEET

Complete the statements by writing the first response that comes to mind.

1. My peers describe me as _____

2. I get frustrated with _____

3. One way I relax is _____

4. I feel disappointed when _____

5. My parents describe me as _____

6. I get angry when _____

7. A quality I expect in a friend is _____

8. I trust someone if _____

9. I feel discriminated against when _____

10. One way I show respect is _____

11. I control my anger by _____

12. I feel best when _____

13. I am good at _____

14. I am prejudiced toward _____

15. I will be an effective peer mediator because _____

2. Tell students to share the information on the worksheet with those in their small groups. To process the activity ask, in the larger group:

▼ What did your group have in common?

▼ What were some of the differences?

▼ Were you surprised about anything?

▼ What qualities will help you be an effective peer mediator?

3. Present and discuss the five characteristics of the peer mediator, one at a time, as given in the Student Manual. Follow up the statement of each characteristic with the specified demonstration or expanded explanation.

Qualities of the Peer Mediator

The peer mediator is impartial.

A mediator is neutral and objective, a person who does not take sides.

Demonstrate by balancing the yardstick on your forefinger. Say:

The mediator is responsible for maintaining balance and, to be fair, must not be influenced by the emotions and stories of either side. If the mediator moves to one side or the other, the balance is lost, and the mediation process will not work.

Show how shifting the balance point will make the yardstick fall.

It is often very difficult for a mediator to be impartial. Situations may arise when the program coordinators assign you to be the mediator but, because you have information they do not have, you should advise them that it would be best to assign another mediator.

Ask the following questions:

▼ Could you be impartial if you were having a problem similar to the problem one of the disputants is having?

▼ Could you be impartial if one of the disputants is your best friend?

▼ What other situations can you think of in which being impartial would be a challenge?

The peer mediator is an empathic listener.

A mediator is skilled at listening with the intent of understanding what each disputant thinks and feels.

Demonstrate by placing the cowboy boots and the ballet slippers on the floor and by standing first behind one pair of shoes and then behind the other while stating:

> The mediator must listen with empathy to be able to understand what it's like to stand in each disputant's shoes. Because the disputants likely will not practice effective communication with each other, the mediator practices active listening not only to hear and understand for himself or herself but also so the disputants can hear and understand each other.

The peer mediator is respectful.

A mediator is able to treat both parties with respect and understanding, and without prejudice.

Demonstrate by saying:

> The essence of being respectful is not that you agree with someone; it is that you understand the person's emotions and beliefs. You might not like the way the person's shoes fit—you may know you would never agree to dance in a pair of cowboy boots or ride a horse in ballet slippers—but as a mediator you do need to show disputants you understand that the shoes they wear are important to them and to their situation.

To illustrate that the mediator must not have prejudices, stand by the cowboy boots and say, "Tell me some of your assumptions about someone who would wear these boots." Allow the students a minute or so to share their ideas. Then repeat, using the ballet slippers.

After the students share their ideas, tell them the cowboy boots belong to a grandmother and the ballet slippers belong to a professional athlete. Explain that the key to being respectful is knowing that all people are different and that you run the risk of blocking communication, trust, and cooperation if you stereotype them.

The peer mediator is trustworthy.

A mediator builds the confidence and trust of the disputants in the mediation process by keeping information private. A mediator does not discuss the problem with other peers. Also, a mediator allows the disputants to solve their own problem rather than imposing his or her own favored solution.

Instruct groups of six to eight students to form a line, with each student placing his or her hands on the shoulders of the person in front. Instruct everyone except the person at the rear of the line to close his or her eyes. The person at the end of the line is to give directions to the first person in the line for moving about the room without running into furniture or other people. Allow about 4 or 5 minutes. Process by asking:

▼ Did the individuals with their eyes closed trust the person directing them?

▼ What might this experience have to do with maintaining privacy in a peer mediation session?

Tell students that if certain information surfaces in a mediation the peer mediator may be responsible for reporting that information to an adult. The peer mediator must report any information about illegal activities, including weapons or drugs. The peer mediator must report any threats or actions by a disputant that are harmful to self or others. Under no circumstances should a peer mediator report any information revealed in a mediation to another student.

The peer mediator helps people work together.

A mediator is responsible for the mediation process, not the solution to the problem. The solution to the problem is the responsibility of the disputants. When the disputants cooperate, they are able to find their own solution.

Demonstrate by taking the length of rope and asking for two volunteers. Have the two volunteers tug on opposite ends of the rope while you hold the rope in the middle. (You will be pulled first one way, then the other.) Next ask the two students to hold the ends of the rope while they sit face to face on the floor. Encourage them to figure out a way to raise themselves to a standing position by pulling on the rope. (It will be necessary for them to work together to do this.) Tell students:

It is very important as a mediator to know that your success or lack of success is separate from whether or not the disputants reach an agreement. What is expected of you is that you use these qualities and the process you will soon learn about to help the disputants problem-solve with each other. It is possible, although unusual, that even if you do your very best job conducting a mediation the disputants will not find a solution to their problem.

OVERVIEW OF THE PEER MEDIATION PROCESS

PURPOSE

Students will receive an overview of the six-step mediation process and see the steps demonstrated.

TIME

30 minutes

MATERIALS

Student Manual (pages 30–38)

The Peer Mediation Video: Conflict Resolution in Schools (Schrumpf & Crawford, 1992) *(optional)*

PROCEDURE

1. Refer students to pages 21–22 of the Student Manual and review the four principles of conflict resolution. Tell them that in this activity they will learn how the four principles of conflict resolution are incorporated into the six-step mediation process.

2. Present the following section of the Student Manual.

STEPS IN PEER MEDIATION

STEP 1 Agree to Mediate

STEP 2 Gather Points of View

STEP 3 Focus on Interests

STEP 4 Create Win-Win Options

STEP 5 Evaluate Options

STEP 6 Create an Agreement

PREPARING FOR PEER MEDIATION

By preparing properly, you demonstrate a sense of control and establish a secure climate in which the disputants are able to communicate. You prepare for the session by arranging the physical environment and assembling materials.

Arranging the Physical Environment

Arrange the physical environment in the mediation room so that no one is at any kind of disadvantage. Doing so will help the disputants see you as not taking sides and will help them communicate better.

It is important to decide who will sit where before a mediation session begins and to arrange the chairs before the disputants arrive. In arranging the chairs, follow two guidelines:

▼ Position the disputants face-to-face across from each other.

▼ Position yourself at the head of the table between the disputants and nearest to the exit.

Assembling Materials

Before beginning a session, collect and have available the following items:

▼ **Peer Mediation Request**

One of the disputants (or another party, such as a teacher) completes this form before the mediation takes place. The form tells the mediator a little about the conflict and helps in scheduling the mediation.

▼ **Brainstorming Worksheet**

This is the form on which the mediator records all the disputants' ideas for solving the conflict. (You can use an easel pad instead of this worksheet.)

▼ **Peer Mediation Agreement**

When the disputants reach an agreement, the mediator fills out this form to show exactly what they have agreed to do. The disputants and mediator sign the agreement.

▼ **Pen or pencil**

▼ **Marker** (if using an easel pad)

The mediation forms you will need start on page 87 of this manual.

3. Refer students to the Peer Mediation Forms section beginning on page 87 in the Student Manual and briefly explain the use of each form. (Copies of these forms are also provided in Appendix A of this Program Guide.)

4. Select volunteers to conduct a practice mediation. Designate the mediator and the disputants. Demonstrate several poor ways to arrange the seating before illustrating the preferred arrangement:

   ▼ Seat the two disputants on the same side of the table and the mediator on the other.

   ▼ Seat the mediator and one disputant on one side of the table across from the other disputant.

   ▼ Seat the mediator closer to one of the disputants, then closer to the other.

   ▼ Show the preferred seating arrangement, with disputants sitting face-to-face and the mediator at the head of the table.

   Stress that the disputants' chairs should be facing each other, even though the disputants may choose, at least in the beginning, not to look at each other.

   If you are using The Peer Mediation Video, *cue the video to the start of the mediation segment. Pause the video and point out that Mac is seated properly between Michael and Rodney. Ask:*

   ▼ What might the disputants believe if Mac were seated closer to Rodney?

   ▼ Closer to Michael?

   ▼ If Mac and Rodney were on the same side of the table?

   ▼ How about Michael and Rodney on the same side of the table?

5. Instruct students to refer to the Peer Mediation Process Summary on page 32 of the Student Manual. Explain that this page is a condensed summary of the entire mediation process and that it can serve as a quick reference reminder whenever they conduct a mediation.

PEER MEDIATION PROCESS SUMMARY

STEP 1: AGREE TO MEDIATE
▼ Make introductions and define mediation.
▼ State the ground rules:
>   Mediators remain neutral; they do not take sides.
>   Mediation is private.
>   Take turns talking and listening.
>   Cooperate to solve the problem.
▼ Get a commitment from each disputant to mediate and follow the ground rules.

STEP 2: GATHER POINTS OF VIEW
▼ Ask each disputant (one at a time) to tell his or her point of view about the problem.
▼ Listen to each disputant and summarize following each disputant's statement.
▼ Allow each disputant a chance to clarify by asking:
>   Do you have anything to add?
>   How did you feel when that happened?
▼ Listen and summarize.

STEP 3: FOCUS ON INTERESTS
▼ Determine the interests of each disputant. Ask:
>   What do you want? Why do you want that?
▼ Listen and summarize. To clarify, ask:
>   What might happen if you don't reach an agreement?
>   What would you think if you were in the other person's shoes?
>   What do you *really* want?
▼ Summarize the interests. Say: "Your interests are _____ ."

STEP 4: CREATE WIN-WIN OPTIONS
▼ Explain brainstorming and state its rules:
>   Say any idea that comes to mind.
>   Do not judge or discuss ideas.
>   Come up with as many ideas as possible.
>   Try to think of unusual ideas.
▼ Write disputants' ideas on the Brainstorming Worksheet.

STEP 5: EVALUATE OPTIONS
▼ Ask disputants to nominate ideas or parts of ideas. Circle these on the Brainstorming Worksheet.
▼ Evaluate options by applying criteria:
>   Is this option fair?
>   Can you do it?
>   Do you think it will work?

STEP 6: CREATE AN AGREEMENT
▼ Help disputants make a plan of action. Get specifics from each disputant: Who, what, when, where, how?
▼ Write the Peer Mediation Agreement. To complete the agreement, have each disputant summarize by asking: "What have you agreed to do?"
▼ Close the mediation.

6. Conduct a demonstration of the peer mediation process. Three volunteers—co-trainers or training assistants—are needed for the demonstration. Volunteers should act out the case example given on pages 33–38 of the Student Manual. Tell students to follow along with the Peer Mediation Process Summary and pay close attention to the behavior of the mediator as he or she follows the six steps.

If you are using The Peer Mediation Video, *instead of having volunteers demonstrate the process, show the second part of the video, "Putting It All Together." In this segment, Mac mediates a dispute between Michael and Rodney (a 15-minute simulation of the six steps). As for the live demonstration, students should follow along with the Peer Mediation Process Summary.*

Case Example

The following case example illustrates how a peer mediator uses the six steps to help two students reach an agreement. In this situation, the mediation between Michael and Sondra has been requested by the school principal, Mr. Thomas.

Step 1: Agree to Mediate

Mediator: Hello, my name is _____, and I am the mediator assigned to conduct this session today. What are your names?

Sondra: My name is Sondra.

Michael: Michael.

Mediator: Michael and Sondra, I welcome you both to the mediation center. Mediation is a communication process in which the two of you will work together, with my assistance, cooperating to peaceably resolve your conflict. For mediation to work, there are ground rules to follow. First, I remain neutral—I will not take sides. Mediation is private—I will not talk about your problem with other students. Each of you will take turns talking, and when one talks, the other should listen. Last, you are expected to cooperate to solve the problem. Sondra, do you agree to mediate and follow the rules?

Sondra: Yes.

Mediator: Michael, do you agree to mediate and to follow the rules?

Michael: OK!

149

Step 2: Gather Points of View

Mediator: Sondra, tell me your point of view.

Sondra: Michael and I were arguing in the hallway. I got mad and threw my books at him. Then he shoved me against the lockers and was yelling at me when Mr. Thomas saw us. Mr. Thomas suspended Michael. I never fight with anyone—I just got so frustrated with Michael, I lost control.

Mediator: You were frustrated and threw your books at Michael. Mr. Thomas saw Michael shove you and suspended him. What did you think when that happened?

Sondra: I felt bad that Michael got in trouble because I started the fight. We aren't talking, and nothing I do seems to help.

Mediator: Sondra, you're sorry Michael was suspended, and you're still frustrated. Michael, tell me your point of view.

Michael: Sondra is always getting mad at me. She tells everyone on the tennis team I'm rude and selfish. I missed a practice, and she turns it into a war.

Sondra: You're irresponsible. You're either late for practice, or you don't even bother to come.

Mediator: Sondra, it's Michael's turn to talk. Please don't interrupt. Michael, you missed a tennis practice, and Sondra got angry. Tell me more about that.

Michael: Well, we're doubles partners. She takes the game much too seriously. She needs to lighten up. She thinks just because she's my tennis partner, I belong to her. She calls me a lot, but I don't want to be with only one girl all the time. I need my space.

Mediator: Michael, are you saying that you are concerned Sondra wants more from you than just being your tennis partner?

Michael: Yes. She doesn't want me to be with other girls.

Mediator: Sondra, do you have anything else you want to add?

Sondra: Michael takes me for granted. I want him to consider how I feel when he stands me up at practice.

Mediator: Sondra, you want Michael to understand your feelings when he doesn't come to practice and doesn't tell you he won't be there.

Sondra: Yes, that's what I want.

Mediator: Michael, do you have anything to add?

Michael: No.

Step 3: Focus on Interests

Mediator: Sondra, why do you think Michael doesn't tell you when he is not going to make practice?

Sondra: Well . . . he probably doesn't want to hear me yell and cry in front of his friends.

Mediator: Sondra, do you think yelling at Michael will help him get to practice?

Sondra: No, I guess not.

Mediator: Michael, what do you want?

Michael: I want her to stop getting so angry.

Mediator: You don't want Sondra to be mad at you. Michael, if Sondra stood you up for practice, how would you feel?

Michael: Oh, I would be worried she got hurt or something. I probably would be mad if I found out she did it on purpose.

Mediator: You'd be concerned that she was all right and upset if she did it on purpose. Michael, what do you really want?

Michael: What do you mean?

Mediator: Do you want to be Sondra's friend?

Michael: I want to be her friend, and I want to be her tennis partner. I don't want to be her boyfriend.

Mediator: You want to be Sondra's friend and tennis partner? Is standing her up for practice helping you get what you want?

Michael: No, it's not helping.

Mediator: Sondra, what do you want?

Sondra: I guess I've wanted Michael to be my boyfriend, and the more I try to make that happen the worse things get.

Mediator: Sondra, can you make Michael be your boyfriend?

Sondra: No, not if he doesn't want to be.

Mediator: Sondra, do you want to be Michael's tennis partner?

Sondra: Yes.

Mediator: Do you want to be his friend?

Sondra: I think so.

Step 4: Create Win-Win Options

Mediator: It sounds like you both want to be friends and tennis partners. Now I want you both to think about what you can do to help solve your problem. We'll make a list of possible solutions by brainstorming. The rules for brainstorming are to say any ideas that come to mind, even unusual ideas. Do not judge or discuss the ideas, and look for as many ideas as possible that might satisfy both of you. Ready? What can you do to solve this problem?

Michael: I could stop skipping practice . . .

Sondra: And let me know if you can't make it.

Michael: We could practice before school if we miss a practice.

Sondra: I could stop yelling at Michael.

Mediator: What else can you both do to solve the problem?

Michael: We could play tennis on Saturday mornings and then have lunch together.

Sondra: I could stop calling Michael just to talk.

Michael: I could take the tournament that's coming up more seriously . . . I really didn't think it mattered.

Mediator: Can you think of anything else?

Michael: No.

Sondra: No.

Step 5: Evaluate Options

Mediator: Which of these ideas will probably work best?

Michael: Well, practicing before school would work.

Sondra: If I don't yell at Michael and stop calling him all the time, he probably would like practice better.

Mediator: Can you do this?

Sondra: If I get upset about something, I could write Michael a note to explain . . . and then we could talk about the problem instead of arguing. Michael could do the same if he's upset about something.

Mediator: Michael, would this work for you?

Michael: It would be better than yelling.

Mediator: What else are you willing to do?

Michael: Well, we have this tournament coming up . . . I would be willing to practice before and after school and on Saturday mornings to make up for the times I've missed.

Mediator: Sondra, are you willing to do that?

Sondra: That practice schedule would be hard work, but I'll do it. I think we can win if we practice real hard. We also need to let each other know if we need to cancel.

Mediator: How would that work?

Michael: We could either call each other or leave notes in each other's lockers.

Mediator: Sondra, do you agree that would help?

Sondra: Yes.

Step 6: Create an Agreement

Mediator: You both seem to have agreed to practice before school, after school, and on Saturday. If either of you needs to cancel practice you will either call the other or leave a note. What time?

Sondra: How about at 7:30 in the morning and 4:00 after school and, say, 10:00 on Saturday?

Michael: OK.

Mediator: Where will you leave the notes for each other and when?

Michael: If we are canceling after-school practice we can put a note in the other person's locker at lunch. I guess we should call if we are canceling before school or on Saturday.

Sondra: That's good.

Mediator: Is there anything else you can agree to?

Sondra: I think that if we have a problem in the future we should write the other person a note explaining the problem and then talk about it.

Michael: I think that's fair.

Mediator: Is the problem solved?

Sondra: I think so.

Michael: Yeah.

Mediator: Michael, what have you agreed to do?

Michael: I've agreed to get serious about tennis and practice every day at 7:30 and at 4:00 and on Saturday morning, and to always show up unless I tell Sondra in advance. Also, I agree to talk with Sondra when there is a problem rather than just ignoring her.

Mediator: Sondra, what have you agreed to do?

Sondra: Practice before and after school every day and on Saturday, at 10:00, I think. I will stop calling Michael just to talk, and I will let him know when something is bothering me without yelling at him or trying to embarrass him.

Mediator: Please look over this agreement to be sure it is correct, and if it is, sign it.

(Sondra and Michael sign, and the mediator signs. The mediator shakes hands with Sondra, then Michael.)

Mediator: Thank you for participating in mediation. If you encounter other problems, please think about requesting mediation to help you. Would the two of you like to shake hands?

(Sondra and Michael shake hands.)

7. Following the demonstration (either live or videotaped), discuss any questions students might have about what they saw.

8. Explain that the next several activities will describe each step of the mediation process in detail and that each student will have an opportunity to practice the process, step by step. Tell students that before doing a "for real" mediation it might be especially useful for them to refer to the case example in the Student Manual.

STEP 1: AGREE TO MEDIATE

PURPOSE

Students will learn how to open the peer mediation session by practicing Step 1.

TIME

15 minutes

MATERIALS

Student Manual (page 39)

PROCEDURE

1. Divide the students into triads. Explain that they each will have an opportunity to be the mediator and practice opening the mediation session. Instruct each group of three to set up for the mediation. Two members of each group will be the disputants, and the other will be the mediator. Remind students about the preferred seating arrangement by telling them you should be able to determine, without asking, which student is the mediator.

2. Present the following section of the Student Manual.

STEP 1: AGREE TO MEDIATE

An effective opening to a mediation session sets the stage for the remainder of the session. You open the session by making introductions, defining mediation, stating the ground rules, and getting a commitment from each disputant to mediate and follow the ground rules.

1. Make introductions.

▼ Introduce yourself: "Hi! My name is _____ , and I will be your mediator."

▼ Ask each disputant for his or her name.

▼ Welcome disputants to mediation.

2. Define mediation.

▼ Use your own words to explain mediation to the disputants. For example: "Mediation is a communication process in which the people with the problem work cooperatively, with the assistance of a neutral third party, to resolve their conflict peaceably."

---

3. State the ground rules.

▼ Mediators remain neutral: "I will not take sides."

▼ Mediation is private: "I will not talk about you or your problem with other students. It is OK for you to tell others that you reached an agreement and what you agreed to, but don't talk about each other and the problem between you."

▼ Take turns talking and listening: "This means that while one of you is talking the other is expected to listen, and also that you will each have an equal opportunity to talk."

▼ Cooperate to solve the problem: "You will do your best to reach an agreement that considers both your interests."

4. Get a commitment from each disputant to mediate and follow the ground rules: "Do you agree to mediate and to follow the rules?"

3. Instruct the triads to practice Step 1. Start with the triad member who is already in the mediator position. After that person has practiced Step 1, each of the other members, in turn, should move to the mediator chair and practice serving as the mediator for Step 1. Have training assistants serve as coaches for each of the triads.

4. In the larger group, discuss any questions about Step 1. Summarize by stressing the following points:

▼ An effective opening sets the stage for the rest of the peer mediation session. It establishes that the mediator is in charge and sets expectations for how all are to behave.

▼ The ground rules structure a win-win climate.

▼ A clear understanding of the ground rules is necessary for the success of the peer mediation process.

▼ It is important for disputants to know that the peer mediator is there to help them create a solution to their problem and not to judge who is right or wrong.

STEP 2: GATHER POINTS OF VIEW

PURPOSE

Students will learn how to gather points of view from both parties in order to better define the problem or conflict.

TIME

30 minutes

MATERIALS

Student Manual (pages 40–43)

Peer Mediation Simulations 1, 2, and 3 (from Appendix E; one copy of each for every group of three students)

PROCEDURE

1. Arrange for volunteers from among your co-trainers and assistant trainers to demonstrate the following mediation, beginning on page 40 in the Student Manual. Have volunteers set up for the mediation in the front of the room. Instruct students to watch the demonstration, paying particular attention to the mediator.

RED RIDING HOOD AND THE WOLF

Mediator: Hello, I am _____. I am your mediator. What is your name?

Red: I'm Red Riding Hood. They used to call me Little Red Riding Hood, but they don't anymore. You see, the Wolf and I have had this problem a long time, and I grew up.

Mediator: What is your name?

Wolf: I'm the Wolf.

Mediator: Welcome to the mediation center. I'm sorry it took you so long to find us. Mediation is a communication process where you, Red and Wolf, can work together, with my help as your mediator, to cooperate to solve the problem between you. The ground rules that make mediation work are as follows: I remain neutral—I do not take sides. Everything said in mediation is private. Each person takes turns talking without interruption. Finally, you will do your best to reach an agreement that considers both your needs. Red Riding Hood, do you agree to the ground rules?

Red: Yes.

Mediator: Wolf, do you agree to the ground rules?

Wolf: Yes, I do.

Mediator: Red Riding Hood, please tell what happened.

Red: Well, you see, I was taking a loaf of fresh bread and some cakes to my grannie's cottage on the other side of the woods. Grannie wasn't well, so I thought I would pick some flowers for her along the way. I was picking the flowers when the Wolf jumped out from behind a tree and started asking me a bunch of questions. He wanted to know what I was doing and where I was going, and he kept grinning this wicked grin and smacking his lips together. He was being so gross and rude. Then he ran away.

Mediator: You were taking some food to your grandmother on the other side of the woods and the Wolf appeared from behind the tree and frightened you.

Red: Yes, that's what happened.

Mediator: Wolf, please tell what happened.

Wolf: The forest is my home. I care about it and try to keep it clean. One day, when I was cleaning up some garbage people had left behind, I heard footsteps. I leaped behind a tree and saw a girl coming down the trail carrying a basket. I was suspicious because she was dressed in this strange red cape with her head covered up as if she didn't want anyone to know who she was. She started picking my flowers and stepping on my new little pine trees. Naturally, I stopped to ask her what she was doing and all that. She gave me this song and dance about going to her grannie's house with a basket of goodies.

Mediator: You were concerned when you saw this girl dressed in red picking your flowers. You stopped her and asked her what she was doing.

Wolf: That's right.

Mediator: Red Riding Hood, is there anything you want to add?

Red: Yes. When I got to my grannie's house the Wolf was disguised in my grannie's nightgown. He tried to eat me with those big ugly teeth. I'd be dead today if it hadn't been for a woodsman who came in and saved me. The Wolf scared my grannie—I found her hiding under the bed.

Mediator: You are saying the Wolf put on your grannie's nightgown so you would think he was your grannie and that he tried to hurt you?

Red: I said he tried to eat me.

Mediator: So you felt he was trying to eat you. Wolf, do you have anything to add?

Wolf: Of course I do. I know this girl's grannie. I thought we should teach Red Riding Hood a lesson for prancing on my pine trees in that get-up and for picking my flowers. I let her go on her way, but I ran ahead to her grannie's cottage. When I saw Grannie, I explained what happened, and she agreed her granddaughter needed to learn a lesson. Grannie hid under the bed, and I dressed up in Grannie's nightgown. When Red Riding Hood came into the bedroom, she saw me in the bed and said something nasty about my big ears. I've been told my ears are big before, so I tried to make the best of it by saying big ears help me hear her better. Then she made an insulting crack about my bulging eyes. This one was really hard to blow off because she sounded so nasty. Still, I make a policy to turn the other cheek, so I told her my big eyes help me to see her better. Her next insult about my big teeth really got to me. You see, I'm quite sensitive about them. I know when she made fun of my teeth I should have had better control, but I leaped from the bed and growled that my teeth would help me to eat her.

Mediator: So you and Grannie tried to play a trick on Red Riding Hood to teach her a lesson. Explain more about the eating part.

Wolf: Now, let's face it. Everyone knows no wolf could ever eat a girl, but crazy Red Riding Hood started screaming and running around the house. I tried to catch her to calm her down. All of a sudden the door came crashing open, and a big woodsman stood there with his axe. I knew I was in trouble . . . there was an open window behind me, so out I went. I've been hiding ever since. There are terrible rumors going around the forest about me. Red Riding Hood calls me the Big Bad Wolf. I'd like to say I've gotten over feeling bad, but the truth is I haven't lived happily ever after. I don't understand why Grannie never told my side of the story.

Mediator: You're upset about the rumors and have been afraid to show your face in the forest. You're also confused about why Grannie hasn't set things straight and has let the situation go on for this long.

Wolf: It just isn't fair. I'm miserable and lonely.

Mediator: Red Riding Hood, would you tell us more about Grannie?

Red: Well, Grannie has been sick—and she's been getting a little forgetful lately. When I asked her how she came to be under the bed she said she couldn't remember a thing that had happened.

Mediator: Grannie seems lately to have trouble remembering things, and she couldn't explain why she was under the bed.

2. After the demonstration, discuss by asking the following questions:

> ▼ What did you learn by watching this role-play?

> ▼ How would you define Red Riding Hood's problem?

> ▼ How would you define the Wolf's problem?

> ▼ What did the mediator do to get this information?

3. Present the following section from the Student Manual.

STEP 2: GATHER POINTS OF VIEW

In this step, you will use the communication skills of active listening—attending, summarizing, and clarifying—to help you understand the disputants' situation and feelings and to help the disputants understand how each perceives the problem. Disputants may see the problem pretty much the same way or, more likely, they will have different points of view because they each perceive the problem differently and have different positions, or ideas, about how to solve the problem. In this step, you are not trying to get each disputant to agree on what happened but rather to share his or her own point of view and hear the point of view of the other.

1. Ask each disputant (one at a time) to tell his or her point of view about the problem:

> ▼ Please share your point of view.

> ▼ Please tell what happened.

2. Listen to each disputant and summarize following each disputant's statement.

3. Allow each disputant a chance to clarify by asking:

> ▼ Do you have anything to add?

> ▼ How did you feel when that happened?

4. Listen and summarize by asking for additional information if needed.

4. Stress the importance of using the communication skills of active listening while gathering points of view. It is especially important to summarize facts and feelings. Ask, "What will you think if one of the disputants does not respond to your question? What will you do?" Tell students that sometimes individuals who are inclined to have a soft response to conflict may not want to tell their point of view. When that happens, it is important for the mediator to help them to share, perhaps by asking different questions.

5. Present the following section of the Student Manual.

Additional questions to help gather points of view:

▼ How did you feel about the other person?

▼ What did you do?

▼ What were you thinking at the time?

▼ How long has the problem existed?

▼ What do you feel is the major problem?

▼ What are you doing now about the situation?

▼ How has your relationship changed?

▼ What did you want the other person to do that he or she didn't do?

▼ What did you want to do that you didn't do?

Since perceptions are reality, you need not be concerned with whether
or not disputants are telling the "truth."

---

6. Discuss the idea that, at other times, especially when you think the disputant has more to say, it may be more effective to ask the disputant to respond to a statement—for example, "Were you afraid you were going to be injured when that happened?"

7. Point out that the speed with which one responds to a question may be related to the person's culture. In the white culture, long silences often make people uncomfortable. In nonwhite cultures, pausing and taking time to think before responding is not uncomfortable at all; hurrying a response is uncomfortable. For others, not responding quickly is a strategy for controlling anger. As a peer mediator, it is important to be patient when silence occurs; you need not be in a hurry.

8. Have the students reassemble their triads. Tell them that they will practice Steps 1 and 2 of the mediation process, using Peer Mediation Simulations 1, 2, and 3. Each member of the triad will be the mediator for one of these simulated problems; the other two members will be the disputants.

9. Give the Peer Mediation Request and the Role-Play Instructions for Simulation 1 to the student seated in the mediator's position. Tell the mediator to give one of the disputants the Student A instructions and the other disputant the Student B instructions. Instruct the mediators to allow disputants time to read their roles, then to perform Steps 1 and 2 of the process.

The following training strategy will be helpful in conducting this and all subsequent simulations: Have all the Disputant As meet together, outside the room if possible, with one of the training assistants. The training assistant facilitates a discussion in the group about how best to play that role in the mediation. Have another training assistant coach all the Disputant Bs in a different location. While the training assistants provide coaching, instruct the mediators about the conflict situation and remind them of key things to accomplish during the mediation. When the group reconvenes, training assistants coach the triads as needed during the simulation.

10. After each mediation practice, have the training assistants ask the peer mediators the following questions to process the activity:

   ▼ What did you do well in the simulation?

   ▼ What could you do differently?

   Training assistants and disputants may give mediators constructive feedback.

11. Repeat this process with a different mediator for Peer Mediation Simulations 2 and 3.

STEP 3: FOCUS ON INTERESTS

PURPOSE

Students will learn to find interests underlying disputants' positions and to focus on those interests for the rest of the mediation process.

TIME

Part 1: 30 minutes

Part 2: 60 minutes

MATERIALS

Student Manual (pages 44–45)

An orange and knife

Peer Mediation Simulations 4, 5, and 6 (from Appendix E; one copy of each for every group of three students)

PROCEDURE

Part 1

1. Hold up the orange and tell the following story:

    Sam and Ben were twins who usually got along fine. One day, however, they got into a terrible fight about who would have the last orange in the bag. Finally, they went to their mother for help in solving their problem. Being a fair mother, she cut the orange in half and gave one half to Sam and the other half to Ben. *(Cut the orange in half to illustrate.)* The children began to argue again, each demanding the other's half of the orange. The mother could not figure out why. She thought cutting the orange in half was a good compromise.

2. Stop and ask the students the following questions:

    ▼ What did Sam want?

    ▼ What did Ben want?

    ▼ Why did the mother's solution not work?

3. Continue with the story:

> When the mother finally realized that she had made a mistake, she asked Ben what was wrong. Ben sobbed that half an orange was not enough to make orange juice. Then Sam cried that there was not enough peel in half an orange to use in the orange rolls he planned to bake.

4. Stop and ask the following questions:

   ▼ What are Ben's interests?

   ▼ What are Sam's interests?

   ▼ What have you learned from this story?

5. Explain that people often take a *position* when in a conflict. In most cases, it is nearly impossible to find a solution to a problem between two people by focusing on positions. Any agreement based on positions probably will not last because the *interests*, or what the people really want, have not been addressed. For lasting solutions, the peer mediator must get the disputants to focus on their interests, especially those they have in common or those that are compatible.

6. Stress that during Step 3, the peer mediator continues to practice active listening, being especially alert to expression of interests and summarizing any common interests revealed. Refer students to the Identifying Interests Worksheet on page 44 in the Student Manual.

The Identifying Interests Worksheet given here includes sample responses. The version presented in the Student Manual is blank.

IDENTIFYING INTERESTS WORKSHEET

SITUATION	POSITION	INTERESTS
1. Marcus shouts at Tyrone, "You can't apply for the same job I did. There's only one opening, and I was there first!" Tyrone yells, "I deserve that job, too!"	*Marcus wants the job. Tyrone wants the job.*	*Marcus and Tyrone want money because money will give them freedon. They may need the money to do things with their friends. They may want to be friends with each other.*
2. Lisa yells at her sister, Kara, "You can't ride my bike to school anymore. It's never here when I want it!" Kara yells, "I'm riding your bike—you almost never use it!"	*Lisa won't let Kara ride her bike. Kara will ride the bike.*	*Lisa and Kara both want transportation. Riding a bike can be fun, especially with friends.*
3. Diana is mad at her boyfriend, Jerome, and says, "If you go out with Rachel, I'll never speak to you again." Jerome yells back, "Rachel is a friend. I'm not her boyfriend!"	*Diana wants Jerome to go out only with her. Jerome wants to be friends with Rachel.*	*Diana and Jerome want to continue their relationship.*
4. Juan is upset with Malcolm: "If you keep asking me for answers in math class, I'll report you to the teacher." Malcolm shouts, "Go ahead—I'll report you when you ask me answers in science!"	*Juan will report Malcolm. Malcolm will report Juan.*	*Both Juan and Malcolm want to achieve in math class. They may want to be friends.*
5. Keisha says to Natalie, "You can't go on the canoe trip because you can't swim like the rest of us." Natalie cries, "I don't need to swim like you. I'm going anyway!"	*Keisha says Natalie can't go on the trip. Natalie is going on the trip.*	*Both Keisha and Natalie want to be part of the group, especially when the group does fun activities.*

7. Discuss the first situation as an example for the large group. Instruct students to work in groups of six to identify the possible positions and common interests the disputants have in the remaining examples. Remind them that interests are related to satisfying the basic psychological needs of belonging, power, freedom, and fun.

8. When students have completed the exercise, have them reassemble as a large group. Ask each group to share what they feel are the disputants' positions and potential interests. Point out that many disputes involve multiple interests and that, when disputants are able to acknowledge that each other's interests are part of the problem, they can begin to cooperate.

Part 2

9. Present the following from the Student Manual.

STEP 3: FOCUS ON INTERESTS

In this step, your goal is to search for interests that join both disputants. Common or compatible interests serve as the building blocks for an agreement. Unless interests are identified, disputants probably will not be able to make an agreement they can both keep. Do not move on to Step 4 until you find out what the interests are.

1. Determine the interests of each disputant. Ask:

▼ What do you want? Why do you want that?

2. Listen and summarize. To clarify, ask:

▼ What might happen if you do not reach an agreement?

▼ What would you think if you were in the other person's shoes?

▼ What do you *really* want?

▼ Is (*Example: fighting*) getting you what you want?

▼ Why has the other disputant not done what you expect?

3. Summarize the interests. Say:

▼ Both of you seem to agree that _____ .

▼ Your interests are _____ .

10. In this portion of the activity, demonstrate Step 3 by role-playing with your co-trainers the first example from the Identifying Interests Worksheet. Before presenting the dialogue, give the following background: Tyrone found out about the job because he saw Marcus dressed up for the interview and asked him where he was going. Marcus is mad because there is only one job opening and he applied first. Marcus has threatened to fight Tyrone if Tyrone doesn't call and say he is no longer interested in the job.

Mediator: Marcus, why do you think Tyrone has not withdrawn his application for the job?

Marcus: He really wants a job.

Mediator: Tyrone, if you were in Marcus's shoes, why would you want this job so much?

Tyrone: For the money. We both really need spending money.

Mediator: Marcus, is fighting over this one job helping you get spending money?

Marcus: No.

Mediator: Is fighting helping your friendship?

Tyrone: No, it isn't.

Mediator: What do you really want?

Marcus: I want a job so I'll have spending money.

Tyrone: I want the same.

Mediator: It sounds as though each of you agrees that fighting and getting mad isn't good for your friendship or helping you get a job. You both agree that you want a job so you'll have spending money.

11. Form student triads different from the ones formed before and tell the groups that they will practice Steps 1, 2, and 3 of the mediation process, using Peer Mediation Simulations 4, 5, and 6. Each member of the triad will be the mediator for one of these simulated problems; the other two members will be the disputants.

12. Give the Peer Mediation Request and Role-Play Instructions for Simulation 4 to the student seated in the mediator's position. Tell the mediator to give one of the disputants the Student A instructions and the other disputant the Student B instructions. Have training assistants coach the groups of disputants separately on their roles while you instruct the mediators to perform Steps 1, 2, and 3 of the process.

13. Reassemble the triads and conduct the simulation. During the simulation, training assistants provide coaching to the triads as needed.

14. After each mediation practice, have the training assistants ask the peer mediators the following questions to process the activity:

> ▼ What did you do well in the simulation?

> ▼ What could you do differently?

> ▼ What questions helped you uncover the disputants' interests and find common or compatible interests?

Training assistants and disputants may give mediators constructive feedback.

15. Repeat this process with a different mediator for Peer Mediation Simulations 5 and 6.

16. Reiterate the ideas that common or compatible interests are the building blocks of a resolution and that the peer mediator does not move on to Step 4 until common or compatible interests are found. If the disputants' answers do not reveal common or compatible interests, the mediator may need to return to Step 2. The mediator may do so by asking, "Is there something about this problem you haven't yet shared?"

STEP 4: CREATE WIN-WIN OPTIONS

PURPOSE

Students will learn to use the conflict resolution technique of brainstorming to create as many options as possible to solve the identified problem.

TIME

30 minutes

MATERIALS

Student Manual (page 46)

Newsprint

Markers

Brainstorming Worksheet (from Appendix A; one copy for every group of four to six students)

PROCEDURE

1. Briefly describe the purpose of the activity and define *brainstorming* as a technique of conflict resolution in which disputants generate as many ideas as possible for solving a problem.

2. Present the following section from the Student Manual.

STEP 4: CREATE WIN-WIN OPTIONS

Many possible ideas exist for resolving a conflict. However, when we are upset or frustrated, we often do not consider all of our options. In this step, you will help disputants create, through brainstorming, a number of options that could potentially solve their problem.

1. Explain that brainstorming will help disputants find solutions that satisfy both parties.

2. State the rules for brainstorming:

▼ Say any ideas that come to mind.

▼ Do not judge or discuss the ideas.

▼ Come up with as many ideas as possible.

▼ Try to think of unusual ideas.

---

3. Tell disputants to try to think of ideas that will help both of them. Write their ideas on a Brainstorming Worksheet.

Additional questions to help the brainstorming process along:

- ▼ What other possibilities can you think of?

- ▼ In the future, what could you do differently?

- ▼ What could be done to resolve this dispute?

3. To demonstrate how brainstorming works, form student groups of four to six members each. Give each group a sheet of newsprint and a marker and ask them to draw a brick at the top of their newsprint. Tell them that they have 3 minutes to conduct a "brick brainstorm"—that is, to come up with as many uses for a brick as they can.

4. After the time is up, ask each group to share the number of ideas they came up with and their two or three most unusual uses for the brick. (If desired, you can repeat this exercise with another object, such as a paper clip or a marshmallow.)

5. Next distribute a copy of the Brainstorming Worksheet to each group. Assign each group one of the six mediation simulation situations already practiced; have groups come up with 7 to 10 possible options for resolving the conflict.

- ▼ Simulation 1: Two students are in conflict because one of them keeps cutting into the lunchline.

- ▼ Simulation 2: Two locker partners are arguing about missing things.

- ▼ Simulation 3: Two students had a loud disagreement in class.

- ▼ Simulation 4: Two students were ready to fight in the cafeteria.

- ▼ Simulation 5: Two students were fighting in the locker room.

- ▼ Simulation 6: Two students are very mad at each other because of a lost library book.

6. Ask each small group to report to the larger group on the options they generated to solve their assigned conflict. Discuss the following questions.

- ▼ Was it hard to follow the rules for brainstorming?

- ▼ Did some of the options seem ridiculous?

- ▼ When did the best ideas come out?

- ▼ Was there much silence? If so, how did you handle it?

STEP 5: EVALUATE OPTIONS

PURPOSE

Students will learn to help disputants choose the best options from those generated in Step 4 by applying objective criteria.

TIME

30 minutes

MATERIALS

Student Manual (page 47)

Brainstorming Worksheets (completed during Activity 12)

PROCEDURE

1. Present the following section from the Student Manual.

STEP 5: EVALUATE OPTIONS

Your main task in this step is to help disputants evaluate and improve on the ideas they created during brainstorming in Step 4. It is also important that the disputants apply objective criteria when deciding whether to keep or reject an option. This helps to ensure that they will be able to reach an agreement that both are likely to honor.

1. **Ask disputants to nominate ideas or parts of ideas they are willing to do in order to help solve the problem. Circle their responses on the Brainstorming Worksheet.**

2. **Evaluate the circled options and invent ways to improve the ideas by using one or more questions (criteria). Ask:**

   ▼ Is this option fair?

   ▼ Can you do it?

   ▼ Do you think it will work?

   ▼ Does the option address the interests of each of you? Of others?

   ▼ What are the consequences of deciding to do this?

   ▼ What if one person did _____? Could you do _____?

   ▼ What are you willing to try?

---

2. After reviewing Step 5 procedures, have the students return to the brainstorming groups they formed in Activity 12 and review the previously completed Brainstorming Worksheets. Instruct the groups to choose one or more options that they believe would resolve their assigned conflict: Tell students that the idea of combining options or parts of options may create a new idea acceptable to each disputant because the options or parts are compatible—they do not interfere with each other.

3. To process the activity, ask each group to share with the larger group the options they chose as possible ideas for resolving the conflict and the reasons they had (criteria) for making their selection.

4. Tell students that *fairness* is often the most powerful criteria for judging options. Discuss fairness in the larger group by asking:

   ▼ What is fair?

   ▼ What are some standards for fairness?

   ▼ Can there be more than one standard?

   ▼ What is the relationship between fairness and rights and responsibilities?

5. Summarize by telling students that in Step 5, the peer mediator helps the disputants decide on what they are willing to do to solve the problem. The peer mediator insists that they examine the ideas generated according to specific criteria in order to create a sound agreement in Step 6.

STEP 6: CREATE AN AGREEMENT

PURPOSE

Students will learn to formalize an agreement between the disputants and to obtain a commitment to the agreement.

TIME

30 minutes

MATERIALS

Student Manual (pages 48–49)

Brainstorming Worksheets (from Activities 12 and 13)

Peer Mediation Agreement Form (from Appendix A; one copy for each group of four to six students)

PROCEDURE

1. Present the following section of the Student Manual.

STEP 6: CREATE AN AGREEMENT

In this step, the peer mediator helps disputants create a sound agreement. A sound agreement is:

- ▼ Effective: It fairly resolves the major issues for each disputant.

- ▼ Mutually satisfying: Both disputants think it is fair.

- ▼ Specific: Answers who, what, when, where, and how.

- ▼ Realistic: The plan is reasonable and can be accomplished by the disputants.

- ▼ Balanced: Each person agrees to be responsible for something.

1. Help disputants make a plan of action. Get specifics from each disputant: Who, what when, where, how. Ask:

- ▼ What are you willing to do to solve this problem?

- ▼ Is the problem solved?

- ▼ What have you agreed to do?

---

2. Write the Peer Mediation Agreement. To complete the agreement, have each disputant summarize by asking: "What have you agreed to do?"

3. Close the mediation:

▼ Review the agreement form with both parties and make any changes.

▼ Sign the form and ask each party to sign.

▼ Thank disputants for participating in mediation, congratulate each for working to reach an agreement, and invite them to use mediation in the future.

▼ Shake hands with each disputant and invite disputants to shake hands with each other.

2. Refer students to the Sample Peer Mediation Agreement on page 49 of the Student Manual. Explain that Rodney Anderson and Rachel Sharp co-mediated a conflict between Andrew and Heather. Andrew had borrowed Heather's Gameboy and took it into school, even though Heather asked him not to do so. The principal confiscated the Gameboy. Discuss the sample agreement.

SAMPLE PEER MEDIATION AGREEMENT

Date _____11/13/96_____

We voluntarily participated in a mediation. We have reached an agreement that we believe is fair and that solves the problem between us. In the future if we have problems that we cannot resolve on our own, we agree to come back to mediation.

Name _____Heather_____   Name _____Andrew_____

Agrees to act calmer and not yell at Andrew if a problem happens in the future.

Agrees to talk with Andrew first to check things out and will try not to jump to conclusions.

Agrees to talk with the principal today to see if he can get Heather's Gameboy.

If the principal refuses to return the Gameboy, Andrew agrees to ask the principal to accept Andrew's Gameboy in place of Heather's.

Agrees to return Heather's Gameboy to her or give her his Gameboy until such time as the principal agrees to release Heather's.

Signature _____Heather_____   Signature _____Andrew_____

Mediator signature _____Rodney Anderson_____

Mediator signature _____Rachel Sharp_____

3. Ask students to return to the brainstorming groups they formed in Activities 11 and 12. Give each group a blank copy of the Peer Mediation Agreement and ask them to work together to write up the agreement they chose as a solution to their assigned conflict. Coach as necessary.

4. Ask small groups to share their agreements in the larger group and critique the agreements.

5. Ask students what they might think if a disputant refuses to shake hands with the mediator. With the other disputant? Tell students that shaking hands may have cultural implications: In some cultures it is taboo for women to shake hands. There may be valid reasons why a person would choose not to shake hands. In mediation, it is a gesture that is offered, not required. Further, handshakes can come in a variety of forms: the formal shake, the high five, the low five, the slap, the finger touch, and so on.

ACTIVITY 15

CO-MEDIATION PRACTICE

PURPOSE

Students will become acquainted with the recommended co-mediation model and practice the complete mediation process.

TIME

Part 1: 60 minutes *(required)*

Part 2: 45 minutes *(recommended)*

MATERIALS

Student Manual (page 50)

Brainstorming Worksheet (from Appendix A; one copy for each student)

Peer Mediation Agreement Form (from Appendix A; one copy for each student)

Peer Mediation Simulations 7, 8, 9, and 10 (from Appendix E; one copy of each for every group of four students)

Part 1

1. Tell students that because mediation is a complicated problem-solving process that must be custom tailored to each dispute, co-mediation is used to enhance the probability of success. Co-mediation also helps to assure impartiality when the mediation pair is matched with the disputants according to characteristics like age, gender, and race.

2. Refer students to the following section of the Student Manual.

WHAT IS CO-MEDIATION?

In **co-mediation,** two mediators work as a team to facilitate the mediation process. Co-mediators act as a single mediator, managing the process while supporting each other. In the co-mediation model, the team members perform two responsibilities:

▼ One member of the team actively facilitates the six-step mediation process.

▼ The other member of the team observes the process and supports the teammate.

Supporting a teammate involves monitoring the process to help make sure that the mediator is remaining neutral, that he or she is summarizing the statements of the disputants, that the ground rules are being followed, and so on. It also involves paying close attention to what is happening and being prepared at all times to help your teammate if he or she seems to be stuck. Often someone who is only observing can more easily think of a question that might help move the mediation toward a resolution because that person is not thinking about what has to be done in the particular step of the process.

Co-mediation works best when the two team members equally share these two responsibilities. One member of the team facilitates Steps 1, 3, and 5 while the other member observes and supports. For Steps 2, 4, and 6, the facilitation and support responsibilities are exchanged.

In co-mediation, the two mediators must decide in advance how they will work together. Co-mediators should decide the following questions:

▼ Who will facilitate Steps 1, 3, and 5, and who will facilitate Steps 2, 4, and 6?

▼ How will the observer help the facilitator? (How will he or she tell the facilitator he or she forgot to do something important, how will he or she offer suggestions, and so forth.)

Remember, as co-mediators your job is to help each other.
The two of you will model cooperation for the disputants.

178

3. Discuss any questions students have about co-mediation. Indicate that most adults think mediation is a process that works best with co-mediation and therefore choose not to mediate alone.

4. Ask each student to find a partner who is someone he or she has not already been in a twosome or triad with during the training. Instruct each pair to join another pair. Indicate that this group of four will practice co-mediation and that each pair will have an opportunity to assume the co-mediation role. When one pair are co-mediators, the other pair role-play the disputants in the simulation.

5. Ask the group to set up for the mediation. After they have set up, ask, "Are you set up properly for the mediation?" Remind them that co-mediators sit together between the disputants, who should be facing each other.

6. Give the Peer Mediation Request and Role-Play Instructions for Peer Mediation Simulation 7 to the students seated in the mediator position. Tell the mediators to give one disputant the Student A instructions and the other disputant the Student B instructions.

7. Have training assistants take the groups of disputants aside and coach them separately on their roles while you give each co-mediation pair a copy of the Brainstorming Worksheet and the Peer Mediation Agreement. Instruct the co-mediators to decide how they will co-mediate the problem; tell them they are to work effectively through all six steps of the mediation process. Instruct them to have available the Peer Mediation Process Summary from page 32 of their Student Manuals as a reference. Allow 2 to 3 minutes for the co-mediators to decide who will do what.

8. Reassemble the mediation groups. Tell them that their goal is not to see how fast they can solve the problem but rather to have the disputants cooperate and reach a sound agreement. Mediators should not proceed to brainstorming until they have identified interests underlying the conflict.

9. Have students conduct the simulation. Allow 12 to 15 minutes, or enough time for most of the groups to finalize an agreement. During the simulation, have training assistants provide coaching as needed.

10. Have each training assistant help his or her group process the completed mediation by asking the mediators to self-evaluate and encouraging the disputants to provide constructive feedback.

11. Ask that some of the solutions be shared in the large group. When each solution is shared, ask, "What did you identify as the interests?"

12. Ask each group to rearrange the seating so that the other pair assumes the co-mediation role. Using Peer Mediation Simulation 8, repeat the preceding co-mediation procedures.

13. Instruct each student to find a different partner and each pair to join another pair. Repeat the co-mediation procedures, using Peer Mediation Simulations 9 and 10.

If time does not permit you to repeat co-mediation practice during basic training, this activity makes a good follow-up experience. Bring the group together within 2 weeks, conduct practice mediations, and review skills.

ACTIVITY 16

SUPPORT FOR PEER MEDIATION AND PEER MEDIATORS

PURPOSE

Students will achieve closure on basic training, have the opportunity to ask questions and concerns, go over the peer mediator contract, and receive certification and congratulations.

TIME

55 minutes

MATERIALS

Student Manual (page 51)

Peer Mediator Contract (from Appendix A; one copy for each student)

T-shirts, buttons, or certificates *(optional)*

PROCEDURE

1. Refer students to the following section of the Student Manual and discuss.

Things to Remember

Being a peer mediator is not always easy. Mediation is always a challenge. It is important to be positive and optimistic, even though a mediation is difficult or the outcome is not as you expect. Remember, you are there only to offer your skilled assistance.

❖

The problem belongs to the disputants—they own it and are the only ones who can solve it.

The times when mediation seems difficult or frustrating can become times of growth and change for everyone. Take the opportunity to talk with other peer mediators or adult staff members and share your thoughts and feelings. Remember that you promised to keep the information of the mediation private and that you must respect that promise when you have these discussions.

If there is honest communication, thinking will be expanded
and boundaries will be broken.

Encouraging another's efforts, sharing perspectives, and cooperating to solve human problems is a lifelong challenge. Through mutual support and respect, everyone will become stronger and better able to reach common goals. As Gandhi said, "If we are to reach real peace in this world, we shall have to begin teaching cooperation to the children."

You have the knowledge and skills to teach peace to others through
your assistance and your example.

2. Refer students to the Peer Mediation Forms section of the Student Manual, beginning on page 87. Review each form to help the students understand what is expected.

3. Give each student a copy of the Peer Mediation Contract. Read it aloud; have students ask any questions and then sign it as their formal agreement to the basic expectations of the program.

4. Give students time to ask questions about any problems they may be concerned about. Some typical questions and their answers are as follows.

Q. What happens if the disputants keep interrupting and getting mad at each other?

A. If disputants are interrupting each other, remind them that they agreed to follow certain ground rules for peer mediation, one of which is to take turns talking and listening. The process will not work if communication and mutual respect are not practiced.

Q. What should I do if the disputants have no idea how to solve their problem? Can I give them ideas?

A. You will need to encourage both disputants to work together to come up with ideas. They probably have some ideas but just aren't comfortable saying them. It is all right to give a suggestion to get the ball rolling. However, if after you make a second suggestion the disputants still haven't shared any of their ideas, ask them how serious they are about solving the problem.

Q. What happens if no agreement is reached?

A. You could try several things. First, you might ask questions to determine whether the problem is really significant or whether a solution has already been worked out. Second, you might try to find out more about the conflict and better define the disputants' interests. Third, you could recognize that resistance is common in peer mediations and just keep talking—a solution might be close. If after a reasonable amount of time no agreement is reached, you might ask disputants to continue another time. If none of these solutions works, don't feel you have failed. Giving disputants the chance to engage in the process is important.

Q. What if during a peer mediation things aren't going well and I'm not sure what to do next?

A. Not every mediation goes as planned. You and your co-mediator can confer at any time to determine what to try next. When there is a problem, you should return to the basic steps and ask the process questions you have learned. If that doesn't help, ask an adult supervisor for help or suggestions.

Q. What happens if a mediation agreement is broken?

A. There will be times when an agreement will be broken. Disputants should be encouraged to try to mediate a second time. Often if an agreement is broken it means that the original resolution did not meet the needs of each disputant.

5. Congratulate the peer mediators on their hard work and their skill. Pronounce them PEACEMAKERS. Distribute any certificates or recognition items. Shake hands with each peer mediator.

CHAPTER 8

ADVANCED TRAINING

The basic training activities in chapter 7 help students understand conflict, the principles of conflict resolution and peacemaking, and the mediation process. They also provide for the development of the skills to use the six-step process and prepare peer mediators to conduct most mediations requested. When peer mediators have had some hands-on experience conducting mediation sessions, interest in additional skills will surface. The activities in this chapter are designed to be used for additional ongoing training and support of peer mediators.

Specifically, Activities 17 through 22 help students who have completed basic training to develop appreciation and understanding of diversity and the potential impact in conflict of social, cultural, and gender differences. This sensitivity correlates with peacemaking and is essential for mediators' continued growth as peacemakers. Also included here are training activities for individuals who have already conducted mediations. Activities 23 through 26 are designed to develop advanced mediation skills, as well as to expand and extend the ability of peer mediators to use the mediation process effectively. Activities 27 and 28 help teach mediators the other two common conflict resolution strategies—negotiation and group problem solving. Mediators will learn to apply their knowledge of the mediation process to use these strategies. Activities 29 and 30 provide ideas for peer mediators to extend the influence of their peacemaking beyond conducting mediation sessions.

These activities can be used in any order. Each school peer mediation program will be unique, and different schools will prioritize these activities differently to address their needs. In any event, continued practice and feedback are crucial for mediators to internalize the understandings and skills developed in the basic training.

Appendix E provides mediation and negotiation simulations that may be used in advanced training. Trainers can develop other simulations by adapting actual conflicts students have mediated or other conflicts characteristic of the school. If such simulations are developed, it will be important to alter them so the real individuals involved in the conflict cannot be identified.

SOCIAL AND CULTURAL DIVERSITY

PURPOSE

Students will learn about different types of diversity, discrimination, and the feelings evoked by discrimination.

TIME

45 minutes

MATERIALS

Student Manual (pages 55–56)

Easel pad or chalkboard

Newsprint and markers

PROCEDURE

1. Remind the peer mediators that in Activity 4 of the basic training they learned that conflicts often are between individuals with differing values and that one's values are largely rooted in issues of social diversity—the gifts he or she has received.

2. Ask the students to form a large circle. Instruct the students that you will, one at a time, name some characteristics people have. Students who possess that characteristic—that is, if the statement is true for them—are to take two steps forward into the circle. If they are not sure if the statement is true for them or if they do not want to identify themselves as having that characteristic, they may continue to stand in the outer circle. After moving forward in response to a given statement, all return to the original large circle.

    Tell students to step forward if:

    ▼ You are left-handed.

    ▼ You wear an earring or other body ring.

    ▼ You like the Beatles.

    ▼ You were raised Catholic.

    ▼ You play a musical instrument.

    ▼ You are being raised by a single parent.

    ▼ At least one of your parents is a person of color.

▼ You play on an organized sports team.

▼ You are of Jewish heritage.

▼ You have a regular job outside of school.

3. Ask students which of these characteristics are preferences: something they choose. Ask students which of these characteristics are based on the gifts they received: something they did not choose.

4. Present the following from the Student Manual.

UNDERSTANDING INDIVIDUAL DIFFERENCES

To be an effective mediator you need to know yourself and your own biases. We all have certain preferences about food, music, clothes, sports, movies, and so on. There are also people and personalities we like more than others. These are examples of differences that we choose. There are also differences that we do not choose. Your gender, skin color, social status, religion, abilities, and national origin make you different from everyone else.

As a mediator, it is important to reflect on and understand individual differences. How do you view and interact with individuals who are different from you?

Think of all the different types of students who go to your school. Think of their different backgrounds, values, and interests. The diversity of your school will occur in any or all of the following categories:

▼ Diversity of culture
>   Skin color
>   Religion
>   National origin

▼ Diversity of social status

▼ Diversity of gender

▼ Diversity of ability
>   Physical
>   Mental

5. In the large group, ask for some examples of the diversity in your school. Have students form groups of four, with each group of four balanced as much as possible by gender. Instruct each group of four to develop a list of all the ways their group represents the diversity of the school. Allow 5 minutes.

6. Share the small-group lists in the larger group. Ask one of the small groups for their complete list, then ask each of the other groups to add types of diversity that are not already listed. Write the types of diversity identified on the easel pad or chalkboard. Ask individuals to share with the larger group

how it feels to be a member of certain diverse groups (for example, the group of cheerleaders, the group of honor roll students, the group of African American students, the group of students who ride the bus, the group of Jewish students, the group of students who speak English as a second language, the group that comprises a certain sports team).

7. Write the words *prejudice, bias,* and *discrimination* on the easel pad or chalkboard. Ask students for their definitions of these terms. Present the following from the Student Manual.

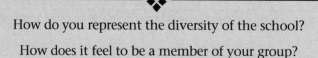

How do you represent the diversity of the school?

How does it feel to be a member of your group?

8. Ask students to return to their small groups and discuss the preceding questions from the Student Manual. Point out that the purpose is not to blame or accuse but to examine how diversity might affect us as mediators. Allow 10 to 15 minutes.

9. Process by asking if the small groups have any insights to share with the total group. Conclude by asking, "What would you do in a mediation situation if you felt you could not remain neutral due to the situation or to the attitude of either or both of the disputants?"

10. To summarize, present the following from the Student Manual.

PREJUDICE, BIAS, AND DISCRIMINATION

Usually, personal differences contribute to personal conflicts. If we are judged or judge others based on age, race, gender, abilities, social class, religion, or sexual orientation, that is **prejudice** or **bias**. When we act on our prejudice it becomes **discrimination**, which is harmful to others and keeps people from meeting their basic needs.

▼ Can you think of a time when you felt you were discriminated against?

▼ Can you think of a time when you discriminated against another person?

▼ As a mediator, in what conflict situations might it be hard for you to remain neutral?

▼ As a mediator, what type of person or what attitude held by a person might make it hard for you to remain neutral?

In your role as a peer mediator you help disputants understand individual differences—this understanding is essential to finding common interests. Further, through your sensitivity, you can become a powerful model to help others learn to respect individual differences. This respect promotes cooperation and in turn makes resolution possible.

BIAS AWARENESS

PURPOSE

Students will learn how different values and personal bias affect tolerance and understanding.

TIME

45 minutes

MATERIALS

Student Manual (page 57)

Chalkboard or easel pad

PROCEDURE

1. Place at one end of the room a sign that reads *AGREE*, and at the other end, a sign that reads *DISAGREE*. Explain that you will read statements and that each student is to stand anywhere along the line between these two signs— one end is for those who absolutely agree with the statement; the other end is for those who absolutely disagree with the statement. Where students choose to stand should best reflect how they feel about the statement. Suggest that students talk to those around them to be sure they have positioned themselves correctly before choosing a final position along the line.

2. Read the first statement in the following list and ask students, "Where do you belong on the agree-disagree continuum?" After the students have positioned themselves on the continuum and are satisfied that they are where they should be, have them discuss their position with those clustered around them. Instruct them to share at least two or three reasons why they took the position they did. Repeat the procedure with each of the other statements.

  ▼ Girls are smarter than boys.

  ▼ Handguns should be illegal.

  ▼ Men are better drivers than women.

  ▼ I would vote for a woman president.

  ▼ The death penalty is right and helps stop murders.

These statements create some conflict in the group, but that is the idea. Don't debate the points—just have each group seek understanding of why others took the positions they did.

3. Process the experience by discussing the following questions:

▼ Could you explain your point of view to those who disagreed with you? If not, why not?

▼ Could you understand another's point of view, even when you didn't agree? If not, why not?

4. Write the word *tolerance* on the easel pad or chalkboard. Ask for definitions and examples of tolerance:

▼ What is an example of something that is hard to tolerate?

▼ What is something that you will not tolerate?

▼ What is something that our school will not tolerate?

▼ What is an area of your life where you think you should show more tolerance?

▼ What is the connection between tolerance and bias?

Remind the peer mediators that often a conflict is over different values, which sometimes are reflections of prejudice. It is important for us to reflect on our biases both as people and as mediators.

5. Instruct students to complete the Bias Self-Evaluation Worksheet on page 57 of the Student Manual.

BIAS SELF-EVALUATION WORKSHEET

Here are some statements to reflect on about biased and nonbiased behaviors.
Rate each of the following items as follows:

1 = I have not thought about this.
2 = I do not do this.
3 = I do this to some extent.
4 = I do this consistently.

1 2 3 4   I do not put down or joke about people because of their culture, skin color, religion, country of origin, gender, or social class.

1 2 3 4   I do not put down or joke about people because of their abilities, disabilities, or physical appearance.

1 2 3 4   I avoid making generalizations about people that become stereotypes for all, such as "Fat people are lazy" or "Females are irrational."

1 2 3 4   I question books, movies, and the media when they present sexist and racist statements or assumptions.

1 2 3 4   I bring it to the attention of my peers if I hear negative comments or jokes about people based on individual differences (skin color, ability, sexual orientation, and so on).

1 2 3 4   I bring it to the attention of adults or peers if I see sexual harassment or gender discrimination.

6. Form small, gender-balanced groups of four students each and instruct students to discuss their responses to the worksheet.

7. Process in the large group by asking students to share one thing they learned about themselves by completing the statement "I learned that I _____."

CULTURAL DIVERSITY AND CLIQUES

PURPOSE

Students will identify the connection between cliques and social diversity in their school and learn about the potential impact of clique membership on the mediation process.

TIME

60 minutes

MATERIALS

Student Manual (page 58)

Newsprint and markers

PROCEDURE

1. Present the following information from the Student Manual.

A CLIQUE IS . . .

▼ A circle or set of friends

▼ To associate together

▼ To act with others of common interests

---

2. Form small groups of five or six students each. Give each group a marker and a sheet of newsprint. Instruct the groups to:

   ▼ Identify and list as many school cliques as you can.

   ▼ Write a descriptive phrase for each clique.

3. Allow about 10 minutes, then have each group post their list and descriptive phrases. Examine and compare the lists. Ask students if they see any connections between the cliques identified and social diversity. Have any of the cliques formed because of skin color, socioeconomic status, abilities, religion, and so on?

4. Present the following from the Student Manual.

There are many **cliques** in every school. Groups of students join together in friendships due to similar interests. Some of these groups are easily identified.

If you are in a certain clique, you feel like an "insider." If you are not in a certain clique, you may feel like an "outsider." Often people feel like outsiders because they are different from the dominant group or they do not have access to that group.

Many conflicts arise because of insider/outsider status. Often insider groups make outsiders feel they do not belong. Groups or cliques are often based on preferences and common interests, and exclusion is natural. But exclusion may also be based on discrimination. If so, the group or clique is not defensible in a school.

5. Ask students to think of a time when they were, or felt like, an insider. How did they feel? Then have students think of a time when they were, or felt like, an outsider or a situation in which they did not feel welcome. Why were they not welcome? How did they feel?

6. Formulate two lists to compare by asking students to share, in the large group, situations when they felt like an outsider. Write responses on the easel pad or chalkboard under the heading *OUTSIDER*. Ask students for examples of situations when they felt like an insider. Write these on the easel pad or chalkboard under the heading *INSIDER*.

7. Brainstorm a list of thoughts or feelings that accompany being an insider. Brainstorm a list of thoughts or feelings that accompany being an outsider.

8. Present the following information from the Student Manual.

Mediators often deal with conflicts between insiders and outsiders. Mediators can facilitate an exchange of feelings and help disputants differentiate between issues of preference and issues of discrimination.

9. Ask students for examples of conflict situations they have either mediated or observed that were caused by exclusion or discrimination from insiders. List several examples: who can sit at a certain lunch table, what group controls a certain hallway, exclusion of a certain person because of gender, skin color, or class.

10. Ask for volunteers—two disputants and a team of co-mediators—to conduct a mock mediation between two disputants representing one of the conflicts listed between an insider and outsider. Conduct the mediation in the large group.

11. Process the mediation demonstration by focusing on feelings of exclusion and discrimination that did surface or might have surfaced.

◀ ACTIVITY 20 ▶

STEREOTYPES

PURPOSE

Students will understand stereotyping as the basis for prejudice.

TIME

45 minutes

MATERIALS

Student Manual (page 59)

Newsprint and markers

PROCEDURE

1. Start the activity with a general discussion by asking students the following questions:

    ▼ Do you think girls or boys have it easier in this world? Why?

    ▼ If you were to be born today, would you rather be born a girl or a boy? Why?

2. Form two groups, one male and the other female. Give the male group a marker and a sheet of newsprint with the heading *GIRLS ARE* ____. Tell the group to brainstorm a list of as many female traits as they can think of. Give the female group a marker and a sheet of newsprint with the heading *BOYS ARE* ____. Tell the group to brainstorm a list of as many male traits as they can think of. Allow about 5 minutes, or until each group has a list of 15 to 20 traits.

3. Return to the large group and have the male group read their list. Ask one of the females in the large group to choose one of the traits that is not true for her. Cross it off the list. Ask another female to choose one trait on the list that is not true for her and cross it off the list. Repeat 8 to 10 times, or more.

4. Follow the same procedure for the list compiled by the female group, asking different boys to eliminate traits that are not true for them.

5. Point out that what the group has just done is take a general notion about a group of people and show that these notions are not true for each individual in that group.

6. Present the following from the Student Manual.

STEREOTYPING IS . . .

▼ A fixed notion or idea about a person or group—
an oversimplified generalization about a person
or group

▼ The basis for prejudice

▼ Limiting

▼ Not true for all individuals

Stereotypes usually play out in the form of discrimination. Ask yourself:

▼ Why has a woman never been President of the
United States? An African-American?

▼ Do you think Franklin D. Roosevelt would have
been elected president if he had been in a wheelchair
during his first campaign?

Stereotypes are a factor in many conflicts.

7. In the large group, hold a general discussion of these questions:

    ▼ What are some of the stereotypes of the various racial
or ethnic groups in our school?

    ▼ Does harassment or prejudice ever occur to an individual
because of membership in a given group?

    ▼ Do certain attitudes—student or adult—make it difficult
for some groups in the school?

    ▼ Have you personally felt stereotyped because of your
membership in a group?

8. Form groups of five or six students each and instruct each group to design a
program, event, or activity that would be a celebration honoring and appreciating differences in the school.

9. Allow the groups to share their ideas in the larger group. Ask the entire group
of mediators if they would be willing to select one of the ideas for further development and present the idea to the school administration. Form an action task
force and do it!

RESOLVING CROSS-CULTURAL CONFLICTS

PURPOSE

Students will learn about different cultural characteristics that can affect the mediation process and learn ways to facilitate the process in the presence of these factors.

TIME

60 minutes

MATERIALS

Student Manual (pages 60–61)

Peer Mediation Simulations 11 and 12 (from Appendix E; one copy for every group of four students)

Peer Mediation Agreement (from Appendix A; two copies for every group of four students)

PROCEDURE

1. Tell students that because we come from different worlds and different cultures we have different beliefs about how conflicts are resolved. Say, "Think about yourself and your expectations for resolving a conflict."

    ▼ What would be important to you in an agreement?

    ▼ Do you expect something very specific in terms of what and when, or can you accept something general and flexible?

    ▼ Do you expect an apology or an admission of wrongdoing or error?

    ▼ Do you wish for payback?

    ▼ Are you willing to talk directly about the problem, or do you prefer to be indirect or nonverbal?

    ▼ Do you express your feelings easily?

    ▼ Are facts important to you?

2. Have students complete the Cultural Traits Worksheet on page 60 of the Student Manual.

CULTURAL TRAITS WORKSHEET

For each item, circle the number on the continuum that indicates where you fit with regard to each cultural trait.

Rational (stick to the facts)	1	2	3	4	5	**Emotional** (feelings are most important)
Competitive	1	2	3	4	5	**Cooperative**
Willing to admit error	1	2	3	4	5	**Interested in saving face**
Open to change	1	2	3	4	5	**Reluctant to change**
On task/on time (want specific details)	1	2	3	4	5	**Flexible** (general commitment OK)
Forgive easily	1	2	3	4	5	**Want payback/restitution**
Prefer direct communications	1	2	3	4	5	**Prefer nonverbal/indirect communications**

These are just some of the differences in how people view conflict or act in conflict situations. Different extremes of different traits might be more associated with one gender or with certain cultural groups, but remember what you have learned about stereotypes—there are always exceptions to such generalizations. As a mediation session proceeds, you will usually be able to determine what is important to each disputant.

3. Instruct students to find a "divergent" partner (for example, a different gender, race, religion). Tell each pair, "Discuss your responses on the worksheet by explaining to your partner what your placement on each trait means to you."

4. Remind students about what they learned in the basic training—that conflicts involving differing values or beliefs are often the most difficult to resolve. Values or belief systems are developed in the environment in which the people grew up. Some of the values and beliefs people hold may arise from situations and events that caused personal hurts or injury. Mediators

attempt to make these beliefs, the environments, and the personal hurts explicit. Only through an open and trusting process can understanding between parties be achieved. Certain questions are likely to help disputants gain a better understanding of each other's perspective.

5. Present the following information from the Student Manual.

QUESTIONS FOR RESOLVING CONFLICT

The following questions may help resolve conflict between disputants with obvious cultural diversity. The step or steps in the process where the question is likely to be appropriate are suggested.

1. What needs to happen to resolve the conflict?

   (Ask during Step 2 and/or Step 5.)

2. What have you gained or lost as a result of the conflict?

   (Ask during Step 2 and/or Step 3.)

3. What are your reasons for taking the position you did?

   (Ask during Step 3.)

4. What needs to happen to reestablish communication and trust?

   (Ask during Step 3, Step 4, Step 5, and/or Step 6.)

5. What would be a fair solution for you?

   (Ask during Step 5.)

6. What different attitudes or new actions would help improve the relationship between the two of you?

   (Ask during Step 4, Step 5, and/or Step 6.)

6. Seek four volunteers to conduct a mock mediation of a conflict between two students of different genders or from different cultural groups. Two of the volunteers will co-mediate; two will serve as the disputants. Choose a conflict over some type of harassment based on name-calling, rumor, and exclusion from a group. Coach one of the disputants to be concerned about emotions and to insist upon bringing out feelings. This person wants mostly for the other person to have a chance to hear his or her feelings. If that happens, this person is willing to forgive and forget. Coach the other disputant to insist upon dealing with the facts and sticking to the task of solving the problem. This person wants some kind of restitution (payback) from the other disputant. Conduct the mediation before the large group.

7. Process the demonstration by discussing what the mediators did that worked. Ask, "What else could the mediators have tried?"

8. Form groups of four, with as much diversity as possible. Instruct students to form pairs and to decide which pair will co-mediate Peer Mediation Simulation 11. Give the co-mediators the Peer Mediation Request and the disputants their respective Role-Play Instructions.

9. Have students conduct the mediation and fill out a Peer Mediation Agreement. Process as a large group when complete.

10. Have the pairs switch roles and conduct Peer Mediation Simulation 12 in the same fashion. Process the experience when complete.

ACTIVITY 22

CONFRONTING PREJUDICE

PURPOSE

Students will learn to use their communication skills to deal with prejudice.

TIME

30 minutes

MATERIALS

Student Manual (pages 62-63)

Index cards (two for each student)

Pencils

PROCEDURE

1. Remind the students that in the basic training they learned that diversity involves cultural and social differences. They learned that we are from different worlds and have received different gifts. Present the following information from the Student Manual.

ABOUT PREJUDICE

As a trained peer mediator, you have become aware of the **social** and **cultural diversity** that exists in your school. You are aware that differences can be either celebrated or used to separate and isolate people.

Every day, you probably hear remarks and see actions that discriminate and devalue certain people or groups of people in your school. Often you may feel uncomfortable or "on the spot" when you hear a harassing statement.

▼ When and how do you confront these statements?

▼ How do you communicate with a peer without causing him or her to feel attacked or put down?

▼ How do you communicate across differing beliefs without escalating a conflict?

---

2. Ask students to give examples of statements they have heard (or actions they have observed) that express prejudice or show discrimination. Ask students if and how they responded when they heard those statements and what the outcome was. Direct students to the examples in the Student Manual.

Following are examples of typical statements that might be heard in a school:

1. As a group of girls are walking down the hall past your locker, you hear this comment from two guys standing nearby: "Look at Mary—she is definitely a 10, but her friend Andrea is more like a 4."

2. After school, while waiting at the bus stop you hear someone say: "That other bus has all those low-life trailer park kids."

3. In history class, during a discussion about the presidency someone says: "A woman should never be President of the United States. Women are too emotional and irrational to be President."

4. In the cafeteria you hear someone at your table say: "Black students in this school aren't very smart. Hardly any of them make the honor role."

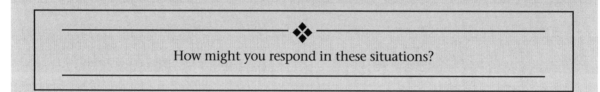

How might you respond in these situations?

3. Present the Steps for Confronting Prejudice on page 63 of the Student Manual. Point out similarities between these steps and the steps of the mediation process.

STEPS FOR CONFRONTING PREJUDICE

1. Stay calm.

2. Summarize what you heard.

   ▼ "Did I hear you say _____?"

3. Seek clarification.

   ▼ "Can you tell me more about what you meant by _____?"

4. Share your point of view and why you believe this.

   ▼ "Well, the way I think about it is _____."

   ▼ "When you made that comment, I felt _____."

5. Ask the reasons for the person's point of view.

   ▼ "On what do you base your opinion?"

   ▼ "Is what you believe true for everyone?"

6. Try to find common ground.

   ▼ "It seems we both think that _____."

7. Thank the other person for listening.

4. Ask for four volunteers to help you as you demonstrate these steps before the large group. Assign each volunteer one of the example statements gathered previously in this activity or use the typical statements given on page 62 of the Student Manual. Ask for the group's reactions and constructive feedback after each example.

5. Give each student two index cards. Instruct students to write on each card an example of a prejudicial or discriminatory comment similar to the examples they have heard. Collect the cards, shuffle them, and draw one. Ask for a volunteer to confront the statement by using the steps. Process each comment by asking for reactions and constructive feedback; do as many as time permits.

CAUCUSING

PURPOSE

Students will learn when and how to caucus in a mediation session.

TIME

60 minutes

MATERIALS

Student Manual (pages 64–65)

Peer Mediation Simulations 13 and 14 (from Appendix E; one copy for every group of four students)

Peer Mediation Agreement (from Appendix A; two copies for every group of four students)

PROCEDURE

1. Present the following information from the Student Manual.

WHAT IS CAUCUSING?

Caucusing is a tool that mediators may use in certain situations in order to help disputants work toward an agreement. Caucusing may be viewed as a "time-out" in the mediation process. In the mediation process, the disputants work face-to-face to reach an agreement. In a caucus, the mediators meet individually with each disputant.

A caucus may take place anytime during the mediation process and, although this is not usually the case, may occur more than once. Normally, caucusing will not be used at all, but it can be very effective if needed. It is the mediators' responsibility to decide whether or not a caucus is necessary.

REASONS FOR CAUCUSING

Caucusing can be used in a number of ways:

▼ To uncover information or clarify details that disputants
  may be willing to reveal only in private

▼ To move beyond an impasse

▼ To deal with issues of diversity or reduce tensions
  between disputants

▼ To explore options or the consequences of choosing
  particular options

▼ To help disputants understand the best outcome they
  can hope for if they choose not to work together to achieve
  a mutually satisfactory agreement

▼ To allow disputants time to think alone and reflect

▼ To build trust in the peer mediators and/or the
  mediation process

GUIDELINES FOR CAUCUSING

1. Meet individually with each disputant. (Co-mediators stay together as a team.)

   ▼ "We want to meet with each of you alone."

2. During the individual meetings, use the procedures in Step 2 (Gather Points of View),
   Step 3 (Focus on Interests), and Step 4 (Create Win-Win Options), depending on the
   situation.

3. Before returning to the joint session, be sure you have a clear understanding of what
   information the disputants do not want revealed. All statements made during caucusing
   are private unless the disputant agrees that the information can be shared.

   ▼ "Everything said when we are alone is private.
   I will not share anything said with the other disputant
   unless you give me permission."

4. When the mediation session resumes, summarize what happened in the mediation
   prior to the caucus, reveal or cause to be revealed any information the disputants
   want revealed from the caucus, and resume the mediation at the point you called
   for the caucus.

2. Tell the peer mediators to find a partner, preferably someone with whom they have not co-mediated previously, and then join with another pair. Each group of four should decide which pair will serve as the co-mediators for Peer Mediation Simulation 13. Give the co-mediators the Peer Mediation Request for the simulation. The other pair will be the disputants for the simulation; give them their respective Role-Play Instructions.

3. The disputants meet separately with the training assistants, who will coach them about playing their roles so the mediators will need to call a caucus. Disputants may be argumentative, resisitive (by refusing to provide a point of view), insistant (by demanding that the other disputant do or say something, such as offer an apology), rejecting of the other disputant's ideas or explanations, and so forth. While the disputants are meeting with their respective training assistants, instruct the mediators that they will be expected to use the caucusing strategy during the simulation to help the disputants work toward an agreement.

4. Allow time for the mediation to proceed. After the mediation, the training assistant for each group helps students process the experience by asking the following questions:

   ▼ What went well in this mediation?

   ▼ What could you do differently?

   ▼ Was the caucus effective? Why or why not?

5. Repeat the process with the other pair serving as co-mediators for Peer Mediation Simulation 14.

6. Reconvene as a large group and ask the students to discuss the circumstances in which they might use the caucusing strategy. Point out that, although caucusing is rarely necessary in peer mediation, it is a good strategy to use in mediations where disputants are not effectively communicating and where resolution does not otherwise appear possible.

● ACTIVITY 24 ●

UNCOVERING HIDDEN INTERESTS

PURPOSE

Students will practice identifying the origins of conflicts and learn more about unmet basic needs as the underlying interests involved in most conflicts.

TIME

45 minutes

MATERIALS

Student Manual (pages 66–70)

Index cards (two for each student)

Pencils

Newsprint and markers

PROCEDURE

1. Present the following information from the Student Manual.

ABOUT HIDDEN INTERESTS

You might think determining what is at the bottom of a conflict is an easy matter, but often what the conflict appears to be about is not the only issue involved. People sometimes have **hidden interests** in a conflict situation—and often these hidden interests are unmet basic psychological needs for belonging, power, freedom, or fun.

During the basic training, you learned that conflicts frequently appear to be about limited resources or different values, perhaps involving diversity issues. However, the conflict is often really about unmet basic needs. For example:

> Suppose Robert is upset because his friend LaToya has not repaid some money she borrowed. Here it appears that the conflict between Robert and LaToya is caused by limited resources (in other words, a lack of money). But when LaToya offers to pay the money back in installments over a few weeks, Robert refuses to accept her solution. In actuality, Robert may view LaToya's failure to repay the loan as demonstrating a lack of respect for him and a lack of appreciation for their friendship. His needs for power and belonging are threatened. The conflict is unlikely to be resolved until Robert's unmet needs are recognized.

207

Suppose Angela places a high value on honesty in friendships. She is angry with her friend Maria because Maria lied to her. In mediation, Angela will not accept Maria's explanations. She may make statements about Maria's ethnicity. Is this conflict the result of different values about honesty? Maybe yes and maybe no. Angela may be bothered less by the clash of values than by the idea that she feels she must cut herself off from Maria because Maria lied. In other words, Angela's need for belonging may be threatened. Any resolution to this problem will likely involve helping Angela decide if she wants to accept Maria as a friend.

Suppose Greg and Dimitri, who have been the best of friends, suddenly appear to be adversaries. Dimitri seems not to want to associate with Greg, an idea Greg has difficulty understanding. Actually, Dimitri likes Greg but feels that Greg does not consider his ideas or wishes. When they are together, having fun, Dimitri believes they always do what Greg wants to do. Dimitri increasingly has come to see this as both a lack of respect for him and as Greg's controlling their relationship. A resolution that would reunite these friends would need to consider Dimitri's concerns about freedom and respect.

Looking Below the Surface

Think about an iceberg in the ocean. We know that what is visible of the iceberg is only part, actually a small part, of the whole iceberg. The tip or visible part of the iceberg is like that part of a conflict that is not hidden—what the dispute seems to be about or what the disputants tell us the problem concerns. In the conflict, we see the positions people take and the demands that they make. Underneath the surface of the ocean is the major part of the iceberg. If ships are not aware of what lies under the tip of the iceberg, the ship will crash. (Remember the Titanic!) Just as with an iceberg, in a conflict the mediator often must probe below the surface of the conflict to explore what is underneath.

Hidden interests are often layered. The first layer may be fears or beliefs founded in prejudice or stereotypes. This layer often offers little to bring the disputants together because the fears and beliefs are rarely shared. Under this layer are the real interests, which are based on the psychological needs for belonging, power, freedom, and fun.

To resolve a conflict, a peer mediator helps disputants look under the surface for the real reasons for the problem. An important part of your job as mediator is to help disputants determine what is really causing the conflict. If you do not, the agreements you help disputants reach are unlikely to be lasting because they do not solve the REAL problem.

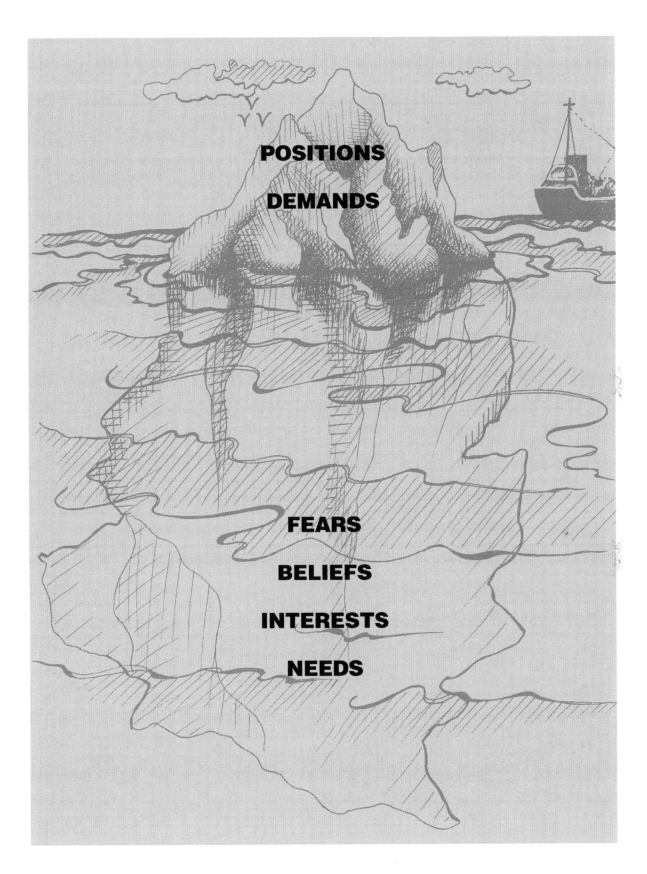

POSITIONS

DEMANDS

FEARS

BELIEFS

INTERESTS

NEEDS

2. Give two index cards to each student. Tell students to write a brief description of a conflict they have mediated or experienced, one on each card.

3. Form groups of five or six students each; give each group a sheet of newsprint and a marker. Tell them reproduce the Hidden Interests Diagram shown on page 70 of the Student Manual.

HIDDEN INTERESTS DIAGRAM

Belonging

Fun

UNMET BASIC NEEDS

Power

Freedom

4. Instruct each group to pool their index cards, then have group members take turns drawing cards from the stack and leading the discussion. As a group, they must decide whether the conflict in any way concerns limited resources or different values, then write on the card *resources* or *values*, as appropriate. They must determine whether the hidden interest is an unmet need for belonging, power, freedom, or fun, then tape the index card to the appropriate area on the Hidden Interests Diagram. (Cards may overlap areas.)

5. Reconvene as a large group and use the following questions to process the activity:

   ▼ What were some conflicts identified by your group as being related to limited resources?

   ▼ What were the unmet needs associated with these conflicts?

   ▼ What were some conflicts identified by your group as being related to different values? Were any of these based on prejudice?

   ▼ What were the unmet needs associated with these conflicts?

   ▼ Were there some conflicts related to unmet needs in which resources or values were not involved?

   ▼ Were there conflicts that concerned more than one unmet need?

   ▼ What were some conflicts you had difficulty classifying?

   ▼ How did you identify the unmet needs?

   ▼ What have you learned from this exercise?

6. Remind students that in the basic training they learned to ask questions in Step 3 of the mediation process to uncover interests. Review those questions, as presented on page 45 of the Student Manual. Point out that mediators also learned in the basic training that it is futile to brainstorm options before interests have been clearly identified.

UNDERSTANDING ANGER

PURPOSE

Students will learn various ways anger can be expressed and how to identify and deal with angry disputants in a peer mediation session.

TIME

60 minutes

MATERIALS

Student Manual (pages 71–75)

Newsprint and markers

Peer Mediation Agreement (from Appendix A; two copies for every group of four students)

Any two Peer Mediation Simulations (from Appendix E; one copy for every group of four students)

Peer Mediation Simulations 1, 4, 5, 7, or 9 work well in this activity. Alternatively, students may create their own conflict situation.

PROCEDURE

1. Explain to students that the first step in learning how to help others manage their anger is to learn about our own anger. Present the following information from the Student Manual.

ABOUT ANGER

Everyone gets angry, upset, frustrated, or irritated by something. Have you ever heard someone remark that "She really knows how to push my buttons" or "He makes me so hot (angry)"? This means that the other person seems to know exactly what to do or say to trigger the speaker's anger. We might think of the words, actions, or both that provoke our anger as our personal **hot buttons**.

Often the people closest to us, our family and/or friends, can really push our hot buttons and really bug us. Sometimes it is people in charge or what they do with that authority that makes us angry.

The first step in learning to help others manage their anger
is to learn about our own anger.

2. Have students complete the Anger Worksheet on page 72 of the Student Manual.

ANGER WORKSHEET

Answer the following questions to help you understand your own personal anger.

1. Who are the people who really bug you, who push your hot buttons? Make a list of names, and after each name indicate what the person does or does not do that irritates you.

2. Describe the circumstances for the last three times you remember being angry.

3. Describe how you responded in each of those circumstances. Did your response escalate or deescalate the situation?

3. Ask students to share some of their answers to the questions in the large group. Share examples from your own life experiences, as appropriate.

4. Form groups of four students each and give each group a piece of newsprint and a marker. Stress that in order to mediate or otherwise resolve conflicts it is necessary to control our anger. Instruct the groups to brainstorm a list of ways to push their "cool buttons" (defuse anger, cool off). Allow 5 minutes, then share the lists in the larger group.

5. Present the following from the Student Manual. Point out any ideas for pushing our own cool buttons that are not already on students' lists of suggestions and have them add any of their own ideas; discuss the final question as a group.

COOL BUTTONS: CONTROLLING YOUR ANGER WORKSHEET

1. Breathe deeply.

2. Count to 10.

3. Keep on counting and breathing deeply.

4. Visualize a calm and relaxing place.

5. Use positive self-talk and affirm yourself.

6. _____

7. _____

8. _____

9. _____

10. _____

❖

Why is it important to cool off before you mediate or negotiate a conflict?

6. Remind the peer mediators that strong emotions often accompany conflict and that anger will frequently be expressed during mediation sessions. Peer mediators must deal with anger to help the disputants work together cooperatively. Present the following from the Student Manual.

PROCESSING ANGER

Anger is a strong human emotion signaling that one or more of our basic needs (belonging, power, freedom, fun) are not being met. Although most people think of anger as being a negative feeling, it is really neither good nor bad. The way people choose to process their anger can have either positive or negative outcomes, however.

Nonassertion

One way to process anger is by turning it inward, or **nonassertion**. People who behave this way are often depressed. In addition, because they never express their anger, no one ever knows what they think or want. As a result, they rarely get their needs met.

Aggression

Another way to process anger is **aggression**. Being aggressive means verbally or physically attacking another individual. This includes fighting, yelling, name-calling, put-downs, and so forth. Generally, aggression turns people off, or they choose to react in a similarly aggressive way, and the problem just gets worse.

Passive Aggression

A third way to process anger is **passive aggression**. People behaving this way look calm on the outside but are really angry inside. They might show anger by rolling their eyes, interrupting, or refusing to cooperate. Others tend to avoid passive aggressive people or choose to get angry in return.

Assertion

Still another way to process anger is **assertion**. Assertive people know they are angry and choose to express that feeling in an appropriate way. They know what they want and need, and can ask for it without showing disrespect for other people's wants and needs. Dealing with anger by being assertive makes it much more likely that people will be able to cooperate and reach a mutually satisfying solution.

As a peer mediator, you can help people process their anger through assertion—not nonassertion, aggression, or passive aggression.

7. In the large group, discuss the following questions:

   ▼ Why do you think people become angry?

   ▼ When one person expresses anger or acts in a passive aggressive manner, what does the other person do?

   ▼ How does anger relate to the basic psychological needs for belonging, power, freedom, and fun?

8. Instruct students to return to the small groups they formed earlier and brainstorm a list of ways to handle angry people in a mediation session. Share the lists in the larger group, asking for consensus as to whether each idea is likely to escalate or deescalate most conflicts.

HOW DO YOU DEAL WITH ANGRY PEOPLE?

▼ Listen to them.

▼ Affirm their feelings.

▼ Clarify their interests and needs.

▼ Don't take their anger personally.

9. Remind peer mediators that their communication skills and the mediation process itself are tools to help disputants handle their anger in appropriate, assertive ways. Present the following information from the Student Manual.

SUGGESTIONS FOR DEALING WITH ANGER IN MEDIATION

1. Remind disputants of the ground rules.

   ▼ "You both agreed to take turns talking and listening."

2. Remind disputants that they agreed to cooperate to solve the problem.

   ▼ "You agreed to cooperate to solve the problem.
     Is what you are saying or doing helping you to cooperate?"

3. Use your active listening skills: Attend to the speaker, summarize what you hear to let the disputant know that he or she has been heard, and affirm or reflect the feelings expressed.

   ▼ "When _____ happened, you were very upset with _____."

4. Ask disputants to relax and take a few deep breaths.

5. Take a break to allow disputants to cool off and return to the mediation at a later time, perhaps even the next day.

6. Clarify interests and focus the mediation session on finding a plan to satisfy those interests rather than focusing on what happened.

7. Caucus with each disputant. Try to find out what the individual disputants want and if they think the anger is helping them get what they want. Coach them how to express their interests to each other.

---

10. Form co-mediation groups of four. Each group of four should decide which pair will serve as the co-mediators for the first Peer Mediation Simulation selected. Give the co-mediators the Peer Mediation Request for the simulation. The other pair will be the disputants for the simulation; give them their respective Role-Play Instructions. Coach the disputants to use aggressive and/or passive aggressive behaviors.

11. Process each mediation by discussing what seemed to work and not work in managing or diffusing the anger. Provide constructive criticism.

12. Have co-mediators and disputants reverse roles. Conduct and process the second Peer Mediation Simulation in the same way as the first.

ADVANCED COMMUNICATION SKILLS

PURPOSE

Students will learn to apply three communication skills in the mediation process: reframing, common ground statements, and challenging.

TIME

45 minutes

MATERIALS

Student Manual (pages 76–78)

Index cards

Pencils

PROCEDURE

1. Explain that sometimes the message one intends to communicate is not heard by the other person because the message is sent in a manner that is difficult for the other person to receive. Angry statements tend to be difficult to hear because often the listener has an emotional reaction that interferes with receiving the message. In mediation sessions, a disputant may deliver his or her message in a hostile, angry, negative, accusing, or demanding way, either through actual words and gestures or through tone of voice. Present the following information from the Student Manual to explain the use of *reframing* in such situations.

REFRAMING

Reframing means listening to one disputant's hostile, angry, negative, accusing, or demanding statement and translating that statement into a productive statement of concern to which you as the mediator and the other disputant can respond. Often reframing means focusing the statement on the problem, not on the persons involved. The mediator offers the disputants a different way of viewing the situation. Reframing helps to tone down an emotional response (often name-calling or put-downs) and make communication more constructive. Reframing is based on the idea that every strong statement contains some underlying interest or concern that prompted the strong statement. Also, the speaker usually wants to be heard and expects a constructive response to his or her statement.

How to Reframe

1. Listen to the statement.

2. Remove the "garbage" (the inflammatory language).

3. Recognize the emotions involved and state who owns these emotions.

4. Try to understand the speaker's interest(s) or concern(s).

5. Restate the message as a concern about the problem, especially about meeting basic needs.

For example:

> **Disputant:** She's got a big mouth, and she's a dirty liar.
>
> **Mediator:** You seem upset, and you have a concern about people knowing the truth.
>
> **Disputant:** Right, she has been telling everyone that I'm cheap and tight with my money, when in fact for the past 2 months she has owed me $20.00.
>
> **Mediator:** It sounds like you're frustrated and would like a fair settlement of the money issue as soon as possible.

Practice Statements

1. I'm sick of her always telling me what to do. She acts like my mother all the time.

2. He and his friends are jerks. They always put me and my friends down. They think they own the school. They better stop, or else I'm gonna mess up their stuff.

3. Every time he sees me in the hall he just stares at me like he wants to get into it with me. He is not as great as he thinks he is. I want him outta my space.

2. In the large group, ask for volunteers to reframe the practice statements given in the Student Manual. Allow three or four peer mediators to try reframing each of the statements.

3. Tell the peer mediators that two other communication skills or strategies may be useful in some mediations: *common ground statements* and *challenging*. Present the following information from the Student Manual.

COMMON GROUND STATEMENTS

Especially in Step 3 of the mediation process (Focus on Interests), the basic psychological needs for belonging, power, freedom, and fun often surface as interests the disputants have in common. It is important that disputants understand this common ground in order to come up with **win-win** solutions. It is often necessary for the mediator to make this common ground known because the disputants are focused on their differences and do not hear the common needs expressed. The mediator does this by making **common ground statements**.

For example:

▼ It sounds like you are both angry with a lack of respect shown towards each other, and also both of you don't want to get into any further trouble.

▼ You have both stated that fair treatment and acceptance of your school group is important to you.

▼ I hear you both saying that you have been friends in the past. Do you still want to be friends?

▼ You have each stated that you think the other person is trying to control you. Is it important for you to make your own choices?

CHALLENGING

In some circumstances, it is appropriate for the mediator to question the ideas or attitudes of one or both of the disputants. This might occur if a disputant's statements are put-downs of the other, expressions of prejudice, threats, or unrealistic demands that could escalate the conflict. When the mediator believes the disputant is out of line, he or she will need to **challenge** certain statements respectfully and maintain neutrality.

Wondering

Wondering is a gentle way to challenge:

Disputant: His hair is so messy, and he dresses so sloppy; I can see why he keeps losing things—you should see his locker.

Mediator: I'm wondering how a discussion of clothes and hairstyles will help settle this conflict.

Reality Testing

Reality testing can be used to check the feasibility of ideas or plans:

Disputant: I am going to the Board of Education, and I am going to sue the school.

Mediator: You have every right to be upset and to threaten the board with a lawsuit. However, going to court takes time and may involve spending money. Are there other steps to consider first?

4. Tell students to write, on the index cards provided, statements that are attacking and inflammatory. These might be made-up statements or statements that they have heard during the heat of a conflict, while conducting mediations, in the media, and so on. Choose two or three cards and allow volunteers to reframe and/or challenge the statements before the large group.

5. Instruct students to work in groups of four. In each small group, a student should read a statement from one of his or her index cards. Other students in the group either reframe or challenge the statement. Do as many as time permits.

6. In the large group, ask whether the mediators remember any times they used reframing, common ground statements, or challenging during the simulations or in actual mediations. Share as time permits.

NEGOTIATION

PURPOSE

Students will apply what they have learned in mediation training to negotiation without the presence of a neutral third party.

TIME

45 minutes

MATERIALS

Student Manual (pages 79–80)

Chalkboard or easel pad

Negotiation Simulations 2 and 3 (from Appendix E; one of each simulation for every two students)

PROCEDURE

1. Tell the peer mediators that it would be unrealistic and unfair to expect that just because they have been trained in conflict resolution (mediation) they will not experience conflict. What is reasonable to expect is that when they do experience conflict they will use their skills to seek resolution, including requesting mediation for their disputes. However, there are times when mediation might not be an option—maybe the other person refuses to mediate, or the conflict is with someone outside of the school.

2. Ask students for some examples of times when, even if available, they probably would not have made use of mediation to resolve a conflict. List on the chalkboard or easel pad according to the following categories: *PEERS, TEACHERS,* and *PARENTS.*

3. Present the following information from the Student Manual.

CHOOSING NEGOTIATION

Sometimes you will want to try to resolve conflict without a mediator, either because mediation is not available or because it is not an option you and the other person agree to choose. It is possible to resolve conflicts peacefully by working face-to-face with the other party and without the assistance of a neutral third party. The process is called **negotiation.**

Your understanding of mediation will help you in this process because the six steps are the same. However, negotiation is more difficult than mediation because there is no neutral third party helping disputants work through the steps, communicate with each other, control their anger, or identify common interests. When you serve as a mediator, you are concerned only with the process. When you negotiate, you have a vested interest in the outcome.

You and another student trained as a peer mediator might choose to negotiate a conflict between you. Because you both know how to mediate, you will understand what takes place in each step of the process. But many of your conflicts will be with peers, teachers, or parents who have not received mediation training. When the person you wish to negotiate with does not know the process, these questions and statements will help you begin negotiating:

▼ Can we try to talk about this calmly?

▼ Do you want to work out this problem between us?

▼ Can we cooperate?

▼ Can we make sure we understand the problem before we take action?

▼ I'll listen to you if you will agree to listen to me.

▼ I want to understand your point of view, and I want you to understand my point of view.

These "starter lines" establish the ground rules for the negotiation—take turns talking and listening and cooperate to solve the problem.

Once two individuals agree that they want to negotiate, the steps of the process are the same as they are for mediation. The challenge is for each person to seek to understand the other's point of view and to speak so that his or her point of view can be understood without the help of a neutral third party.

4. Point out that negotiation is a communication process in which the people with the problem work together to solve the problem:

> As for mediation, communication is the essence of the negotiation strategy. Because as a mediator you understand active listening, you can effectively listen for both yourself and the other party. For example, if you are the person trained as a mediator, you should let the other disputant present his or her point of view first, then summarize what you heard, using your reframing skill as needed. Follow by presenting your point of view, then summarize yourself by saying, "The most important idea I wanted you to hear was _____." Summarize the other party's and your own statements throughout the process until you are confident that you are listening to each other and cooperating.

5. Demonstrate negotiation with a volunteer, using one of the conflict examples generated earlier. Use a "starter line" to engage the volunteer and have observers follow along with the Negotiation Process Summary on page 80 of the Student Manual as you negotiate a win-win solution.

NEGOTIATION PROCESS SUMMARY

STEP 1: AGREE TO NEGOTIATE

▼ I agree to take turns talking and listening and to cooperate to solve the problem.

STEP 2: SHARE POINTS OF VIEW

▼ My view of the problem is _____, and I feel _____.

STEP 3: FOCUS ON INTERESTS

▼ What I want is _____ because _____.

STEP 4: CREATE OPTIONS

▼ Some ideas to solve the problem could be _____.

STEP 5: EVALUATE OPTIONS

▼ Which options will work and be fair for both of us?

STEP 6: CREATE AN AGREEMENT

▼ I am willing to _____.

6. Ask students to pair up and have the pairs use Negotiation Simulations 2 and 3 to practice. Ask students to alternate being Disputant A and Disputant B, and for each simulation to assume that Disputant B does not know the process.

7. To process the experience, ask students to share their negotiated outcomes. Ask each one what the interests were that led to the outcome.

ACTIVITY 28

GROUP PROBLEM SOLVING

PURPOSE

Students will use their mediation skills and the mediation process
to assist a group in resolving conflict.

TIME

45 minutes

MATERIALS

Student Manual (pages 81–83)

PROCEDURE

1. Present the following information from the Student Manual.

CONFLICT AND GROUPS

There are times when conflicts involve groups of people. Organizations, clubs, teams, and cliques can have conflicts internal to the group. Even students in a certain class can have conflicts. Conflicts also occur between different groups. For example:

The drama club might be preparing for a school play, and there are conflicts between cast members as to practice time and frequency.

The newspaper staff might be in conflict with the Multicultural Club for publishing an editorial or cartoon that lacked cultural sensitivity.

Three major school groups have representatives on a planning committee to decide the next school fund-raiser. Each group has its own self-interests and agenda, and these are causing conflict in the planning committee.

There are conflicts between students in the biology class over scheduling lab times and stations in order to complete the required experiments.

Have groups in this school experienced internal conflict?

What was the conflict?

Was the conflict ever resolved?

Have there been conflicts between groups in the school?

What was the conflict?

Was the conflict resolved?

2. In the large group, brainstorm a list of conflicts within or among groups in the school. Ask the peer mediators, remembering what they know about the importance of the disputants' solving their own problems in mediation, which of the disputes described in the Student Manual could be resolved through cooperative group problem solving.

3. Present the following information from the Student Manual.

CHOOSING GROUP PROBLEM SOLVING

Group problem solving is multi-party dispute resolution involving a process of shared decision making. It can be used when the conflict involves more than two people and more than two points of view. The group works to find a consensus decision, or the best solution that the group can make at the time to solve the problem and that can be supported by all members.

The six steps of group problem solving are the same as the six steps of mediation. The group composition in the problem solving can vary from two or three designated spokespersons representing each group or faction of the group to a large group with open participation.

Group problem solving can be very effective, but it is usually more complicated than a two-party mediation, and therefore more time is required. Generally, there will be several points of view and multiple interests. At least two peer mediators, and preferably three or four for large groups, should work together, following the mediation steps, to facilitate problem solving in the group.

GROUND RULES FOR GROUP PROBLEM SOLVING

Managing problem solving in a group is often complex because of the number of participants. Establishing ground rules for the problem-solving session is very important. The following five ground rules are helpful.

1. Participants sit in a circle. This gives no one special status and allows each person to have visual contact with each of the other participants.

2. Every member of the group is responsible for communication—listening and speaking. This means that each person is responsible for sharing his or her point of view if it has not already been shared by another group member and that each person is responsible for working to understand others' points of view.

3. The **rule of focus** applies to all discussions. This means that a speaker will be allowed to talk without being interrupted by other group members.

4. Participants show respect for others. This means no criticism or sarcasm toward group members or their ideas.

5. Each time someone in the group presents a point of view, a group member summarizes that point of view before anyone else can present another point of view.

---

4. Answer any questions from the peer mediators about the reasons for or meaning of the ground rules. Stress that these ground rules serve the same purpose as the ground rules for mediation: They help people work together to solve the problem. The last ground rule—to summarize each person's point of view before moving on—is perhaps the most important, and the peer mediators facilitating the problem solving effort should be sure this rule is followed. It is usually best if the mediators allow other group members to summarize rather than summarize each statement themselves. The mediators may be more skilled, but group members will listen more carefully if all are expected to summarize what has been said. The mediators can best serve by reframing when needed.

5. Present the following information from the Student Manual.

GROUP PROBLEM SOLVING PROCESS SUMMARY

STEP 1: AGREE TO PROBLEM SOLVE

▼ Group members establish and agree on ground rules.

STEP 2: GATHER POINTS OF VIEW

▼ Group members tell what happened; the problem is identified.

STEP 3: FOCUS ON INTERESTS

▼ Group members tell what they want and why.

STEP 4: CREATE WIN-WIN OPTIONS

▼ Group members brainstorm ideas that will help the whole group.

STEP 5: ESTABLISH CRITERIA AND EVALUATE OPTIONS

▼ Is the solution within the rules?

▼ Is this a decision the group is empowered to make?

▼ Is it fair to all involved?

STEP 6: CREATE AN AGREEMENT

▼ Can each member support this agreement?

▼ What are the specifics of the plan of action?

The questions used in each step of the group problem solving process
will generally be the same questions used in the corresponding step
of the mediation process.

6. Discuss in the large group how group problem solving is likely to be similar to mediation and how it is likely to be different. What should the peer mediators facilitating the group problem solving be on the alert for? Emphasize the following ideas:

   ▼ Not everyone is required to speak.

   ▼ Some group members may try to dominate the discussion.

   ▼ Some points of view may not be given at first; keep asking if there are any other points of view.

   ▼ Establish criteria to use in selecting options before arriving at a *consensus solution*. A consensus solution is the best solution that the group can make at this time to solve the problem and that can be supported by all members. Don't settle for majority rule.

   ▼ Develop a specific plan—who is doing what and when.

7. Ask for three peer mediators to volunteer to work together to facilitate a group problem solving session. The others will be members of the group. Use one of the examples of group conflict given earlier and conduct a group problem solving simulation.

As an alternative, you may choose to do Activity 29 before practicing group problem solving and use the following as the group problem: "As the peacemakers of our school you have been asked to develop and orchestrate a peace promotion for the entire school. The administration wants it to have a single focus that will involve everyone. You must decide today what your general theme and plan will be so they can be submitted to the administration for approval."

8. Process the experience by asking the following questions:

   ▼ What worked?

   ▼ What didn't work?

   ▼ Were the peer mediators effective in facilitating the group discussion and the problem-solving process?

   ▼ What could they have done differently that might have improved the session?

◖ ACTIVITY 29 ◗

PROMOTING PEACE

PURPOSE

Students will think about what peace is and how it can be promoted at home, at school, and in the community.

TIME

20 minutes

MATERIALS

Student Manual (pages 84–85)

Chalkboard or easel pad

PROCEDURE

1. Ask students to think about the topic "How Do You Promote Peace in Your School?" Generate a list of actions students have taken or actions they have witnessed others taking to promote peace. Ask which of the ideas they believe are most effective in getting others involved in peacemaking. Summarize that promoting peace means to teach peace, talk peace, demonstrate peace, recognize peace, and celebrate peace.

2. Present the following information from the Student Manual, then have students fill out the Peace Wheel on page 85.

YOUR VIEW OF PEACE

What does Peace mean to you?

What words, images, and feelings do you associate with PEACE?

Where does PEACE occur?

Who is involved when PEACE happens?

3. Organize students into groups of three. Instruct each group to brainstorm activities to promote peace throughout the school community.

4. Have each small group select one peace promotion idea and make a plan to put it into action for the school. The plan should include a timeline, activities, resources, and a description of who is responsible for what. Allow about 10 minutes.

5. Share the plans in the larger group.

PEACE WHEEL

Record your own ideas about peace on the Peace Wheel.

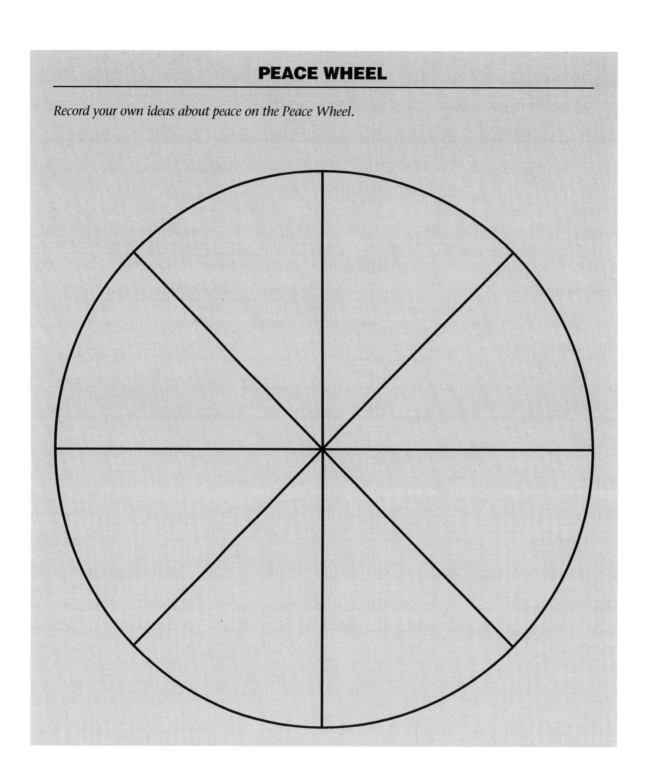

ACTIVITY 30

FOCUSING ON CONFLICT AND PEACE

PURPOSE

Students will learn more about conflict resolution and peace.

Each of these short experiences has a peace and conflict theme. These activities could be used in a classroom or could supplement mediation training. Peer mediators might find these ideas useful in getting students who have not been trained in mediation interested in peacemaking and conflict resolution.

TIME

15–30 minutes each

MATERIALS

Specified in each activity

PROCEDURE

1. Read the newspaper and keep track of how often you find the words *peace* and *conflict*. With which news events are these words associated?

2. Watch the evening news and determine how often the words *mediator* or *negotiator* are used. What are the conflicts about?

3. Make a "Peace and Conflict" collage out of weekly news magazines. Display it on your wall or in your locker.

4. Think about a conflict in a film or video you have seen recently. Discuss with a friend: What was the conflict? What escalated the conflict? Was it resolved? How? Were all parties satisfied?

5. With a group of friends, think about a conflict that exists in your school, such as two groups that don't get along or a group that isn't widely accepted. What is underlying the conflict? What can you or your friends do to change the situation?

6. Discuss with a family member: What would be needed for there to be peace in the world? If we had peace, what would it look like? Do we need war to make peace?

7. Interview senior citizens: What does peace means to them? What have they found to be the best way to resolve conflicts? What do they think would bring about world peace?

8. Do one unusual (for you) thing to foster peace with your best friend. Now choose an individual you have generally avoided and direct a peaceful action toward that person.

APPENDIX A

Program Forms

Answer each question by providing the response that most accurately reflects your personal view of your school.

1. I am a: ☐ student ☐ staff member ☐ parent ☐ other

2. Conflicts interfere with the teaching and learning process:

   ☐ Often ☐ Sometimes ☐ Rarely

3. Problems between people at this school are caused by:

a. expectation to be competitive	☐ Often	☐ Sometimes	☐ Rarely
b. intolerance between adults and students	☐ Often	☐ Sometimes	☐ Rarely
c. intolerance between students	☐ Often	☐ Sometimes	☐ Rarely
d. poor communication	☐ Often	☐ Sometimes	☐ Rarely
e. anger and/or frustration	☐ Often	☐ Sometimes	☐ Rarely
f. rumors	☐ Often	☐ Sometimes	☐ Rarely
g. problems brought to school from somewhere else	☐ Often	☐ Sometimes	☐ Rarely

4. Without exceeding 100% as the total, what percentage of the problems referred for disciplinary action are problems:

a. between students	_____ %
b. between student and classroom teachers	_____ %
c. between student and other staff members	_____ %
d. between student and school rules	_____ %
e. other:_____	_____ %

   Total 100%

5. Indicate the types and frequency of conflicts experienced by students in this school:

a. put-downs/insults/teasing	☐ Often	☐ Sometimes	☐ Rarely
b. threats	☐ Often	☐ Sometimes	☐ Rarely
c. intolerance of differences	☐ Often	☐ Sometimes	☐ Rarely
d. loss of property	☐ Often	☐ Sometimes	☐ Rarely
e. access to groups	☐ Often	☐ Sometimes	☐ Rarely
f. rumors	☐ Often	☐ Sometimes	☐ Rarely
g. physical fighting	☐ Often	☐ Sometimes	☐ Rarely
h. verbal fighting	☐ Often	☐ Sometimes	☐ Rarely
i. schoolwork	☐ Often	☐ Sometimes	☐ Rarely
j. other: _____	☐ Often	☐ Sometimes	☐ Rarely

6. Indicate the effectiveness of each of the following actions in causing a student

to change a problem behavior:

a. time-out   ☐ Very effective ☐ Somewhat effective ☐ Not effective

b. detention   ☐ Very effective ☐ Somewhat effective ☐ Not effective

c. conference with an adult   ☐ Very effective ☐ Somewhat effective ☐ Not effective

d. suspension   ☐ Very effective ☐ Somewhat effective ☐ Not effective

e. contacting parent(s)   ☐ Very effective ☐ Somewhat effective ☐ Not effective

f. expulsion   ☐ Very effective ☐ Somewhat effective ☐ Not effective

7. Without exceeding 100% as the total, what percentage of influence do the following groups have in the way the school operates?

    a. students   _____ %

    b. teachers   _____ %

    c. parents   _____ %

    d. principals and school administrators   _____ %

    e. superintendents and district administrators   _____ %

    f. Board of Education   _____ %

    g. other:_____   _____ %

                                                      Total 100%

8. In this school, I am generally:

    a. treated fairly

        ☐ Most of the time ☐ About half the time ☐ Not very often

    b. treated with respect

        ☐ Most of the time ☐ About half the time ☐ Not very often

    c. given equal opportunity

        ☐ Most of the time ☐ About half the time ☐ Not very often

    d. treated with compassion

        ☐ Most of the time ☐ About half the time ☐ Not very often

    e. accepted

        ☐ Most of the time ☐ About half the time ☐ Not very often

9. I am allowed to solve problems that affect me:

        ☐ Nearly always ☐ Sometimes ☐ Hardly ever

10. This school should do a better job teaching students to:

    a. tell other people how they feel   ☐ Definitely yes ☐ Maybe ☐ Definitely no

    b. disagree without making
       other people angry   ☐ Definitely yes ☐ Maybe ☐ Definitely no

    c. respect authority   ☐ Definitely yes ☐ Maybe ☐ Definitely no

    d. control anger   ☐ Definitely yes ☐ Maybe ☐ Definitely no

    e. ignore someone who is bothersome   ☐ Definitely yes ☐ Maybe ☐ Definitely no

    f. solve problems with other students   ☐ Definitely yes ☐ Maybe ☐ Definitely no

11. When I need help, I ask for it: ☐ Nearly always   ☐ Sometimes   ☐ Hardly ever

12. If I needed help, I think I could get it from:

    a. a parent   ☐ Definitely yes ☐ Maybe ☐ Definitely no

    b. a brother or sister   ☐ Definitely yes ☐ Maybe ☐ Definitely no

    c. another family member   ☐ Definitely yes ☐ Maybe ☐ Definitely no

    d. a teacher   ☐ Definitely yes ☐ Maybe ☐ Definitely no

    e. a counselor   ☐ Definitely yes ☐ Maybe ☐ Definitely no

    f. another school staff member   ☐ Definitely yes ☐ Maybe ☐ Definitely no

    g. another adult   ☐ Definitely yes ☐ Maybe ☐ Definitely no

    h. another student   ☐ Definitely yes ☐ Maybe ☐ Definitely no

13. I think this school has:

        ☐ more problems than most other schools

        ☐ about the same number of problems as most other schools

        ☐ fewer problems than most other schools

PHASE 1: DEVELOP PROGRAM TEAM AND COMMITMENT TO PROGRAM

Create program team

Train program team

Designate program coordinator(s)

Conduct needs assessment

Build faculty consensus for program development

PHASE 2: DESIGN AND PLAN PROGRAM

Develop implementation timeline

Establish advisory committee

Develop policies and procedures

Identify and develop funding sources

PHASE 3: SELECT AND TRAIN MEDIATORS

Conduct student orientation

Select peer mediators

Train peer mediators

Recognize peer mediators

PHASE 4: EDUCATE A CRITICAL MASS OF THE SCHOOL POPULATION

Conduct staff inservice

Conduct student workshops

Provide family and community orientation

Offer parent workshops

PHASE 5: DEVELOP AND EXECUTE PROMOTIONAL CAMPAIGN

Design and implement initial campaign

Conduct ongoing promotional efforts

PHASE 6: OPERATE AND MAINTAIN THE PROGRAM

Develop process for requesting mediation

Schedule mediations and mediators

Supervise mediation sessions

Provide mediators with ongoing training and support

Evaluate program

Peer Mediator Application

Name _____ Grade _____

Address _____

1. I want to be a peer mediator because:

2. List your personal qualities that will help you be a good mediator.

If selected, as a peer mediator I agree to the following terms:

▼ To complete all required training sessions

▼ To serve as a mediator as scheduled

▼ To request mediation to resolve my own personal conflicts

▼ To make up class assignments missed during peer mediation training or duty

Signature _____ Date _____

Peer Mediator Student Nomination

I would like to nominate the following students to be peer mediators because I would respect and trust them to help me resolve a conflict:

1. _____

2. _____

3. _____

Signature _____ Date _____

- -

Peer Mediator Staff Nomination

I would like to nominate the following students to be peer mediators because they show leadership potential within their group:

1. _____

2. _____

3. _____

Signature _____ Date _____

Parent Permission Letter

Date_____

Dear_____ :

It is my pleasure to inform you that _____ has been selected to be trained to become a peer mediator. Peer mediators are students who, with adult supervision, mediate conflicts between their peers.

Conflicts between students are a normal part of daily life. Conflicts that are most common in school include name-calling, rumors, threats, and relationship or friendship issues. Mediation is a conflict resolution process that provides students the opportunity to talk and effectively resolve their conflicts. Peer mediators conduct the mediation process. They do not take sides or make decisions for their peers in conflict. Peer mediators help the students in conflict listen to each other's points of view, focus on the problem, and create their own solutions.

In mediation training, students learn communication, problem-solving, and critical thinking skills and how to apply those skills in the six-step mediation process. Peer mediators participate in both basic and advanced training. Advanced training sessions will be scheduled throughout the school year during and after school. Basic training is scheduled for

Date(s) _____

Time(s) _____

Place _____

Please give permission for_____ to participate in the peer mediation program by signing the permission form below.

If you have any questions, please call me at _____ .

Sincerely,

- -

Please detach and return to_____ by _____ .

I give my permission for _____ to participate in peer mediation training to become a peer mediator.

Parent/guardian signature _____ Date _____

Peer Mediation Certificate

This is to certify that

_____

**has successfully completed basic training
in peer mediation.**

_____

Date of completion

_____

Program sponsor

Peer Mediator Contract

As a peer mediator, I understand my role is to help students resolve conflict peacefully. As a peer mediator, I agree to the following terms.

1. To complete basic and advanced training sessions at the scheduled times

2. To maintain privacy for all mediations

3. To be a responsible peer mediator by conducting mediation sessions according to the process, completing all necessary forms, and promoting the program

4. To maintain satisfactory school conduct (this includes using mediation services for interpersonal conflicts)

5. To make up any class work missed during training or mediation sessions

6. To serve as a peer mediator for the year

Student signature _____ Date _____

Peer Mediation Request

Date _____

Names of students in conflict:

_____ Grade _____

_____ Grade _____

_____ Grade _____

_____ Grade _____

Where did the conflict occur? *(check one)*

☐ Bus   ☐ Outdoors

☐ Cafeteria   ☐ Gym/locker room

☐ Classroom   ☐ Bathroom

☐ Hallway

☐ Other *(specify)* _____

Briefly describe the problem:

_____

_____

_____

_____

Mediation requested by *(check one)*

☐ Student   ☐ Social worker

☐ Teacher   ☐ Dean/assistant principal

☐ Counselor   ☐ Principal

☐ Other *(specify)* _____

Signature of person requesting mediation _____

DO NOT WRITE BELOW THIS LINE
TO BE COMPLETED BY A PROGRAM COORDINATOR

What is the conflict about? *(check one)*

☐ Rumors   ☐ Fighting or hitting

☐ Harassment   ☐ Bias or prejudice

☐ Threats   ☐ Relationship

☐ Name-calling   ☐ Property loss or damage

☐ Other *(specify)* _____

Peer Mediator Classroom Release

Student _____ Grade _____

Teachers: There are times when a peer mediator might be asked to conduct a mediation during class. The student will be released from class only with your permission. Please indicate on this form if you approve an occasional release for this student.

Period	Subject	Room Number	Approval (Y/N)	Teacher Signature
1				
2				
3				
4				
5				
6				
7				
8				
9				

OPTIONS LIST

▼ What are some possible options that address both of your interests?

▼ What other possibilities can you think of?

1. _____

2. _____

3. _____

4. _____

5. _____

6. _____

7. _____

8. _____

9. _____

10. _____

Peer Mediation Agreement

Date_____

We voluntarily participated in a mediation. We have reached an agreement that we believe is fair and that solves the problem between us. In the future if we have problems that we cannot resolve on our own, we agree to come back to mediation.

Name _____   Name _____

_____   _____

_____   _____

_____   _____

_____   _____

_____   _____

_____   _____

_____   _____

_____   _____

_____   _____

_____   _____

_____   _____

Signature _____   Signature _____

Mediator signature _____

Mediator signature _____

Post-Mediation Session Assessment

Name _____ Date_____

Please check the boxes that represent your honest thoughts and feelings.

1. I am a: ☐ Student ☐ Teacher ☐ Administrator ☐ Parent ☐ Counselor

   ☐ Other _____

2. Have you ever participated in a mediation before? ☐ Yes ☐ No

   If yes, how many times? _____

3. Do you think that the mediators:

   Listened to you? ☐ Yes ☐ No

   Understood your interests? ☐ Yes ☐ No

   Acted fairly? ☐ Yes ☐ No

4. Describe your relationship with the other person before this conflict occurred. *(check as many as you like)*

   ☐ Friend ☐ Acquaintance ☐ Stranger

   ☐ Relative ☐ Boyfriend/girlfriend ☐ Other

5. What were your feelings about the other person when you came into the mediation session?

6. How do you feel about the other person now?

7. If you reached an agreement, are you satisfied with your agreement? ☐ Yes ☐ No

8. If you did not reach an agreement, what are your alternatives for dealing with this problem? What will you do next?

Date _____

Mediator _____

Mediator _____

Place a check mark (✓) by each step where you did quality work. Place an asterisk (*) by each step where you think the quality could improve. Co-mediators complete this form as a team.

STEP 1: AGREE TO MEDIATE

☐ Welcomed both people and introduced yourself as the mediator.

☐ Explained the mediation process.

☐ Explained ground rules.

☐ Asked each person: "Are you willing to follow the rules?"

STEP 2: GATHER POINTS OF VIEW

☐ Asked each person to tell what happened.

☐ Listened, summarized, clarified.

STEP 3: FOCUS ON INTERESTS

☐ Found real interests.

☐ Listened, summarized, clarified.

☐ Summarized interests before going to the next step.

STEP 4: CREATE WIN-WIN OPTIONS

☐ Explained brainstorming rules.

☐ Asked for ideas that address the interests of both parties.

STEP 5: EVALUATE OPTIONS

☐ Asked parties to combine options or parts of options.

☐ For each option, asked:

Is this option fair?

Can you do it?

Do you think it will work?

STEP 6: CREATE AN AGREEMENT

☐ Asked disputants to make a plan of action: Who, what, when, where, how?

☐ Wrote the plan.

☐ Asked each person to read the plan and sign the agreement.

☐ Closed the session with a handshake.

OTHER

☐ Remained neutral—did not take sides.

☐ Avoided making suggestions to solve the problem.

☐ If parties did not reach an agreement, knew what to say to end the session.

☐ Worked together with co-mediator.

☐ Gave each party a turn to talk without interruption.

Answer the following questions.

1. What did you do well?

2. If you could do this mediation again, what might you do differently?

3. Were certain steps more difficult for you than others? If so, what could you do to strengthen these steps?

4. Do you have any other concerns or questions?

Staff supervisor_____ Date _____

Comments:

Peer Mediation Record

Month_____ Year_____ Page_____ of_____

Mediation Case Number	Date	Grade	Sex (M/F)	Race	Location	Requested By	Type	Time	Signed (Y/N)	Kept (Y/N)

KEY

Location

B = Bus
C = Cafeteria
R = Classroom
H = Hallway
G = Gym/locker room
D = Outdoors
B = Bathroom
O = Other

Requested By

S = Student
T = Teacher
C = Counselor
W= Social worker
D = Dean/assistant principal
P = Principal
O = Other

Type

R = Rumors
H = Harassment
T = Threats
N = Name-calling
F = Fighting or hitting
B = Bias or prejudice
RL = Relationship
P = Property loss or damage
O = Other

Time: To the nearest 5 minutes.

Signed: Was agreement signed?

Kept: Was agreement still in force at 1-month follow-up interview with selected disputants?

Circle the number that best corresponds to how you think the school staff should respond to conflict in the school or classroom.

	Always	Often	Sometimes	Never
1. Tell the students to "knock it off."	1	2	3	4
2. Try to smooth over the situation.	1	2	3	4
3. Help students understand different points of view.	1	2	3	4
4. Separate the students and keep them away from each other.	1	2	3	4
5. Refer the conflict to the administration.	1	2	3	4
6. Determine who started it.	1	2	3	4
7. Try to find the cause of the problem.	1	2	3	4
8. Try to work out a compromise between those in conflict.	1	2	3	4
9. Mediate the dispute using a six-step mediation process.	1	2	3	4
10. Ask students to apologize to each other.	1	2	3	4
11. Encourage students to brainstorm solutions to the problem.	1	2	3	4
12. Refer the students to peer mediation.	1	2	3	4
13. Assign a punishment or consequence.	1	2	3	4
14. Let students have it out, as long as no one gets physically hurt.	1	2	3	4
15. Tell students they will be sent to the discipline office.	1	2	3	4
16. Get everyone busy doing something else.	1	2	3	4
17. Tell students to settle it after class.	1	2	3	4

Circle the number that best describes how much you agree or disagree with each of the following statements.

	Strongly Agree	Agree Somewhat	Disagree Somewhat	Strongly Disagree
1. Conflicts among students have no place in the school.	1	2	3	4
2. Conflict is a natural, vital opportunity of life.	1	2	3	4
3. To resolve values conflicts means the disputants must change or align their values.	1	2	3	4
4. When students fight over property, the equitable distribution of resources is usually an effective solution.	1	2	3	4
5. In a dispute, there is typically a student who is right and a student who is wrong.	1	2	3	4
6. Avoiding conflict helps students build productive relationships.	1	2	3	4
7. Bargaining over positions to achieve a compromise is important for the resolution of conflict.	1	2	3	4
8. Every problem has both substance and relationship issues.	1	2	3	4
9. Students can peacefully resolve conflicts involving bias and prejudice.	1	2	3	4
10. Conflict provides real opportunity to learn and grow.	1	2	3	4
11. Students are effective peacemakers.	1	2	3	4
12. Mediation is a process that could be used to resolve disputes between teachers and students.	1	2	3	4

Circle the number that best corresponds to your response to conflict in the school or classroom.

	Always	Often	Sometimes	Never
1. Tell the students to "knock it off."	1	2	3	4
2. Try to smooth over the situation.	1	2	3	4
3. Help students understand different points of view.	1	2	3	4
4. Separate the students and keep them away from each other.	1	2	3	4
5. Refer the conflict to the administration.	1	2	3	4
6. Determine who started it.	1	2	3	4
7. Try to find the cause of the problem.	1	2	3	4
8. Try to work out a compromise between those in conflict.	1	2	3	4
9. Mediate the dispute using a six-step mediation process.	1	2	3	4
10. Ask students to apologize to each other.	1	2	3	4
11. Encourage students to brainstorm solutions to the problem.	1	2	3	4
12. Refer the students to peer mediation.	1	2	3	4
13. Assign a punishment or consequence.	1	2	3	4
14. Let students have it out, as long as no one gets physically hurt.	1	2	3	4
15. Tell students they will be sent to the discipline office.	1	2	3	4
16. Get everyone busy doing something else.	1	2	3	4
17. Tell students to settle it after class.	1	2	3	4

Circle the number that best describes how much you agree or disagree with each of the following statements.

	Strongly Agree	Agree Somewhat	Disagree Somewhat	Strongly Disagree
1. Conflicts among students have no place in the school.	1	2	3	4
2. Conflict is a natural, vital opportunity of life.	1	2	3	4
3. To resolve values conflicts means the disputants must change or align their values.	1	2	3	4
4. When students fight over property, the equitable distribution of resources is usually an effective solution.	1	2	3	4
5. In a dispute, there is typically a student who is right and a student who is wrong.	1	2	3	4
6. Avoiding conflict helps students build productive relationships.	1	2	3	4
7. Bargaining over positions to achieve a compromise is important for the resolution of conflict.	1	2	3	4
8. Every problem has both substance and relationship issues.	1	2	3	4
9. Students can peacefully resolve conflicts involving bias and prejudice.	1	2	3	4
10. Conflict provides real opportunity to learn and grow.	1	2	3	4
11. Students are effective peacemakers.	1	2	3	4
12. Mediation is a process that could be used to resolve disputes between teachers and students.	1	2	3	4

Answer the following questions.

1. I have requested a peer mediation. ☐ Yes ☐ No

   If yes, approximate number of requests. _____

2. I have participated as a disputant in a mediation. ☐ Yes ☐ No

   If yes, was an agreement reached? ☐ Yes ☐ No

   If yes, number of mediations in which you participated. _____

3. I have served as a peer mediator using the six-step process. ☐ Yes ☐ No

Circle the number that best corresponds to your response to conflict in the school or classroom.

	Always	Often	Sometimes	Never
1. Tell the students to "knock it off."	1	2	3	4
2. Try to smooth over the situation.	1	2	3	4
3. Help students understand different points of view.	1	2	3	4
4. Separate the students and keep them away from each other.	1	2	3	4
5. Refer the conflict to the administration.	1	2	3	4
6. Determine who started it.	1	2	3	4
7. Try to find the cause of the problem.	1	2	3	4
8. Try to work out a compromise between those in conflict.	1	2	3	4
9. Mediate the dispute using a six-step mediation process.	1	2	3	4
10. Ask students to apologize to each other.	1	2	3	4
11. Encourage students to brainstorm solutions to the problem.	1	2	3	4
12. Refer the students to peer mediation.	1	2	3	4
13. Assign a punishment or consequence.	1	2	3	4
14. Let students have it out, as long as no one gets physically hurt.	1	2	3	4
15. Tell students they will be sent to the discipline office.	1	2	3	4
16. Get everyone busy doing something else.	1	2	3	4
17. Tell students to settle it after class.	1	2	3	4

Circle the number that best describes how much you agree or disagree with each of the following statements.

	Strongly Agree	Agree Somewhat	Disagree Somewhat	Strongly Disagree
1. Conflicts among students have no place in the school.	1	2	3	4
2. Conflict is a natural, vital opportunity of life.	1	2	3	4
3. To resolve values conflicts means the disputants must change or align their values.	1	2	3	4
4. When students fight over property, the equitable distribution of resources is usually an effective solution.	1	2	3	4
5. In a dispute, there is typically a student who is right and a student who is wrong.	1	2	3	4
6. Avoiding conflict helps students build productive relationships.	1	2	3	4
7. Bargaining over positions to achieve a compromise is important for the resolution of conflict.	1	2	3	4
8. Every problem has both substance and relationship issues.	1	2	3	4
9. Students can peacefully resolve conflicts involving bias and prejudice.	1	2	3	4
10. Mediation is a process that could be used to resolve disputes between teachers and students.	1	2	3	4
11. Mediation is a process that could be used to resolve problems between adults in school.	1	2	3	4
12. Managing student behavior without punishment is crucial to the development of cooperative and responsible students.	1	2	3	4

Circle the number that best corresponds to your response to conflict in the school or classroom.

	Always	Often	Sometimes	Never
1. Tell the students to "knock it off."	1	2	3	4
2. Try to smooth over the situation.	1	2	3	4
3. Help students understand different points of view.	1	2	3	4
4. Separate the students and keep them away from each other.	1	2	3	4
5. Refer the conflict to the administration.	1	2	3	4
6. Determine who started it.	1	2	3	4
7. Try to find the cause of the problem.	1	2	3	4
8. Try to work out a compromise between those in conflict.	1	2	3	4
9. Mediate the dispute using a six-step mediation process.	1	2	3	4
10. Ask students to apologize to each other.	1	2	3	4
11. Encourage students to brainstorm solutions to the problem.	1	2	3	4
12. Refer the students to peer mediation.	1	2	3	4
13. Assign a punishment or consequence.	1	2	3	4
14. Let students have it out, as long as no one gets physically hurt.	1	2	3	4
15. Tell students they will be sent to the discipline office.	1	2	3	4
16. Get everyone busy doing something else.	1	2	3	4
17. Tell students to settle it after class.	1	2	3	4

Circle the number that best describes how much you agree or disagree with each of the following statements.

	Strongly Agree	Agree Somewhat	Disagree Somewhat	Strongly Disagree
1. Conflicts among students have no place in the school.	1	2	3	4
2. Conflict is a natural, vital opportunity of life.	1	2	3	4
3. To resolve values conflicts means the disputants must change or align their values.	1	2	3	4
4. When students fight over property, the equitable distribution of resources is usually an effective solution.	1	2	3	4
5. In a dispute, there is typically a student who is right and a student who is wrong.	1	2	3	4
6. Avoiding conflict helps students build productive relationships.	1	2	3	4
7. Bargaining over positions to achieve a compromise is important for the resolution of conflict.	1	2	3	4
8. Every problem has both substance and relationship issues.	1	2	3	4
9. Students can peacefully resolve conflicts involving bias and prejudice.	1	2	3	4
10. Mediation is a process that could be used to resolve disputes between teachers and students.	1	2	3	4
11. Mediation is a process that could be used to resolve problems between adults in school.	1	2	3	4
12. Managing student behavior without punishment is crucial to the development of cooperative and responsible students.	1	2	3	4

APPENDIX B

Evaluation Results for Peer Mediation & Conflict Resolution Programs

Research and evaluation on conflict within schools and on the impact of conflict education programs has not been extensive. One of the most comprehensive studies on conflict within schools was conducted by DeCecco and Richards (1974) over 20 years ago. These investigators interviewed over 8,000 students and 500 faculty members in more than 60 junior and senior high schools in areas of New York City, Philadelphia, and San Francisco. They found that over 90% of the conflicts reported by students were perceived to be either unresolved or resolved in destructive ways. Negotiation of conflicts was practically nonexistent. The researchers concluded that in most situations individuals were either trying to avoid conflict or conquer the opposition.

TEACHING STUDENTS TO BE PEACEMAKERS

More recently, David Johnson and Roger Johnson (1994), of the Cooperative Learning Center at the University of Minnesota, have reported the results of a series of landmark studies they conducted between 1988 and 1994. These studies were designed to examine students' ability to manage conflict before and after peer mediation training. As described in *Teaching Students to Be Peacemakers* (Johnson & Johnson, 1991), the peer mediation program had as its basis the theories of integrative bargaining (Pruitt, 1981), perspective reversal (Johnson, 1971), and constructive conflict (Deutsch, 1973). Student mediation training lasted from 9 to 15 hours for the various studies; students involved were in first through ninth grades. The studies were conducted in both suburban and urban settings. Five studies used control groups, three studies randomly selected classrooms and/or controls from the school, one study randomly assigned students to conditions, and four studies rotated teachers across conditions.

Johnson and Johnson's (1994) research is highly significant because their program is based on the theoretical literature on conflicts of interests, integrative bargaining, perspective reversal, and third-party intervention. These same theories pervade most conflict resolution programs in operation within schools today. Results of these studies provide educators and conflict resolution experts with valuable information about the need for conflict resolution programs and the impact of conflict management training programs on students' ability to manage their conflicts constructively. The following discussion summarizes results of Johnson and Johnson's research and suggests implications for the development of subsequent conflict resolution programs.

Need for conflict resolution programs

Before conflict resolution training, most students were found to be involved in conflicts daily, indicating that conflicts are pervasive within classroom and schools. The conflicts reported most frequently involved put-downs and teasing, playground problems, access or possession, physical aggression and fights, academic work, and turn taking. Before training, students referred the majority of their conflicts to the teacher, used destructive strategies that tended to escalate the conflict rather than resolve it, and lacked knowledge of how to negotiate. If they did not bring their conflict to a teacher, students typically used destructive strategies (such as repeating their request and trying to force the other person to give in) that would escalate the conflict and increase the likelihood that the teacher would have to intervene. Untrained students never indicated that they would negotiate a solution to a conflict. Students had no idea how to negotiate an agreement satisfactory to both. The finding that students were not being taught negotiation procedures and skills in the home or community at large suggested, therefore, that all students could benefit from training in how to manage conflicts constructively.

Impact of conflict resolution training

Johnson and Johnson established some parameters to judge the effectiveness of conflict resolution training. Specifically, they determined that conflict resolution training works if it does as follows:

▼ Reduces the number of student-student conflicts referred to teachers and the principal

▼ Results in students' mastering the negotiation and mediation procedures and skills taught

▼ Results in students' using these procedures and skills in settings other than the classroom

Their research indicated that after negotiation and mediation training, the student-student conflicts that did occur were by and large managed by the students themselves without the involvement of adults. The frequency of student-student conflicts that teachers had to manage dropped 80% after the training, and the number of conflicts referred to the principal was reduced to zero. Such a dramatic reduction of referrals of conflicts to adult authorities changed the discipline program from arbitrating conflicts to maintaining and supporting the peer mediation process. At the end of the academic year, months after students received training in negotiation and mediation, almost all the students who had been trained still knew all the negotiation and mediation steps. This knowledge was assessed by giving students conflict scenarios to respond to in written, interview, and video-taped simulation formats. The high rate of retention was attributed to the fact that students were using the procedures to manage their day-to-day conflicts with classmates and peers. Students who received training could also apply the procedures to actual conflict situations. Trained students were carefully observed, and information was gathered from teachers, principals, and parents to find out whether or not the negotiation and mediation skills transferred to nonclassroom and nonschool settings. Results indicated that students did use the negotiation and mediation procedures in playground, neighborhood, and family settings. A number of parents volunteered to teachers that students used negotiation and mediation procedures and skills with their brothers and sisters, neighborhood friends, and grandparents.

Academic achievement

Johnson and Johnson's findings indicated that learning the negotiation procedure affects students' academic achievement. The peacemaker training was integrated into a 2-week high school English literature unit. Students were randomly assigned to experimental or control groups. Students in the experimental group studied a novel, learned the negotiation procedure, and role-played each of the major conflicts in the novel using the integrative negotiation procedure. Students in the control group spent all their time studying the novel. Students in both conditions took an achievement test the last day of the instructional unit. Students in the experimental condition scored significantly higher on the achievement test than did students in the control condition. This finding suggests that, even though it takes time to teach the negotiation procedure, learning of academic material can be substantially improved.

Link between peer mediation training and negotiation research

Two different approaches to peer mediation exist: school cadre and total student body. The *school cadre approach* is based on the assumption that a few specially trained students can defuse and resolve constructively the interpersonal conflicts taking place among members of the student body. A small number of students are trained to serve as peer mediators, usually in a 1- or 2-day workshop or a semester-long class. The *total student body approach* emphasizes training every student in the school in ways to manage conflicts constructively.

Investigating how students would manage conflicts in which they could use a win-lose strategy or win-win (integrative negotiation) strategy, Johnson and Johnson found that all untrained students used the win-lose strategy. Students who had undergone training primarily used the integrative negotiation strategy. This finding provides an important link between peer mediation training and the research on negotiation. If mediation is to succeed, disputants must be taught how conflicts are managed. This means that if previous training has not taken place, disputants will need to be trained in integrative negotiation as part of the process of mediation. It may well be that destructive conflict management techniques are the result of ignorance of conflict resolution procedures. If so, this would validate the importance of the total student body approach to peer mediation.

Adult perceptions

Johnson and Johnson found adult perceptions of the peer mediation program helpful in their assessment of program effectiveness. Interviews indicated that teachers, principals, and parents believed the program reduced the incidence of destructively managed conflicts and resulted in a more positive classroom climate. When students regulate their own behavior, the need for teachers and administrators to monitor and control student actions declines. Discipline improves, while teachers are freed to devote their energies to teaching. By training the teachers to train the students, both the faculty and the student body learn the same procedures for managing conflict. Schoolwide norms and procedures are thus established for everyone in the school.

Summary

The Johnson and Johnson research demonstrated that even young children can be taught how to negotiate and mediate. This finding has relevance for professionals who work with families, youth programs, or schools. Knowing how to negotiate and mediate conflicts is important for a number of reasons. First, it empowers students to regulate their own behavior. Self-regulation is the ability to act in socially approved ways in the absence of monitoring by others. It is a central and significant hallmark of cognitive and social development. Frequently, adults act as referees and judges in the lives of children. When they take on these roles, adults place children in a dependent position and deprive them of opportunities to learn valuable social skills. Second, children who are able to negotiate and mediate have a developmental advantage over children who do not know how to do so. It may be hypothesized that using one's own competencies to resolve conflicts with others constructivly increases both the child's strength and ability to cope with stress and adversity and the child's ability to build and maintain high quality relationships with peers (Prothrow-Stith, 1987).

HIGHLIGHTS OF OTHER RESEARCH

The Ohio School Conflict Management Demonstration Project

The Ohio School Conflict Management Demonstration Project, conducted in 17 schools between 1990 and 1993, indicated that most students improved their attitudes toward conflict, increased their understanding of nonviolent problem-solving methods, and enhanced their communication skills (Ohio Commission on Dispute Resolution and Conflict Management, 1994).

Clark County Social Service School Mediation Program

The Clark County Social Service School Mediation Program in Nevada reported for the 1992 school year that the amount of conflict among students in two participating elementary schools was reduced and the existence of the program helped prevent fights among students (Carpenter, 1993). Peer mediators mediated 163 conflicts and resolved 138 (a success rate of 85%).

Peer mediators demonstrated a significant increase in conflict management skills, self-esteem, and assertiveness. In addition, the number of teachers who spent less than 20% of their time on discipline increased by 18% after the program. Similar findings occurred in the reported results for the 1993–1994 school year (Carpenter, 1994).

Suburban Chicago

Evaluation of a mediation program in a suburban Chicago high school indicated positive results (Tolsen, McDonald, & Moriarity, 1990). Researchers found that mediation was more effective than traditional discipline in reducing the number of interpersonal conflicts and that the majority of disputants and student mediators were highly satisfied with all aspects of the program.

Resolving Conflict Creatively Program

Evaluation of the impact of the Resolving Conflict Creatively Program (RCCP) in four multiracial, multiethnic school districts in New York City showed that 84% of teachers surveyed reported noticing positive changes in classroom climate (Metis Associates, Inc., 1990). A total of 71% of teachers in the RCCP evaluation reported moderate or great decreases in physical violence in the classroom, whereas 66% observed less name-calling and fewer verbal put-downs. Similar percentages observed that students were showing better perspective-taking skills, greater willingness to cooperate, and more caring behavior. In addition, over 98% of respondents said that the mediation component gave children an important tool for dealing with conflicts. Other changes reported by teachers and administrators in the evaluation included children's spontaneously using conflict resolution skills, increased self-esteem and sense of empowerment, increased awareness and verbalizing of feelings, and more acceptance of differences.

Project S.M.A.R.T.

Project S.M.A.R.T. (School Mediator Alternative Resolution Team), ongoing in six New York City high schools, reported that suspensions for fighting decreased by 46%, 45%, 70%, 60%, and 65% at five participating high schools during the first year of program operation (Lam, 1989).

New Mexico Mediation in Schools Program

An evaluation report for the New Mexico Center for Dispute Resolution's Mediation in Schools Program (Carter, 1994) states that teachers in program schools perceived less violence and hurtful behavior among students, whereas teachers in nonprogram schools reported more violence. Program teachers were likely to use positive, noncoercive conflict resolution strategies (especially mediation) in response to hurtful behavior among students. Nonprogram teachers, on the other hand, were more likely to use coercive, win-lose, adult-authored strategies (especially detention and sending students to the principal's office) in response to problem behavior. As this report suggests, the peer mediation process clearly "belongs to the students." In more than 2,300 mediations, only 250 required some sort of adult intervention. Students trained as mediators had clearer definitions of mediation and conflict resolution strategies and skills than did their untrained peers. Untrained students did not fully grasp the benefits of a win-win situation and creative conflict resolution strategies. Also, untrained students did not show the levels of self-esteem and confidence demonstrated by trained students, nor did they feel as good about school. Finally, the amount of time staff members in program schools spent dealing with conflicts was reduced, as was the number of violent incidents among students.

Program for Young Negotiators

The Harvard Graduate School of Education is undertaking a systematic evaluation of the impact of the Program for Young Negotiators. Preliminary findings from the evaluation team suggest that the majority of participating students are learning the basic messages taught by the program and using them, at least in certain situations (Nakkula & Nikitopoulos, 1996). Most interviewees reported experiencing the program as "fun" because of its use of games and role-plays. This latter point is important in that the "fun" experience keeps the students engaged in the training process and facilitates their recall of the basic messages.

The interviews also revealed that most students could cite concrete examples of using their negotiation skills with peers and, perhaps more unexpectedly, with parents. Several students reported that their parents were caught off guard by their practice of negotiation at home. The shift from arguing, complaining, and resisting to negotiating generally met with a positive response from parents, according to many program graduates. Parent feedback suggests the use of negotiation steps opens up avenues for parent-child discussion.

Peace Education Foundation

In 1991, the Peace Education Foundation initiated conflict resolution and peer mediation programs throughout Dade County, Florida, Region II Public Schools (Hanson, 1994). Training for school staff was provided in order to establish both classroom-based and schoolwide student mediation programs and to infuse school curricula with conflict resolution instruction. A review of mediator reports showed that 86% of conflicts mediated were resolved. A system of incident reporting showed a statistically significant reduction in the rate of referrals for general disruptive behavior in the elementary schools that had the highest levels of implementation. Conflict resolution affected student attitudes toward resolving conflicts positively. Results from student surveys indicated that those who received training were more willing to respond to conflict situations with actions other than threats and violence.

In 1994, staff teams from seven alternative and two middle schools with a high percentage of at-risk students received training in the Peace Education conflict resolution model. Post-intervention surveys showed the following:

▼ Student attitudes toward conflict changed significantly after learning the model.

▼ Students were more inclined to explain, reason, compromise, or share in order to resolve their conflicts.

▼ Students were less likely to appeal to authority figures or to use aggression and threats when in conflict.

▼ Teachers felt more respected and less frustrated as a result of implementing the model.

Evaluations of the Palm Beach County Schools initiative revealed a considerable reduction in student referrals and suspensions. For example, the number of referrals at one elementary school dropped to 5 between September and December of 1994 from 124 during the same period in 1992.

Parents who attended a "Fighting Fair for Families" workshop also reported favorable results. According to 2-month follow-up surveys from 163 participants, 79% reported improvement in the way conflicts were handled at home, 76% reported improvement in the way feelings were treated at home, 70% reported improvement with the way people listen to each other at home, and 80% reported that their "Rules for Fighting Fair" program poster was still displayed in their homes.

St. Mary's University Mediation Project

The Mediation Project of the Public Justice Department of St. Mary's University, San Antonio, Texas, has provided conflict resolution training in middle and high schools. Preliminary studies of this collaborative project among school, university, and community have shown significant decreases in disciplinary problems and student violence on school campuses (Leal, 1993; Leal, Hollis, & Cole, 1996). Smithson Valley Middle School recorded a 57% drop in disciplinary actions in the first year of its peer-based mediation program's operation.

CONCLUSION

Research from the field continues to support the need for conflict resolution programs and legitimizes the contention that effective conflict resolution programs must be based on proven negotiation theory. Such theory must be operationalized into instructional procedures that educators can be trained to use and that students can use to resolve their own conflicts.

Further evaluation is anticipated, but it is unlikely to alter the present view that conflict resolution education is indeed effective. What further research promises is information concerned with strengthening, expanding, and sustaining conflict resolution education.

APPENDIX C

Case Example: Common Ground Peer Mediation Program

This appendix describes actual sponsorship and promotional efforts for Common Ground, the peer mediation program begun in 1988 at the Urbana, Illinois, Middle School. Although a strategy such as this one will not be appropriate for every school, the discussion does illustrate how resources were combined to shape the plan. Many of the techniques used may be adapted in other schools.

The Urbana program was supported by school funds and donations from a corporate sponsor, a local food distribution company. Corporate sponsorship was obtained by a retired teacher who remains active as a community liaison between the school and local businesses. After she discovered that this company had an employee-management mediation center, she approached the personnel director with the school's plan. Her outreach resulted in funding for printing of all of the peer mediation literature; T-shirts for peer mediators, staff trainers, and advisory committee members; and catering for a recognition luncheon. Miscellaneous funds from various school clubs and organizations paid for pins and art supplies.

Three students in a graphic design class were responsible for developing promotional materials. The students were given this special assignment because they were interested and good "idea" people. A parent who is a professional graphic designer and illustrator in the community volunteered to assist them.

After poring over dozens of graphic design and art magazines, the students came up with sketches for logos, color schemes, and suggestions for names and tag lines. According to them, the development of the main concept was the hardest part of the whole campaign, and they worked intensely for 2 weeks before they came up with any designs that they felt were satisfactory. Their plan was designed to convey the images of gentle humor and sincerity.

The peer mediators, program coordinators, and staff involved in the project voted on their favorite options. Once decisions were made, the design students created mock-ups of a brochure for adults, a brochure for students, posters, flyers,

T-shirts, pins, and invitations to a recognition luncheon. The brochures for adults and students are reproduced at the end of this appendix as Figures 18 and 19. A sample promotional poster is shown in Figure 20. The program name (Common Ground), logo, and tag line ("Students helping students") were prepared for presentation to the school administration and the program's corporate sponsor.

Throughout the week prior to the grand opening, morning announcements, written and read by peer mediators on the public address system, helped explain the mediation concept and added to the excitement. A teacher involved in the program volunteered along with other teachers who were supporters of the project to organize a luncheon to recognize the peer mediators. She made arrangements with the catering department of a local grocery store and mailed invitations to mediators and parents, sponsors, administrators, school board members, the school district superintendent, and special guests. Decorations were set up by the peer mediators.

The recognition luncheon took place the day before the grand opening. The luncheon was well attended, and the principal welcomed guests and publicly thanked the school and community sponsors and organizers. After lunch, mediation demonstrations were given by peer mediators, and the school social worker explained the process to parents and sponsors. The peer mediators received special certificates and official T-shirts, and were honored by parents, teachers, friends, and members of the business community.

After the luncheon, selected peer mediators were interviewed by local media reporters. Later that day, after all the other students were gone, the mediators covered the school with flyers and posters that would signal the opening of the Common Ground mediation center. Flyers were posted on most student lockers, and posters were displayed throughout the cafeteria and even in the bathroom stalls. Teachers displayed posters in their classrooms depicting the mediation center's logo and explaining referral procedures.

The morning of the grand opening, students entered the school to find posters and flyers everywhere. Announcements over the public address system noted the official opening of the mediation center. All peer mediators and teachers who were part of the program wore their T-shirts. During first hour, teachers distributed brochures and explained the mediation process, discussed procedures for referrals, and answered questions. At lunch, students were given the chance to meet their grade-level peer mediators at tables set up near the lunch lines. The mediators handed out pins that read "Start Talking—Common Ground Mediation."

The next day after school, the faculty assembled in the library for coffee, after which the principal introduced the peer mediators. The mediators received enthusiastic applause and thanks from teachers and support staff. During the same week, brochures were mailed to all parents, and news releases were sent to the local media. Several requests for mediation were made within the first few days of the center's operation. These requests continued throughout the school year.

When the first group of peer mediators filled out evaluations at the end of the year, they were asked if they had it to do over again whether they would choose to participate. They unanimously answered yes. The campaign had succeeded in establishing an effective alternative for resolving conflicts.

Figure 18. Sample Staff and Community Brochure

Conflicts Are Part of Everyday Life

At Urbana Middle School students have a positive way to settle conflicts called *mediation*. Common Ground is the name of the in-school mediation center where students help students mediate their own disputes.

Student Conflicts Are Common

At Urbana Middle School, the most typical conflicts between students are:

▼ "She said/he said" rumors

▼ Name-calling

▼ Friendships gone amiss

▼ Threats

Student conflicts that are not resolved may end up with loss of friends, verbal attacks, and disruptive behaviors that can make learning more difficult.

Mediation: A Tool to Resolve Conflicts

Mediation has been used in many settings as a positive and structured approach to settle disputes. It is a voluntary and cooperative process where two parties who are having a conflict communicate with each other and look for agreement. It is a problem-solving approach where no one loses.

Mediation at Urbana Middle School is used to resolve student disputes because it empowers students to:

▼ Communicate more effectively across age and cultural differences

▼ Develop empathy and the skills of listening, oral expression, and critical thinking

▼ Address problems of hostility, aggression, and absenteeism in a peaceful way

A select number of students are trained to act as mediators. The student mediators facilitate the process when a request is made. In this way, students are given an opportunity to solve their own problems without an adult's doing it for them.

How the Center Was Established

Steps were undertaken during the fall to establish the center. Highlights of this process were:

Staff orientation: Staff were given an overview of the mediation process and the purpose of the student mediation center. Interested staff were asked to volunteer for the advisory committee.

Student assemblies: Grade-level assemblies were held to explain mediation and the center. At this time any students who were interested in becoming mediators applied.

Mediator selection: A diverse group of students were selected from those who applied. Ten students from each grade level were chosen by the advisory committee.

Figure 18. (continued)

Training of mediators: The selected students were given 1520 hours of training in the skill of conflict resolution.

Procedures for Mediation

The advisory committee established guidelines for the center:

▼ Any student can request mediation.

▼ Students can be referred to mediation by faculty, administration, or parents.

▼ All parties must agree voluntarily to the process.

▼ All parties involved agree to keep the mediation private.

Disputants come up with their own solutions, and an agreement is signed.

Ongoing Training and Evaluation

Records are kept, and the advisory committee will assess the effectiveness of the center. Ongoing training and support are given to the student mediators.

Steps in the Mediation Process

STEP 1: Agree to Mediate

▼ Make introductions.

▼ State the ground rules.

STEP 2: Gather Points of View

▼ Ask each person to tell what happened.

▼ Ask each person whether he or she wants to add anything.

STEP 3: Focus on Interests

▼ Determine and summarize shared interests.

STEP 4: Create Win-Win Options

▼ Brainstorm solutions and ask disputants what can be done to resolve the problem.

STEP 5: Evaluate Options

▼ Ask each person what could be done to resolve the problem.

STEP 6: Create an Agreement

▼ Write up the agreement and have disputants sign it.

▼ Shake hands.

Benefits

Mediation promotes a positive school environment in which students learn a peaceful way to resolve conflicts. This process teaches mutual respect through clear and direct communication. This life skill can be applied to the family, neighborhood, and community.

Students are empowered with a strategy to deal successfully with everyday problems, ultimately resulting in enhanced self-esteem and positive changes in behavior.

Figure 19. Sample Student Brochure

Having a conflict?

▼ Has someone made fun of you or teased you?

▼ Did someone say, "Just wait and I'll get you after school?"

▼ Did "he say" that "she said" that "you said" . . . and a rumor is going around the school?

What is mediation?

Mediation is a chance for you to sit face-to-face and talk, uninterrupted, so each side of the dispute is heard. After the problem is defined, solutions are created and then evaluated. When an agreement is reached, it is written and signed.

What is a student mediator?

A student mediator is one of your peers who has been trained to conduct the mediation meeting. The student mediator makes sure the mediation session is helpful and fair. Your fellow students were selected to help you resolve differences because they might better understand your point of view.

Are there any rules in mediation?

To make the process work, there are a few simple rules.

1. Mediation is a process that both students choose.
2. Everything said during a mediation is kept private. What is said in the room stays in the room.
3. In mediation, students take turns talking, and no one can interrupt.
4. The student mediator does not take sides.

If I have a conflict, how do I go about getting it mediated?

It is very easy to request a mediation. Just pick up a mediation request form from a counselor or a social worker. Take 2 minutes to fill it out and return it to any counselor or social worker. Within a day you will receive notification of the time and place of mediation. Mediation will be scheduled when the least amount of class time is missed.

Why should I try mediation?

There are many reasons why mediation will be helpful to you. Here are a few.

1. Conflicts that do not get resolved often end in fights, which could result in suspension.
2. Conflicts that do not get resolved often result in hurt feelings, which could cause you to lose friends.
3. You will learn to choose a peaceful, responsible way to solve your own problems without an adult's doing it for you.
4. Mediation will help you develop mutual respect and clear communication.
5. Mediation will make school a more positive place to learn and grow.

Check out Common Ground, Urbana Middle School's student mediation center.

Figure 20. Sample Poster

APPENDIX D

Boundary Breakers & Closure Activities

Boundary breakers are activities designed to offer a low-risk way for groups to get acquainted and work together as a team. Based on cooperation and communication, they can be used either to relax or to energize a group. Most involve movement and a high level of participation.

Closure activities are designed to review, summarize, and reinforce what has been learned. They provide an important check on how participants are feeling and thinking about the events of the day and help trainers plan future training activities that will be successful. Finally, closure activities affirm the positive qualities and efforts of each participant and act to structure the support individuals need to learn and grow.

These activities are short, usually 10 to 15 minutes long, and require few materials. The few handouts mentioned appear at the end of this appendix.

BOUNDARY BREAKERS

The Line-Up

1. Have all the students stand, then ask them to line up in a circle around the room in alphabetical order by first name (for example, Alan, Barb, Dinesh, Katina . . . Zoey). The person to the left should have a name beginning with

The Line-Up, Send a Letter, The Knotted Rope, The Telephone Booth, and Connections Closure have been adapted by permission from activities appearing in *Boundary Breakers: A Team Building Guide for Student Activity Advisers*, by J. Schrader, 1990, Reston, VA: National Association of Secondary School Principals. This resource also contains many other good activities.

an earlier letter in the alphabet; the person to the right should have a name beginning with a later letter. Encourage the students to move around the room, talk, and cooperate to make the circle follow the pattern.

2. After the circle is complete, have the students go around and introduce themselves.

3. Have one more line-up. This time, ask students to arrange themselves according to their birthdays. Each student should have someone with an earlier birthday to the left and a later birthday to the right. After the circle is complete, encourage students to go around and tell their birthdays and the number of people in their families.

4. Ask students to return to their seats.

Find Someone Who . . .

1. Give each student a Find Someone Who . . . handout, located at the end of this appendix. Have students circulate around the room to collect a different signature for each statement. After 5 to 10 minutes, ask them to return to their seats.

2. Read the list aloud and have students raise their hands if a statement applies to them. You might want to ask follow-up questions—for example, if a number of students have finished reading books last week, you might inquire which books they read.

Interview Guide

1. Give each student a copy of the Interview Guide, located at the end of this appendix. Next have each one find someone in the class he or she does not know very well and take about 5 minutes to conduct an interview based on the questions given. When one interview is complete, the interviewer and interviewee switch roles.

2. After the interviews are over, have students introduce their partners to the group and share some information they learned.

Sentence Completions

1. Give each student a copy of the Sentence Completions handout, located at the end of this appendix.

2. Next have students get into groups of three or four by drawing their desks or chairs into small circles. Have students share responses by going around the circle, one sentence at a time.

3. After 5 to 10 minutes, reassemble the group and discuss for a few minutes what responses students shared.

What Do We Have in Common?

1. Have students number off so they will be divided randomly into groups of five, then ask these groups to place their desks or chairs together in small circles. Ask each person in the group to introduce himself or herself and share a positive experience that has happened recently.

2. Next have each group make a list of 5 to 10 things that everyone in the group has in common. Encourage groups to be creative and avoid the obvious (for instance, "We are all teenagers"). Some ideas to discuss are food, likes/dislikes, favorite activities or sports, music, and families.

3. After 5 to 10 minutes, reassemble in the larger group and have each small group share their list.

Send a Letter

This activity is best for groups under 25. If your group is larger, you can divide it accordingly.

1. Arrange the desks or chairs in a circle with yourself in the middle. Be sure that everyone has a chair and that there are no extra chairs in the circle.

2. Explain the rules of the activity by saying that the person who is in the middle must first say his or her name, then say, "I'm sending a letter to _____ ." The student will then complete the idea with a specific description like "someone with glasses" or "someone with brown hair."

3. Any group member who fits the description must stand up and sit in another student's chair. The person who is left standing gets to be the next sender.

4. Continue the activity for about 5 minutes.

The Knotted Rope

1. Tie a length of rope with a knot for each group member. (Knots should be approximately 2 feet apart.)

2. Ask each student to hold onto the rope with one hand. After everyone is holding on, ask the group to untie the knots in the rope without anyone's removing his or her hand.

3. After the rope has been untangled, give participants a chance to discuss how it felt to accomplish this task.

The Telephone Booth

1. For each group of 10 students, mark a 3-foot square on the floor with masking tape to indicate the walls of a telephone booth. The object of the game is to get all 10 group members into the telephone booth. Allow groups 2 minutes to figure out the problem.

2. After the time is up, ask students the following questions.

   ▼ Who was the leader?

   ▼ Who gave the most ideas?

   ▼ Whose ideas were accepted?

CLOSURE ACTIVITIES

Closure Lists

1. Have students get into groups of six to eight. Give each group a sheet of newsprint and a marker and instruct them to make two lists. One list should include new things that they learned during the day; the other should list what they believe will be the hardest about being a peer mediator and what they feel they want to learn more about.

2. After 10 minutes, encourage each group to share their lists.

Connections Closure

This activity works best with groups of fewer than 30 students. Divide larger groups as necessary.

1. Have everyone get into a large circle. Hold a large ball of string or twine and start the activity by making one positive statement about the day. The statement could be about something you learned or relearned, or about a person you met or got to know better. After making that statement, hold the end of the string and toss the ball to someone else.

2. The person who catches the ball makes a similar statement, holds the string, and tosses the ball to another person.

3. When everyone has received the string and made a statement, a web will be produced. Have everyone continue to hold the string while you point out that we are all part of the whole and all interconnected.

The Quality Line

1. Have students sit in a circle. Go around the circle and ask each person to give one reason why he or she is a good peer mediator. This could be a quality or skill (for example, "I am a good listener").

2. Have students go around a second time and share something that they have learned from being a peer mediator. Point out that peer mediation is a growth process for both disputants and mediator.

Hear Your Strengths

1. Have students get into a circle of six to eight individuals.

2. Choose one person in the group to focus on. Go around the circle and have everyone give that person a positive message about a strength the person possesses. Ask students to make eye contact with and speak directly to the person.

3. Instruct the identified person not to interrupt or say anything until everyone has spoken. The person can then say thank you.

4. Continue until everyone has had a chance to be recognized.

You're in the Bag

1. Have students form groups of eight, then give each group member a small paper bag, seven slips of paper, and a pencil or pen.

2. Instruct each student to write his or her name on the paper bag and then to write a positive note or message to each other member of the group and place the message in that person's bag.

3. After all the messages have been delivered, let participants read the notes.

4. Finally, have each person read one or two positive notes to the rest of the group.

Affirmation Exercise

1. Explain that an affirmation is a positive message that we give to ourselves or to others. We need as many positive messages as we can get, and we can get them through positive self-talk or by receiving affirmations from others.

2. Write some examples of affirmations on a chalkboard or flip chart. For example:

   ▼ You are a good listener, and others listen to you.

   ▼ You respect people and help them work together.

   ▼ You are trustworthy and honest toward others.

   ▼ You are objective and supportive of others.

   ▼ You accept and respect people for their efforts.

   ▼ You enhance other people's lives.

   ▼ Life is for the taking.

   ▼ Your efforts and energies make a difference.

3. Have half of the students sit in chairs in a circle and the other half stand directly behind the seated individuals. Ask each standing person to think of an affirmation. Have the sitting people relax and close their eyes. (If you have some relaxing music, play it at this point in the activity.)

4. Ask the standing participants to touch the shoulders of their sitting partners, lean down, and softly say their affirmation. This is done simultaneously to all sitting participants.

5. The standing people then move on in a clockwise fashion to the next sitting person and softly send them the same affirmation, proceeding around the circle until they return to their starting places.

6. The sitting persons and standing persons switch places, and the exercise continues as before.

7. After the exercise is complete, ask how it felt to receive one affirmation after the next, as well as how it felt to give affirmations. Finally, ask how students think this exercise can help them become better peer mediators.

Find Someone Who . . .

Find a person in the group who fits one or more of the following statements. Have the person sign his or her name by any statements that are true.

1. Was born in another state _____

2. Likes classical music _____

3. Cries at movies or watching TV _____

4. Refuses to walk under a ladder _____

5. Has a parent who was born in another country _____

6. Finished reading a book last week _____

7. Plays a musical instrument _____

8. Speaks more than one language _____

9. Plays on a sports team _____

10. Is new to this school _____

11. Is the youngest in the family _____

12. Likes to cook _____

13. Has more than three pets _____

14. Likes to play tennis _____

15. Has a family of more than five _____

16. Likes to dance _____

17. Was born on a holiday _____

18. Likes to roller skate or roller blade _____

Find a person you don't know yet and obtain the following information.

1. What is your name?

2. Who are the members of your family?

3. What is your favorite hobby? How did you get interested in it?

4. What is your idea of a perfect Saturday afternoon?

5. What do you like most about school?

6. What would you change about school if you were principal?

7. What would you do with $1,000?

8. What is the best news you could get right now?

9. What is one of the best things that has ever happened to you?

10. Describe your life 10 years from now. Where will you be living? What will be your job? Will you have a family?

Sentence Completions

These are some sentences about you. Please finish them with the first thought that comes to your mind.

1. I like to _____

2. My teachers think I _____

3. One word that describes me is _____

4. I worry when _____

5. I get upset when I hear people say _____

6. I am best at_____

7. I want to learn _____

8. I sometimes wish _____

9. I am afraid of _____

10. I get angry when _____

APPENDIX E

Simulations

This appendix includes 14 Mediation Simulations and 3 Negotiation Simulations (each of which also could be mediated). The Mediation Simulations allow students to experience the peer mediation process during the basic and advanced training. Directions are provided for the use of these simulations in activities described in chapters 7 and 8. The Negotiation Simulations are intended for use as specified in Activity 5 (chapter 7) and Activity 27 (chapter 8).

General instructions

1. When using a Mediation Simulation, give the mediator(s) the Peer Mediation Request. Instruct the mediator(s) to fill in the date and the name and grade level of each disputant.

2. Cut the disputants' Role-Play Instructions in half and give each of the disputants either the Disputant A half or the Disputant B half. Instruct each disputant to fill in the other person's name in the blanks and to study the information to provide a convincing portrayal instead of simply reading the information during the mediation.

A training assistant may be assigned to a group made up of all Disputant A players to coach them in their role portrayal. Other assistants may coach a group of students designated as Disputant B. Such coaching is helpful in either mediation or negotiation practice.

3. Start the simulation.

4. Provide coaching by assistant trainers during the simulation. Coaching can be very helpful, but the coaches must allow the mediator(s) or negotiators to experience the process. Coaches should intervene only if the mediators or negotiators get stuck or are otherwise struggling.

5. End the role-play and have negotiators and mediation groups discuss the results among themselves. The following types of questions will be helpful.

To mediators or negotiators

- ▼ What did you do well in the role-play?

- ▼ What was the hardest part of the process?

- ▼ What could you do differently?

To disputants in mediation

- ▼ What did the mediator(s) do well?

- ▼ Do you think the agreement would hold?

- ▼ What might you have done differently if you were mediating the conflict?

6. Process the simulations with the large group by asking several groups to report the common interests they found. Ask for a few examples of the agreements formulated.

Date _____

Names of students in conflict:

Disputant A _____   Grade _____

Disputant B _____   Grade _____

_____   Grade _____

_____   Grade _____

Where did the conflict occur? (_check one_)

☐ Bus   ☐ Outdoors

☐ Cafeteria   ☐ Gym/locker room

☑ Classroom   ☐ Bathroom

☐ Hallway

☐ Other (_specify_) _____

Briefly describe the problem:

Disputant B cuts in the front of the lunchline every day, and I'm getting mad about it.

I told the person to stop, but she/he won't.

_____

_____

Mediation requested by (_check one_)

☑ Student   ☐ Social worker

☐ Teacher   ☐ Dean/assistant principal

☐ Counselor   ☐ Principal

☐ Other (_specify_) _____

Signature of person requesting mediation ____ _Disputant A_ _____

DO NOT WRITE BELOW THIS LINE
TO BE COMPLETED BY A PROGRAM COORDINATOR

What is the conflict about? (_check one_)

☐ Rumors   ☐ Fighting or hitting

☐ Harassment   ☐ Bias or prejudice

☐ Threats   ☐ Relationship

☐ Name-calling   ☐ Property loss or damage

☐ Other (_specify_) _____

Directions: Write in the other disputant's name in the blank spaces. Tell your point of view first.

Situation: Two students are in conflict because one of them keeps cutting into the lunchline. One of them has requested the peer mediation.

Your point of view: Every day in the lunchline, _____ cuts in front. The lines are really long, and the rule is no cutting in line. You told a lunchroom supervisor last week, but nothing has changed. You are upset that the person is still cutting in.

Background information: You think _____ is a bully, but you are not afraid to speak up because a rule was broken.

Directions: Write in the other disputant's name in the blank spaces. Tell your point of view second.

Situation: Two students are in conflict because one of them keeps cutting into the lunchline. One of them has requested the peer mediation.

Your point of view: You sometimes have stomach problems, so it takes more time for you to eat. Every day you have a friend who saves a place in line for you. _____ keeps telling everyone that you cut in line, but you know it is necessary for you to have more time to eat.

Background information: You think _____ has a big mouth and is always minding everyone else's business. Your mother thinks you might have an ulcer and has made a doctor's appointment to check it out.

Date _____

Names of students in conflict:

Disputant A _____ Grade _____

Disputant B _____ Grade _____

_____ Grade _____

_____ Grade _____

Where did the conflict occur? *(check one)*

☐ Bus   ☐ Outdoors

☐ Cafeteria   ☐ Gym/locker room

☐ Classroom   ☐ Bathroom

☑ Hallway

☐ Other *(specify)* _____

Briefly describe the problem:

Disputant B keeps taking things from my locker. I'm missing books and homework

assignments. I even lost some lunch money, and I want it back!

_____

_____

Mediation requested by *(check one)*

☑ Student   ☐ Social worker

☐ Teacher   ☐ Dean/assistant principal

☐ Counselor   ☐ Principal

☐ Other *(specify)* _____

Signature of person requesting mediation ___ _Disputant A_ _____

DO NOT WRITE BELOW THIS LINE

TO BE COMPLETED BY A PROGRAM COORDINATOR

What is the conflict about? *(check one)*

☐ Rumors   ☐ Fighting or hitting

☐ Harassment   ☐ Bias or prejudice

☐ Threats   ☐ Relationship

☐ Name-calling   ☐ Property loss or damage

☐ Other *(specify)* _____

Directions: Write in the other disputant's name in the blank spaces. Tell your point of view first.

Situation: Two locker partners are arguing about missing things. One of them has requested peer mediation.

Your point of view: Yesterday you opened your locker, and your lunch money and your math book with your completed homework were missing. You received a zero on the homework for the day, and when you asked _____ about it she/he wouldn't say anything.

Background information: You are a messy person, and _____ is very neat. You were friends in the past.

Directions: Write in the other disputant's name in the blank spaces. Tell your point of view second.

Situation: Two locker partners are arguing about missing things. One of them has requested peer mediation.

Your point of view: Last week some of your pictures inside the locker were gone, as well as your math book. The locker is always a mess, and you just take the first book you see. You admit to taking the book and the money from _____ because you were not sure to whom they belonged.

Background information: You are a neat person and have given up on trying to keep the locker clean because _____ is so messy.

Date _____

Names of students in conflict:

_____*Disputant A*_____ Grade _____

_____*Disputant B*_____ Grade _____

_____ Grade _____

_____ Grade _____

Where did the conflict occur? *(check one)*

☐ Bus   ☐ Outdoors

☐ Cafeteria   ☐ Gym/locker room

☑ Classroom   ☐ Bathroom

☐ Hallway

☐ Other *(specify)* _____

Briefly describe the problem:

_____*These two students are always arguing in class and have a lot of hostility toward each other.*_____

_____*They both agreed to mediation before things get out of hand.*_____

_____

_____

Mediation requested by *(check one)*

☐ Student   ☐ Social worker

☑ Teacher   ☐ Dean/assistant principal

☐ Counselor   ☐ Principal

☐ Other *(specify)* _____

Signature of person requesting mediation _____*Teacher*_____

DO NOT WRITE BELOW THIS LINE

TO BE COMPLETED BY A PROGRAM COORDINATOR

What is the conflict about? *(check one)*

☐ Rumors   ☐ Fighting or hitting

☐ Harassment   ☐ Bias or prejudice

☐ Threats   ☐ Relationship

☐ Name-calling   ☐ Property loss or damage

☐ Other *(specify)* _____

Directions: Write in the other disputant's name in the blank space. Tell your point of view first.

Situation: Two students had a loud disagreement in class. A teacher has requested the peer mediation.

Your point of view: Another student in your math class is always bugging you. Today _____ looked at you, kicked your desk, and pushed your books on the floor. You are ready to fight.

Background information: Math class is hard for you, and you feel that people put you down in the class.

Directions: Write in the other disputant's name in the blank spaces. Tell your point of view second.

Situation: Two students had a loud disagreement in class. A teacher has requested the peer mediation.

Your point of view: You think that _____ is always asking dumb questions that disrupt the class. The whole class has to wait around until the teacher answers _____ .

Background information: You think _____ should be in another math class. You are not very patient with people you think are stupid.

Date _____

Names of students in conflict:

Disputant A _____ Grade _____

Disputant B _____ Grade _____

_____ Grade _____

_____ Grade _____

Where did the conflict occur? _(check one)_

☐ Bus ☐ Outdoors

☑ Cafeteria ☐ Gym/locker room

☐ Classroom ☐ Bathroom

☐ Hallway

☐ Other _(specify)_ _____

Briefly describe the problem:

Disputant B keeps bugging me and talking about me. She/he even threw food

at me in the cafeteria yesterday.

_____

_____

Mediation requested by _(check one)_

☑ Student ☐ Social worker

☐ Teacher ☐ Dean/assistant principal

☐ Counselor ☐ Principal

☐ Other _(specify)_ _____

Signature of person requesting mediation _____Disputant A_____

DO NOT WRITE BELOW THIS LINE

TO BE COMPLETED BY A PROGRAM COORDINATOR

What is the conflict about? _(check one)_

☐ Rumors ☐ Fighting or hitting

☐ Harassment ☐ Bias or prejudice

☐ Threats ☐ Relationship

☐ Name-calling ☐ Property loss or damage

☐ Other _(specify)_ _____

Directions: Write in the other disputant's name in the blank spaces. Tell your point of view first.

Situation: Two students were ready to fight in the cafeteria. One of the students has requested the peer mediation.

Your point of view: _____ sits two tables away from you in the lunchroom. _____ keeps making faces and whispering to friends about you. She/he even throws food at you when no teacher is looking. Today you got so mad you accidentally dumped a slice of pizza in _____'s lap as you walked by.

Background information: You were friends with _____ in grade school, but the friendship broke off when _____ began this new school year. You are not sure why the relationship changed.

Directions: Write in the other disputant's name in the blank spaces. Tell your point of view second.

Situation: Two students were ready to fight in the cafeteria. One of the students has requested the mediation.

Your point of view: _____ was your friend until this year. You believe she/he acts superior to everyone else and is always putting other people down. You know it was no accident that the slice of pizza dropped in your lap. You want your pants dry cleaned at _____'s expense.

Background information: You think _____ is acting this way because she/he is in all advanced classes. You still want to be friends.

Date _____

Names of students in conflict:

Disputant A _____ Grade _____

Disputant B _____ Grade _____

_____ Grade _____

_____ Grade _____

Where did the conflict occur? _(check one)_

☐ Bus   ☐ Outdoors

☐ Cafeteria   ☑ Gym/locker room

☐ Classroom   ☐ Bathroom

☐ Hallway

☐ Other _(specify)_ _____

Briefly describe the problem:

These two students were pushing and ready to fight in the locker room.

They are isolated until there is a successful mediation.

_____

_____

Mediation requested by _(check one)_

☐ Student   ☐ Social worker

☐ Teacher   ☐ Dean/assistant principal

☐ Counselor   ☑ Principal

☐ Other _(specify)_ _____

Signature of person requesting mediation ____ _Principal_ _____

DO NOT WRITE BELOW THIS LINE

TO BE COMPLETED BY A PROGRAM COORDINATOR

What is the conflict about? _(check one)_

☐ Rumors   ☐ Fighting or hitting

☐ Harassment   ☐ Bias or prejudice

☐ Threats   ☐ Relationship

☐ Name-calling   ☐ Property loss or damage

☐ Other _(specify)_ _____

Directions: Write in the other disputant's name in the blank spaces. Tell your point of view first.

Situation: Two students were fighting in the locker room. The principal has requested the peer mediation.

Your point of view: You and _____ were playing around in the locker room yesterday, and _____ got mad and started fighting. The PE teacher referred both of you to the principal. You still don't know why _____ got so mad.

Background information: You and _____ have been good friends the last 2 years. Joking around and play fighting is how you often act toward one another.

Directions: Write in the other disputant's name in the blank spaces. Tell your point of view second.

Situation: Two students were fighting in the locker room. The principal has requested the peer mediation.

Your point of view: You have gotten very tired of the way _____ has been treating you. She/he can be such a jerk. _____ is always putting you down and using you as a play punching bag. It was time _____ got some of her/his own medicine.

Background information: You feel everyone is on your case. Your grades were low this semester, you were cut from the basketball team, and your father might be taking a job in another town, so your family might have to move.

Date _____

Names of students in conflict:

Disputant A _____ Grade _____

_____ *Disputant B* _____ Grade _____

_____ Grade _____

_____ Grade _____

Where did the conflict occur? *(check one)*

☐ Bus   ☐ Outdoors

☐ Cafeteria   ☐ Gym/locker room

☐ Classroom   ☐ Bathroom

☐ Hallway

☑ Other *(specify)* _____ *Library* _____

Briefly describe the problem:

_____ *I loaned Disputant B a library book, and she/he lost it. Now I'm supposed to pay for it.* _____

_____

_____

_____

Mediation requested by *(check one)*

☑ Student   ☐ Social worker

☐ Teacher   ☐ Dean/assistant principal

☐ Counselor   ☐ Principal

☐ Other *(specify)* _____

Signature of person requesting mediation _____ *Disputant A* _____

DO NOT WRITE BELOW THIS LINE

TO BE COMPLETED BY A PROGRAM COORDINATOR

What is the conflict about? *(check one)*

☐ Rumors   ☐ Fighting or hitting

☐ Harassment   ☐ Bias or prejudice

☐ Threats   ☐ Relationship

☐ Name-calling   ☐ Property loss or damage

☐ Other *(specify)* _____

Directions: Write in the other disputant's name in the blank spaces. Tell your point of view first.

Situation: Two classmates are very mad at each other because of a lost library book. One of them has requested the peer mediation.

Your point of view: You and _____ are fighting because _____ lost a library book. You are working together on a report, and _____ borrowed the book from you and never returned it. You got an overdue notice. If you don't find the book, you're going to have to pay for it.

Background information: You don't have the money to pay for the book. You've done most of the work on the report, and _____ has been a good friend.

- -

Directions: Write in the other disputant's name in the blank spaces. Tell your point of view second.

Situation: Two classmates are very mad at each other because of a lost library book. One of them has requested the peer mediation.

Your point of view: _____ is saying that you lost the library book. However, you are sure that you returned it before the due date. You feel as though she/he is trying to put the blame of losing the book on you.

Background information: _____ has been a good friend. You have a history of losing and forgetting things, and you don't work very hard at school. However, this time you are sure it isn't your fault the book is missing.

Date _____

Names of students in conflict:

    Disputant A _____ Grade _____

    Disputant B _____ Grade _____

    _____ Grade _____

    _____ Grade _____

Where did the conflict occur? _(check one)_

☐ Bus   ☐ Outdoors

☐ Cafeteria   ☐ Gym/locker room

☐ Classroom   ☐ Bathroom

☐ Hallway

☑ Other _(specify)_ ___ _All over school_ _____

Briefly describe the problem:

    Disputant B is saying she/he is going to kick my butt because I was talking to her/his

    boyfriend/girlfriend. I don't want to fight, but I will.

    _____

    _____

Mediation requested by _(check one)_

☑ Student   ☐ Social worker

☐ Teacher   ☐ Dean/assistant principal

☐ Counselor   ☐ Principal

☐ Other _(specify)_ _____

Signature of person requesting mediation ___ _Disputant A_ _____

DO NOT WRITE BELOW THIS LINE

TO BE COMPLETED BY A PROGRAM COORDINATOR

What is the conflict about? _(check one)_

☐ Rumors   ☐ Fighting or hitting

☐ Harassment   ☐ Bias or prejudice

☐ Threats   ☐ Relationship

☐ Name-calling   ☐ Property loss or damage

☐ Other _(specify)_ _____

Directions: Write in the other disputant's name in the blank spaces. Tell your point of view first.

Situation: Two students are threatening each other because of a rumor about a boyfriend/girlfriend. One of them has requested the peer mediation.

Your point of view: You have heard from several other students that _____ was holding hands with your boyfriend/girlfriend at the mall last night. You don't like the idea of someone else messing around with your boyfriend/girlfriend.

Background information: _____ and you have been friends in the past. You think _____ is a flirt and the cause of your relationship's going bad.

Directions: Write in the other disputant's name in the blank spaces. Tell your point of view second.

Situation: Two students are threatening each other because of a rumor about a boyfriend/girlfriend. One of them has requested the peer mediation.

Your point of view: You have heard from several other students that _____ wants to fight you. You don't want to fight, and you don't want to go with _____'s boyfriend/girlfriend.

Background information: You think _____ doesn't have many friends and is jealous of your popularity.

Date _____

Names of students in conflict:

    Disputant A _____ Grade _____

    Disputant B _____ Grade _____

    _____ Grade _____

    _____ Grade _____

Where did the conflict occur? _(check one)_

☑ Bus   ☐ Outdoors

☐ Cafeteria   ☐ Gym/locker room

☐ Classroom   ☐ Bathroom

☐ Hallway

☐ Other _(specify)_ _____

Briefly describe the problem:

    Disputant B has been telling everybody on the bus something that's none of her/his business.

    The person better shut up or else!

_____

_____

Mediation requested by _(check one)_

☑ Student   ☐ Social worker

☐ Teacher   ☐ Dean/assistant principal

☐ Counselor   ☐ Principal

☐ Other _(specify)_ _____

Signature of person requesting mediation ___ _Disputant A_ _____

DO NOT WRITE BELOW THIS LINE

TO BE COMPLETED BY A PROGRAM COORDINATOR

What is the conflict about? _(check one)_

☐ Rumors   ☐ Fighting or hitting

☐ Harassment   ☐ Bias or prejudice

☐ Threats   ☐ Relationship

☐ Name-calling   ☐ Property loss or damage

☐ Other _(specify)_ _____

Directions: Write in the other disputant's name in the blank space. Tell your point of view first.

Situation: One student is upset because another has been spreading the rumor that her/his 16-year-old sister is pregnant. The first student has requested the peer mediation.

Your point of view: It is true that your sister is pregnant, but you don't think it is anyone else's business.

Background information: You think _____ has a big mouth and loves to gossip.

Directions: Write in the other disputant's name in the blank space. Tell your point of view second.

Situation: One student is upset because another has been spreading the rumor that her/his 16-year-old sister is pregnant. The first student has requested the peer mediation.

Your point of view: You told only one person that the other student's sister was pregnant, and you told because that person asked about it. You heard the rumor from other people.

Background information: You know the sister and think of her as a friend. You think that _____ doesn't need to be so sensitive about her/his sister's situation—a lot of girls get pregnant.

Date _____

Names of students in conflict:

Disputant A _____ Grade _____

Disputant B _____ Grade _____

_____ Grade _____

_____ Grade _____

Where did the conflict occur? _(check one)_

☐ Bus   ☐ Outdoors

☐ Cafeteria   ☐ Gym/locker room

☐ Classroom   ☐ Bathroom

☑ Hallway

☐ Other _(specify)_ _____

Briefly describe the problem:

These two students are ready to fight. They have been loud, rude, and disrespectful

to each other as well as to me when I told them to calm down. I will refer them to

the office if mediation is not successful.

_____

Mediation requested by _(check one)_

☐ Student   ☐ Social worker

☑ Teacher   ☐ Dean/assistant principal

☐ Counselor   ☐ Principal

☐ Other _(specify)_ _____

Signature of person requesting mediation _____Teacher_____

DO NOT WRITE BELOW THIS LINE

TO BE COMPLETED BY A PROGRAM COORDINATOR

What is the conflict about? _(check one)_

☐ Rumors   ☐ Fighting or hitting

☐ Harassment   ☐ Bias or prejudice

☐ Threats   ☐ Relationship

☐ Name-calling   ☐ Property loss or damage

☐ Other _(specify)_ _____

Directions: Write in the other disputant's name in the blank spaces. Tell your point of view first.

Situation: Two students are threatening each other and ready to fight. A teacher has requested the peer mediation.

Your point of view: You are a new student in school. For the past month, _____ has been saying junk about you and giving you dirty looks. Yesterday, _____ bumped into you in the hall and wanted to fight.

Background information: You miss a lot of your old friends and want to make some new friends in this new school.

Directions: Write in the other disputant's name in the blank space. Tell your point of view second.

Situation: Two students are threatening each other and ready to fight. A teacher has requested the peer mediation.

Your point of view: You are angry at _____ because she/he came into the school as a new student and put down all your friends. If that is going to be her/his attitude, there is going to be trouble.

Background information: You are the informal leader of a large group of students. You have the influence to have the new student accepted or rejected by her/his new peers.

Date _____

Names of students in conflict:

___*Disputant A*_____ Grade _____

___*Disputant B*_____ Grade _____

_____ Grade _____

_____ Grade _____

Where did the conflict occur? *(check one)*

☐ Bus   ☐ Outdoors

☑ Cafeteria   ☐ Gym/locker room

☐ Classroom   ☐ Bathroom

☐ Hallway

☐ Other *(specify)* _____

Briefly describe the problem:

___*These two students are angry at each other and calling each other names.*___

___*A rumor is going around the school that they have a drinking problem.*___

_____

_____

Mediation requested by *(check one)*

☐ Student   ☐ Social worker

☐ Teacher   ☐ Dean/assistant principal

☐ Counselor   ☐ Principal

☑ Other *(specify)* ___*Lunchroom supervisor*___

Signature of person requesting mediation ___*Supervisor*___

DO NOT WRITE BELOW THIS LINE

TO BE COMPLETED BY A PROGRAM COORDINATOR

What is the conflict about? *(check one)*

☐ Rumors   ☐ Fighting or hitting

☐ Harassment   ☐ Bias or prejudice

☐ Threats   ☐ Relationship

☐ Name-calling   ☐ Property loss or damage

☐ Other *(specify)* _____

Directions: Write in the other disputant's name in the blank spaces. Tell your point of view first.

Situation: One student has been calling another student an alcoholic. The lunchroom supervisor has requested the peer mediation.

Your position: You were sitting in the school cafeteria, and _____ came up to you and started yelling that you told everybody she/he was an alcoholic.

Background information: You know that _____ gets drunk most every weekend and mentioned to a mutual friend that you think she/he needs some professional help. You want to be friends with _____ .

Directions: Write in the other disputant's name in the blank space. Tell your point of view second.

Situation: One student has been calling another student an alcoholic. The lunchroom supervisor has requested the peer mediation.

Your position: You like to party but do not feel that you have a problem with drinking too much alcohol. Two people today called you a drunk, and you are getting mad. You believe _____ drinks even more than you.

Background information: One of your family members is a recovering alcoholic, and you are sensitive about being called a drunk.

Date _____

Names of students in conflict:

Disputant A _____ Grade _____

Disputant B _____ Grade _____

_____ Grade _____

_____ Grade _____

Where did the conflict occur? _(check one)_

☐ Bus   ☐ Outdoors

☐ Cafeteria   ☐ Gym/locker room

☐ Classroom   ☐ Bathroom

☑ Hallway

☐ Other _(specify)_ _____

Briefly describe the problem:

Two students were in the hall outside the art room, surrounded by a group of students.

These two were in the center of the group and were shouting racial slurs at each other.

I separated them just as they were about to start swinging their fists. They have been

isolated until there can be a mediation.

Mediation requested by _(check one)_

☐ Student   ☐ Social worker

☐ Teacher   ☑ Dean/assistant principal

☐ Counselor   ☐ Principal

☐ Other _(specify)_ _____

Signature of person requesting mediation ___ _Assistant Principal_ _____

DO NOT WRITE BELOW THIS LINE

TO BE COMPLETED BY A PROGRAM COORDINATOR

What is the conflict about? _(check one)_

☐ Rumors   ☐ Fighting or hitting

☐ Harassment   ☐ Bias or prejudice

☐ Threats   ☐ Relationship

☐ Name-calling   ☐ Property loss or damage

☐ Other _(specify)_ _____

Directions:　Write in the other disputant's name in the blank spaces. Tell your point of view first.

Situation:　Two students were in the hallway outside the art room. They were in the center of a large group of students and were shouting racial slurs at each other. They were about to start fighting when the assistant principal broke it up.

Your point of view:　You have known _____ for about 2 years, and she/he has been making racial slurs toward you for some time. You think _____ feels superior to you because she/he has nicer things, gets better grades, and plays on a sports team. You suspect that _____ is mostly upset because you are dating and have dated classmates of _____ 's race.

Background information:　You are from a different racial/ethic group than _____ . You come from a low socioeconomic neighborhood and although you work hard in school, you receive average to poor grades. You and _____ have had relationship problems for a long time. You resent _____ because she/he wears expensive clothes and has a car. _____ seems to flaunt her/his good fortune. Aside from problems with _____ , you are popular with friends and classmates.

Directions:　Write in the other disputant's name in the blank spaces. Tell your point of view second.

Situation:　Two students were in the hallway outside the art room. They were in the center of a large group of students and were shouting racial slurs at each other. They were about to start fighting when the assistant principal broke it up.

Your point of view:　You have known _____ for about 2 years, and you have had problems with each other nearly from the start. You think _____ is jealous of you personally and is always competing with you. _____ puts you down by minimizing your accomplishments and by trying to take over your friends, especially those of the opposite sex.

Background information:　You are from a different racial/ethnic group than _____ . You come from a middle-class background, but your parents work hard to provide you with advantages such as very nice clothes and your own car. You are a good student and you are a successful player on one of the school sports teams. Aside from the problems with _____ , you are popular with friends and classmates, although you have only casual acquaintances with those from other racial/ethnic groups.

Date _____

Names of students in conflict:

Disputant A _____ Grade _____

_____ *Disputant B* _____ Grade _____

_____ Grade _____

_____ Grade _____

Where did the conflict occur? *(check one)*

☐ Bus   ☐ Outdoors

☐ Cafeteria   ☐ Gym/locker room

☐ Classroom   ☐ Bathroom

☐ Hallway

☑ Other *(specify)* _____ *All over school* _____

Briefly describe the problem:

Disputant B has been telling everybody not to associate with me.

She/he wants to punish me by trying to get others to isolate me.

_____

_____

_____

Mediation requested by *(check one)*

☑ Student   ☐ Social worker

☐ Teacher   ☐ Dean/assistant principal

☐ Counselor   ☐ Principal

☐ Other *(specify)* _____

Signature of person requesting mediation _____ *Disputant A* _____

DO NOT WRITE BELOW THIS LINE

TO BE COMPLETED BY A PROGRAM COORDINATOR

What is the conflict about? *(check one)*

☐ Rumors   ☐ Fighting or hitting

☐ Harassment   ☐ Bias or prejudice

☐ Threats   ☐ Relationship

☐ Name-calling   ☐ Property loss or damage

☐ Other *(specify)* _____

Directions:　Write in the other disputant's name in the blank space. Tell your point of view first.

Situation:　One student has requested a mediation because she/he is upset with the behavior of the other. She/he feels that the other student is trying to turn other students in the school against her/him and is trying to get all the other students to ignore and isolate her/him.

Your point of view:　You believe that _____ is trying to use her/his position as President of the Student Council to get other students to "shut you out." She/he talks to anyone who will listen and blames you for causing the school to cancel one of the school's annual events for students.

Background information:　As the only Native American in the school, you have consistently voiced displeasure over the school sports team's nickname and mascot—Redskins. You have especially objected to the school cheerleaders wearing Indian-like costumes and face and body paint. This year you asked permission to address the school board and focused your objection on the annual homecoming celebration, called "Pow-Wow Days." Historically, throughout this day and during the game that evening, students and alumni have dressed as Indians and danced "native" dances. Because of your compelling presentation, the school board voted to continue the homecoming celebration but banned all costumes and any "native" dances. You felt good about this decision because you had stood up for your beliefs and had been able to persuade others to see the situation from your perspective.

Directions:　Write in the other disputant's name in the blank spaces. Tell your point of view second.

Situation:　One student has requested a mediation because she/he is upset with the behavior of the other. She/he feels that the other student is trying to turn other students in the school against her/him and is trying to get all the other students to ignore and isolate her/him.

Your point of view:　You think that _____ is blaming you for something that is her/his problem. If _____ chooses to take an unpopular position, _____ has to face the consequences. You talk to lots of people in the school because of your position as President of the Student Council. You think it is important for you to hear from as many students as you can.

Background information:　Lots of students have complained to you about the changes the administration has ordered for the annual homecoming celebration. Their complaints are that the tradition of "Pow-Wow Days" is meaningless if they and alumni cannot dress as Indians and perform "native" dances. Personally, you "sort of" understand _____'s objections, but you also feel strongly that the will of the majority should not have to yield to the wishes of a few—especially just one. You have not, however, "bad mouthed" _____ . You have simply answered students' questions when they have asked why the changes were made. You have not told anyone to do anything to _____ . You have consistently replied when asked specifically by others what they could do about _____ : "Do what you feel is right." As a student leader, you think what _____ did took a lot of courage, even though you don't agree with what was decided.

Date _____

Names of students in conflict:

    Disputant A _____ Grade _____

    Disputant B _____ Grade _____

    _____ Grade _____

    _____ Grade _____

Where did the conflict occur? *(check one)*

☐ Bus   ☐ Outdoors

☐ Cafeteria   ☐ Gym/locker room

☑ Classroom   ☐ Bathroom

☐ Hallway

☐ Other *(specify)* _____

Briefly describe the problem:

    These two students are mad at each other and want to fight. _____

    I hope they can work out their misunderstanding. _____

    _____

    _____

Mediation requested by *(check one)*

☐ Student   ☐ Social worker

☑ Teacher   ☐ Dean/assistant principal

☐ Counselor   ☐ Principal

☐ Other *(specify)* _____

Signature of person requesting mediation _____*Teacher*_____

DO NOT WRITE BELOW THIS LINE
TO BE COMPLETED BY A PROGRAM COORDINATOR

What is the conflict about? *(check one)*

☐ Rumors   ☐ Fighting or hitting

☐ Harassment   ☐ Bias or prejudice

☐ Threats   ☐ Relationship

☐ Name-calling ☐ Property loss or damage

☐ Other *(specify)* _____

Directions: Write in the other disputant's name in the blank space. Tell your point of view first.

Situation: Two students were found in the hall after PE class arguing and ready to fight. A teacher who saw and heard the dispute has requested the peer mediation.

Your position: In the locker room after PE class _____ came up to you, called you a jerk, and spit on your shirt. You want an apology, and you want the shirt to be cleaned.

Background information: You don't really know this person, but you feel strongly that you want your shirt cleaned. You sometimes have been teased during PE, and this has gone too far.

Directions: Write in the other disputant's name in the blank spaces. Tell your point of view second.

Situation: Two students were found in the hall after PE class arguing and ready to fight. A teacher who saw and heard the dispute has requested the peer mediation.

Your position: In PE class today _____ shoved you during the game. She/he also shoved one of your friends. After class you told _____ to watch out next time. You didn't spit on her/him— you spit on the floor. You're not going to apologize or clean her/his shirt.

Background information: You think that _____ thinks she/he is better than anyone else and is looking for a fight with you and your friends.

Date _____

Names of students in conflict:

    Disputant A _____ Grade _____

    Disputant B _____ Grade _____

    _____ Grade _____

    _____ Grade _____

Where did the conflict occur? *(check one)*

☐ Bus   ☐ Outdoors

☐ Cafeteria   ☐ Gym/locker room

☐ Classroom   ☐ Bathroom

☑ Hallway

☐ Other *(specify)* _____

Briefly describe the problem:

    Disputant B pushed me and hit me in the hall yesterday. I don't want to fight.

_____

_____

_____

Mediation requested by *(check one)*

☑ Student   ☐ Social worker

☐ Teacher   ☐ Dean/assistant principal

☐ Counselor   ☐ Principal

☐ Other *(specify)* _____

Signature of person requesting mediation ___*Disputant A*_____

DO NOT WRITE BELOW THIS LINE

TO BE COMPLETED BY A PROGRAM COORDINATOR

What is the conflict about? *(check one)*

☐ Rumors   ☐ Fighting or hitting

☐ Harassment   ☐ Bias or prejudice

☐ Threats   ☐ Relationship

☐ Name-calling   ☐ Property loss or damage

☐ Other *(specify)* _____

Directions:　Write in the other disputant's name in the blank spaces. Tell your point of view first.

Situation:　One student hit and threatened another student. The student who was hit has requested the peer mediation.

Your position:　In the hall yesterday _____ came up to you and pushed you against the locker and hit you. Your new notebook was damaged. You didn't do anything.

Background information:　You are on probation, and if you fight back you will be "sent up." The current girlfriend/boyfriend of _____ was going with you, and you still want a relationship with that person.

- -

Directions:　Write in the other disputant's name in the blank spaces. Tell your point of view second.

Situation:　One student hit and threatened another student. The student who was hit has requested the peer mediation.

Your position:　For the past week _____ has been looking at, talking to, and putting a move on your girlfriend/boyfriend. There will be trouble if _____ doesn't stay away.

Background information:　You think that _____ likes to threaten and fight with people. You are happy with your new girlfriend/boyfriend and won't take a chance on losing the relationship.

Directions: Write in the other disputant's name in the blank spaces. Tell your point of view first.

Situation: You were sent to the dean's office by the supervisor because you were observed attacking _____ during open gym. After hearing your story, the dean called _____ to the office. At the dean's insistence you and _____ have agreed to try to negotiate your differences.

Your point of view: You asked a group of your classmates if you could join their game during open gym time. _____ immediately said no because "You're not a good player, and you stink." She/he also said the game didn't need any "of your kind." This made you mad, and when you went after _____ , the supervisor saw you, accused you of attacking _____ , and sent you out of the gym and to the office.

Background information: You and _____ have been in mostly the same classes all year, but you have not been very friendly toward each other. _____ does not seem to like you or other students of your race. You are not sure why _____ treats you differently, but you think _____ is probably prejudiced.

- -

Directions: Write in the other disputant's name in the blank spaces. Tell your point of view second.

Situation: _____ was sent to the dean's office by the supervisor because she/he was observed attacking you during open gym. The dean has called you to the office. At the dean's insistence you and _____ have agreed to try to negotiate your differences.

Your point of view: _____ was trying to butt into a game with your friends, and that made you angry. You did not want _____ to play because you were afraid that all her/his friends would also want to play and that would make the game no longer fun for you and your friends. You told _____ she/he couldn't play, and an argument happened. _____ started after you, but the supervisor stopped it and sent _____ to the office. You think _____ should play with her/his friends, not yours, but you also think the supervisor overreacted and first should have tried to find out what the problem was. You do not think _____ should have been sent to the office.

Background information: You think _____ is trying to butt in where she/he doesn't belong. She/he seems to want to "take over" your friends and your activities rather than hang with her/his own friends. Your parents talk about problems like this with people of _____'s race. Your dad says that he lost a chance for a better job because that race gets favored treatment. You and _____ have been in most classes together all year, and she/he seems OK most of the time, but you are afraid to get too close.

Directions: Write in the other disputant's name in the blank spaces. Tell your point of view first.

Situation: You are upset with _____ , your best friend, because something that you shared as a secret with _____ is all over school. You have refused to talk to _____ for a week. At _____'s request, you have agreed to a negotiation.

Your point of view: Last weekend, you confided to your best friend, _____ , that you were planning to break up with your boyfriend/girlfriend because he/she mistreats you and puts you down in front of other friends. You were sick and didn't go to school until Wednesday. You saw your boyfriend/girlfriend in the hall, and he/she refused to look at you. Several other kids asked you about the breakup. Since you had not told anyone, including your boyfriend/girlfriend, you conclude that _____ has been telling everyone your secret. You are very upset.

Background information: You and _____ are of the opposite sex but have been best friends ever since you started elementary school. You have always shared secrets like this. You are really bothered by this problem because you do not have any other really close friends. You are also upset because you had decided that you might have overreacted to what happened between you and your boyfriend/girlfriend last Friday night and wanted to give the relationship another chance. Now he/she is angry with you. You are pretty sure that since lots of others know the situation, he/she will not give you another chance.

Directions: Write in the other disputant's name in the blank spaces. Tell your point of view second.

Situation: _____ is upset with you, his/her best friend, because something that _____ shared as a secret with you is all over school. _____ has refused to talk to you for a week. At your request, _____ has agreed to a negotiation.

Your point of view: You did not know that _____ was sick on Monday. When she/he did not show up at school, you assumed that the breakup was a bad scene and that _____ was really hurt, maybe even physically. You were really upset with the boyfriend/girlfriend for the way _____ had said she/he had been treated. When you confronted the boyfriend/girlfriend about the problem, you realized that he/she did not know about the breakup. You didn't say anything to anyone else and planned to tell _____ about your blunder when she/he came back to school.

Background information: You and _____ are of the opposite sex but have been best friends ever since you started elementary school. You have always shared secrets like this. You are really bothered by this problem because you do not have many other really close friends. You blame the boyfriend/girlfriend for telling everyone else. You don't feel sorry for what you said to the boyfriend/girlfriend anyway. He/she shouldn't have treated your friend badly in the first place. You just want your best friend back. Actually, you really would like for _____ to be your boyfriend/girlfriend, but you are pretty sure he/she has no idea you feel this way.

Directions: Write in the other disputant's name in the blank spaces. Tell your point of view first.

Situation: You and _____ were shouting at each other during art class, and the teacher made you leave the classroom. He told the two of you to work out a plan to behave appropriately and he would check with you at the end of the period. If you didn't have it worked out, he would assign you both to after-school detention. You are trying to work it out with each other.

Your point of view: You are mad about the way you were treated in PE class earlier today and at _____ because she/he was a part of that treatment. To get even, you squirted red oil paint on _____'s watercolors and brushes in art class.

Background information: You are not good at sports—in fact, you are pretty bad. Today you were playing a team game, and one of the good players who has often made fun of your play accidentally knocked you down and ripped your new shirt. She/he said "Oops, sorry." You got really upset and started yelling at the person, then everyone started ripping your shirt and saying "Oops" and laughing. _____ participated with the others. You feel picked on not just because of your lack of athletic prowess but also because of your religion. You have made hardly any friends since coming to this school last year. _____ has been one of the few kids who has been nice to you and not teased you. The two of you often talk at school and seem to have some common interests. _____ seems to think you are smart and funny and often chooses to work with you on class projects. You know that art is important to _____ . She/he has won some contests for watercolor.

- -

Directions: Write in the other disputant's name in the blank spaces. Tell your point of view second.

Situation: You and _____ were shouting at each other during art class, and the teacher made you leave the classroom. He told the two of you to work out a plan to behave appropriately and he would check with you at the end of the period. If you didn't have it worked out, he would assign you both to after-school detention. You are trying to work it out with each other.

Your point of view: You are upset with yourself for your behavior toward _____ in PE today. You don't know what got into you. You tried to talk with _____ before art class, but she/he ignored you. You couldn't believe it when you saw the red oil paint all over your watercolors and brushes. They were all ruined. When _____ said, "We're even," you exploded. She/he had no right to ruin your stuff.

Background information: You have known _____ since she/he came to your school last year. You don't like the way some of the kids have treated her/him, especially the teasing and name calling about _____'s religion. You got involved in the shirt tearing in PE today because everyone else was doing it. You didn't realize that _____ was so upset, and then you wished you had not been involved. You admire _____ because you think she/he is really smart and very funny. She/he makes you laugh, and you like being around her/him. _____ seems to like you also. Art is your best subject, and you have won some contests with watercolors. The paints that were ruined were new, and you cannot afford to replace them. There is an art show next month, and you are working to get a scholarship to a summer art camp.

Glossary

ACTIVE LISTENING: Actively seeking to understand the message of another by using the skills of attending, summarizing, and clarifying

AGGRESSION: Forceful action or attack

APOLOGIZING: To admit error or discourtesy by an expression of regret

ASSERTION: Expressing one's needs and wants in a way that shows respect for others' needs and wants

ATTENDING: Using mostly nonverbal behaviors such as eye contact, gestures, and facial expressions to indicate interest in the speaker's message

AVOID: To keep away from, stay clear of, shun

BASIC NEEDS: Needs that underlie all human behavior (belonging, power, freedom, fun)

BATNA: The Best Alternative to a Negotiated Agreement, or a personal assessment useful in deciding whether to negotiate (mediate) and a standard for determining if an agreement is acceptable

BEHAVE: To act, function, or conduct oneself in a specific way

BELONGING: A feeling of being part of a group or in natural association with others (one of the four basic needs)

BIAS: A predetermined and often prejudiced view

BRAINSTORMING: A technique for helping disputants create as many options as they can for solving their problems

CAUCUS: Meeting with each disputant individually

CHOICE: Option of selection; power of deciding

CLARIFY: To make clearer or easier to understand

CLIQUE: A group of individuals drawn together by some common interest and exclusive of others

COMBINE: To bring into a state of unity, join, merge, or blend; to join forces for a common purpose or enter into an alliance

COMMUNICATE: To express thoughts, feelings, and actions so they are understood

COMMUNITY: A social group having common interests; similarity or identity among people

COMPROMISE: A settlement of differences in which each side makes concessions

CONFIDENTIAL: Secret; communicated to another under the assurance it will not be repeated

CONFLICT: Controversy or disagreement; to come into opposition

CONFRONT: To face with hostility or oppose defiantly

CONSEQUENCE: That which logically or naturally follows an action

CONTROL: To direct, guide, or influence

COOPERATION: Associating for mutual benefit; working toward a common end or purpose

CREATE: To bring into being, originate, or produce

CRITERION: Standard; a basis for judging

CULTURAL DIVERSITY: Differences in individuals attributed to race, religion, or ethnicity

DEESCALATE: To decrease the intensity of

DIFFERENCE: The condition or degree of being unlike, dissimilar, or diverse

DISAGREEMENT: A failure or refusal to agree; a difference of opinion

DISCRIMINATION: An act based on prejudice

DISPUTANT: One engaged in an argument or conflict

DIVERSITY: The fact or quality of being different or distinct

EMOTION: A strong feeling (for example, joy, sorrow, reverence, hate, love)

EMPATHIC: Characterized by understanding so intimate that the feelings, thoughts, and actions of one are easily known by another

ESCALATE: To increase or intensify

ETHNIC: Relating to large groups of people classed according to common racial, national, or cultural background

FREEDOM: The capacity to exercise choice or free will (one of the four basic needs)

FUN: Enjoyment, pleasure, amusement, playful behavior (one of the four basic needs)

Ground Rule: One of several basic rules for conducting peer mediation, spelled out to disputants at the beginning of the session

Hidden Interest: In a conflict situation, a basic need or want people may have that does not appear on the surface to be related to the problem

Hostility: State of being antagonistic; hatred

Interest: Involvement or concern; the aspect of something that enables it to matter

Intolerance: Quality or condition of being unable to grant equal freedom of expression; bigotry

Mediate: To intervene between two or more disputing parties in order to bring about an agreement

Misunderstanding: A failure to understand; a disagreement

Negotiate: To discuss with another or others in order to come to terms or reach an agreement

Option: Something that may be chosen; an alternative course of action

Passive Aggression: An indirect expression of one's anger (for example, by refusing to cooperate)

Peace: A process of responding to diversity and conflict with tolerance, imagination, and flexibility; fully exercising one's responsibilities to ensure that all fully enjoy all human rights

Peacemaking: Honoring self, honoring others, and honoring the environment

Peer Mediation: A process of conflict resolution, facilitated by a neutral, trained peer mediator, in which students work together to solve their own problems

Perception: The process or act of insight, intuition, or knowledge gained through the senses

Position: A mental posture or point of view

Power: The ability to act or perform effectively (one of the four basic needs)

Prejudice: An adverse judgment or opinion formed without knowledge or examination of facts; irrational suspicion or hatred for a particular group, race, or religion; the holding of preconceived judgments

Private: Not available for public knowledge

Reconcile: To reestablish friendship between; to settle or resolve

Resolution: A course of action decided upon to solve a problem

Resource: An available supply that can be drawn upon when needed

Respect: To feel or show esteem for; to honor

RESPONSIBILITY: Personal accountability or the ability to act without guidance

SOCIAL DIVERSITY: Differences in individuals attributed to gender, sexual orientation, social class, or physical/mental abilities

STEREOTYPE: A mental picture that reflects an oversimplified judgment about something or someone

SUMMARIZE: To restate in a brief, concise form

SYNERGY: Action of two or more people working together to achieve something neither could achieve alone

TRUST: To have confidence in or feel sure of; faith

UNDERSTAND: To perceive and comprehend the nature and significance of; to know and be tolerant or sympathetic toward

VALUE: A principle, standard, or quality considered worthwhile or desirable; to regard highly

VIOLENCE: Actual or threatened use of physical force toward another

References & Suggested Readings

American Psychological Association. (1993). *Violence and youth—Psychology's response: Vol 1. Summary report of the Commission on Violence and Youth.* Washington, DC: Author.

Amsler, T. (1994, March). *Educating for citizenship: Reframing conflict resolution work in K–12 schools.* Paper presented at the Community Board Program, Couson Festshrift Meeting, Queenstown, MD.

Bodine, R.J., & Crawford, D.K. (1995). Our school's choice: Creating peace or struggling with violence. *Illinois Principals Association Building Leadership: A Practitioners Bulletin, 9,* 1–4.

Bodine, R.J., Crawford, D.K., & Schrumpf, F. (1994). *Creating the peaceable school: A comprehensive program for teaching conflict resolution.* Champaign, IL: Research Press.

Carpenter, J. (1993). *Clark County social service school mediation program evaluation report.* Clark County, Nevada, Social Service.

Carpenter, J. (1994). *Clark County social service school mediation program evaluation report.* Clark County, Nevada, Social Service.

Carter, S. (1994). *Evaluation report for the New Mexico Center for Dispute Resolution: Mediation in the Schools Program, 1993–94 school year.* Albuquerque: New Mexico Center for Dispute Resolution.

Cohen, R. (1995). *Students resolving conflicts: Peer mediation in schools.* Glenview, IL: Goodyear.

Crawford, D.K., Bodine, R.J., & Hoglund, R.G. (1993). *The school for quality learning: Managing the school and classroom the Deming way.* Champaign, IL: Research Press.

Creighton, A., & Kivel, P. (1992). *Helping teens stop violence: A practical guide for counselors, educators, and parents*. Alameda, CA: Hunter House.

DeCecco, J., & Richards, A. (1974). *Growing pains: Uses of school conflict*. New York: Aberdeen.

DeJong, W. (1994). School-based violence prevention: From peaceable school to the peaceable neighborhood. *National Institute for Dispute Resolution Forum, 25*, 8.

Deutsch, M. (1973). *The resolution of conflict*. New Haven, CT: Yale University Press.

Deutsch, M. (1991, August). *Educating for a peaceful world*. Paper presented at the annual meeting of the American Psychological Association, San Francisco.

Elias, M.J. (1995, August 2). Preventing youth violence. *Education Week*, p. 54.

Fisher, R., Ury, W., & Patton, B. (1991). *Getting to yes: Negotiating agreements without giving in*. New York: Penguin.

Ford, C.W. (1994). *We can all get along: 50 steps you can take to help end racism at home, at work, in your community*. New York: Dell.

Glasser, W. (1984). *Control theory*. New York: Harper and Row.

Haberman, M., & Schreiber Dill, V. (1995, Spring). Commitment to violence among teenagers in poverty. *Kappa Delta Pi Record*, p. 149.

Hamburg, D. (1994). *Education for conflict resolution* (Report of the President). New York: Carnegie Corporation.

Hanson, M.K. (1994). A conflict resolution/student mediation program: Effects on student attitudes and behaviors. *ERS Spectrum, 12*(4), 9–14.

Ho, L. (1990). *Cross-cultural swinging: A handbook for self-awareness and multicultural living*. Honolulu: Cross Cultural Communication.

Johnson, D.W. (1971). Role reversal: A summary and review of the research. *International Journal of Group Tensions, 1*, 318–334.

Johnson, D.W., & Johnson, R.T. (1991). *Teaching students to be peacemakers*. Edina, MN: Interaction.

Johnson, D.W., & Johnson, R.T. (1993). Cooperative learning and conflict resolution. *The Fourth R, 42*, 1.

Johnson, D.W., & Johnson, R.T. (1994). *Teaching students to be peacemakers: Results of five years of research*. Minneapolis: University of Minnesota.

Johnson, D.W., Johnson, R.T., & Holubec, E. (1986). *Circles of learning: Cooperation in the classroom*. Edina, MN: Interaction.

Kreidler, W.J. (1984). *Creative conflict resolution: More than 200 activities for keeping peace in the classroom (K–6)*. Glenview, IL: Scott, Foresman.

Kreidler, W. J. (1994). *Conflict resolution in the middle school.* Cambridge, MA: Educators for Social Responsibility.

Lam, J. (1989). *The impact of conflict resolution programs on schools: A review and synthesis of the evidence* (2nd ed.). Amherst, MA: National Association for Mediation in Education.

Lebow, T. (Ed.). (1994). *Diversity awareness: Tools for schools.* Ann Arbor: University of Michigan, School of Education.

Locke, D. C. (1992). *Increasing multicultural understanding.* Newbury Park, CA: Sage.

Metis Associates, Inc. (1990). *Resolving Conflict Creatively Program: 1988–1989 summary of significant findings.* New York: Author.

Moore, P., & Batiste, D. (1994). Preventing youth violence: Prejudice elimination and conflict resolution programs. *National Institute for Dispute Resolution Forum, 25,* 18.

Myers, S., & Filner, B. (1993). *Mediation across cultures: A handbook about conflict and culture.* Unpublished manuscript.

Ohio Commission on Dispute Resolution and Conflict Management. (1994). *Conflict management in schools: Sowing seeds for a safer society.* Columbus, OH: Author.

Pallas, A. M., Natriello, G., & McDill, E. L. (1989). The changing nature of the disadvantaged population: Current dimensions and future trends. *Educational Researcher, 18*(5), 16–22.

Prothrow-Stith, D. (1987). *Violence prevention: Curriculum for adolescents.* Newton, MA: Education Development Center.

Pruitt, D. (1981). *Negotiation behavior.* New York: Academic.

Raider, E. (1987). *Conflict resolution.* New Paltz, NY: Ellen Raider International, Inc.

Sadalla, G., Henriques, M., & Holmberg, M. (1987). *Conflict resolution: A secondary curriculum.* San Francisco: The Community Board Program.

Schrader, J. (1990). *Boundary breakers: A team building guide for student activity advisers.* Reston, VA: National Association of Secondary School Principals.

Schrumpf, F., & Crawford, D. K. (1992). *The peer mediation video: Conflict resolution in schools* [Video]. Champaign, IL: Research Press.

Schrumpf, F., Crawford, D., & Usadel, H. C. (1991). *Peer mediation: Conflict resolution in schools* (1st ed.). Champaign, IL: Research Press.

Tolsen, E. R., McDonald, S., & Moriarity, A. (1990). *Peer mediation among high school students: A test of effectiveness.* Chicago: University of Illinois, Center for Urban Research and Effectiveness.

Woolner, C. (1990). *Rethinking mediation: Living peacefully in a multi-cultural world.* Amherst, MA: National Association for Mediation in Education.

About the Authors

Fred Schrumpf has practiced school social work for 12 years with children in prekindergarten through twelfth grades and has taught at the university level for many years. He holds master's degrees in both school social work and educational administration. In 1990 he was named Social Worker of the Year by the Illini chapter of the National Association of Social Workers. Currently, he is an independent trainer/consultant and coordinator for the Regional Center for Social Work and Education Collaboration at Eastern Washington University, Spokane. As a consultant for the Illinois Institute for Dispute Resolution, in 1993 he trained more than 1,000 teachers, administrators, and support staff. He has also presented numerous workshops on negotiation skills, conflict resolution and the family, the peaceable school, celebrating self, the teacher as advisor, and team building. He is coauthor of the Research Press titles *Life Lessons for Young Adolescents: An Advisory Guide for Teachers* (1993) and *Creating the Peaceable School: A Comprehensive Program for Teaching Conflict Resolution* (1994).

Donna K. Crawford is Executive Director of the Illinois Institute for Dispute Resolution. She is an experienced school administrator, mediator, reality therapist, and conflict resolution trainer. She holds a master's degree in special education and an advanced certificate of education in administration from the University of Illinois at Urbana-Champaign. She has received training in alternative dispute resolution methods from the Justice Center of Atlanta, Illinois State Board of Education Department of Specialized Services, Divorce Mediation Institute of Ann Arbor, and Harvard University Law School. In addition, she serves as a practicum supervisor for the Institute for Reality Therapy in Los Angeles and is certified in Reality Therapy. In addition, she serves on the National Association of Mediation in Education and National Institute for Dispute Resolution joint committee to bring conflict resolution programs to university colleges of education. She is coauthor of the Research Press titles *The School for Quality Learning: Managing the School and Classroom the Deming Way* (1993) and *Creating the Peaceable School: A Comprehensive Program for Teaching Conflict Resolution* (1994). She is also coauthor of the book *Conflict Resolution Education: A Guide to Implementing Programs in Schools, Youth Serving Organizations and Community and Juvenile Justice Settings* (U.S. Departments of Justice and Education, 1996).

Richard J. Bodine is the Education Program Manager, Illinois Institute for Dispute Resolution, and President of the School for Quality Learning, Inc., both located in Urbana, Illinois. He holds an undergraduate degree in the teaching of mathematics and chemistry and has taught math and science in the upper elementary grades, middle school, high school, and junior college. He has a master's degree in special education and an advanced certificate of education in administration from the University of Illinois at Urbana-Champaign. For 20 years, he served as principal of Leal Elementary School in Urbana. He has consulted with numerous schools throughout the country on gifted education, individualized learning programs, and administrative issues. In addition, he has directed several summer teacher training institutes on innovative practices and has taught administration at the graduate level, including several semesters of the course on principalship. In 1992, he was the recipient of the Illinois State Board of Education's "Those Who Excel" award as outstanding administrator. He holds training certificates from CDR Associates of Boulder, Colorado, for mediation, dispute management systems design, and conflict resolution in organizations. He is a coauthor of the Research Press title *The School for Quality Learning: Managing the School and Classroom the Deming Way* (1993), as well as of the book *Conflict Resolution Education: A Guide to Implementing Programs in Schools, Youth Serving Organizations and Community Juvenile Justice Settings* (U.S. Departments of Justice and Education, 1996).